Strategy and Force Planning

JOSHUA M. EPSTEIN

STRATEGY AND FORCE PLANNING

The Case of the Persian Gulf

THE BROOKINGS INSTITUTION
Washington, D.C.

Library of Congress Cataloging-in-Publication data:

Epstein, Joshua M., 1951–
  Strategy and force planning.
  Includes bibliographical references and index.
  1. Persian Gulf Region—Defenses.   2. United States—
Military relations—Persian Gulf Region.   3. Soviet
Union—Military relations—Persian Gulf Region.
4. Persian Gulf Region—Military relations—United
States.   5. Persian Gulf Region—Military relations—
Soviet Union.   I. Title.
UA830.E67   1987   355′.0330536   85-73160
ISBN 0-8157-2454-3
ISBN 0-8157-2453-5 (pbk.)

9 8 7 6 5 4 3 2 1

THE BROOKINGS INSTITUTION is an independent organization devoted to nonpartisan research, education, and publication in economics, government, foreign policy, and the social sciences generally. Its principal purposes are to aid in the development of sound public policies and to promote public understanding of issues of national importance.

The Institution was founded on December 8, 1927, to merge the activities of the Institute for Government Research, founded in 1916, the Institute of Economics, founded in 1922, and the Robert Brookings Graduate School of Economics and Government, founded in 1924.

The Board of Trustees is responsible for the general administration of the Institution, while the immediate direction of the policies, program, and staff is vested in the President, assisted by an advisory committee of the officers and staff. The by-laws of the Institution state: "It is the function of the Trustees to make possible the conduct of scientific research, and publication, under the most favorable conditions, and to safeguard the independence of the research staff in the pursuit of their studies and in the publication of the results of such studies. It is not a part of their function to determine, control, or influence the conduct of particular investigations or the conclusions reached."

The President bears final responsibility for the decision to publish a manuscript as a Brookings book. In reaching his judgment on the competence, accuracy, and objectivity of each study, the President is advised by the director of the appropriate research program and weighs the views of a panel of expert outside readers who report to him in confidence on the quality of the work. Publication of a work signifies that it is deemed a competent treatment worthy of public consideration but does not imply endorsement of conclusions or recommendations.

The Institution maintains its position of neutrality on issues of public policy in order to safeguard the intellectual freedom of the staff. Hence interpretations or conclusions in Brookings publications should be understood to be solely those of the authors and should not be attributed to the Institution, to its trustees, officers, or other staff members, or to the organizations that support its research.

To My Family and Melissa

Foreword

SINCE WORLD WAR II, American national security policy has faced two fundamental questions: What is the most credible strategy for the deterrence of attack on vital interests? And what military forces are required to execute that strategy? The Iranian revolution, the fall of the shah, and the Soviet invasion of Afghanistan posed these problems anew.

In this book, Joshua M. Epstein sets forth the three basic strategies available to the United States for the deterrence of Soviet conventional aggression and determines which of these strategies would prove most credible in the Persian Gulf region. Using original planning methods, he then derives what he argues is an efficient force structure to execute that strategy. His purpose is broad: to address a defense policy problem of immediate concern to the United States, while shedding light on enduring theoretical questions of strategic choice and the determination of military requirements.

The author, a research associate in the Brookings Foreign Policy Studies program, acknowledges the valuable suggestions of John D. Steinbruner, director of that program. For their insightful reviews of the manuscript, he thanks Ted Greenwood, Richard L. Kugler, and John J. Mearsheimer. The author also benefited from discussions with Barry R. Posen and with analysts at NATO Headquarters in Brussels, and at Supreme Headquarters, Allied Powers Europe (Technical Center) in the Hague.

The book makes substantial use of primary sources, including declassified war plans obtained through the good offices of the Modern Military Branch of the National Archives in Washington. Fred Kaplan generously shared his collection of declassified Draft Presidential Memoranda on theater nuclear forces, documents central to chapter 2.

The author is grateful to Jeanette Morrison, who edited the manuscript; to Ann M. Ziegler, who provided word processing; to Joseph P. Fennell, Carole H. Newman, and Sallyjune F. Kuka of the Brookings Social Science Computation Center, who contributed indispensable programming and computer graphics. The author also thanks Lisa B. Mages for research assistance and Alan G. Hoden, James E. McKee, and Daniel A. Lindley III for verifying the book's factual content.

Earlier versions of chapter 3 and parts of chapter 4 were published in *International Security*, vol. 8 (Winter 1983–84) and vol. 6 (Fall 1981), respectively.

Funding for this book was provided by a Rockefeller Foundation International Relations Fellowship and by grants from the Ford Foundation and the John D. and Catherine T. MacArthur Foundation. The author and Brookings are grateful for that support.

The views expressed in this study are those of the author and should not be ascribed to the persons or foundations whose assistance is acknowledged above, or to the trustees, officers, or other staff members of the Brookings Institution.

BRUCE K. MACLAURY
President

December 1986
Washington, D.C.

Contents

1. Introduction   1
   Background *1*
   The Contingency *2*
   Organization: Three Strategies *6*
   Methodology *8*

2. Strategy I: Vertical Escalation   11
   Tripwire Postures by Default and Design *11*
   Nuclear Targeting Options and the Romeo Tradition *13*
   Battlefield Nuclear Exchanges: Who Benefits? *18*
   Escalatory Pressures *20*
   The Price of Success *27*
   Credibility *28*

3. Strategy II: Horizontal Escalation   30
   The Question of Wartime Operational Goals *33*
   Target Selection Problems: Soviet Value, U.S. Diversion,
       and Vertical Escalation *35*
   The Risk of Counterhorizontal Escalation *39*
   Diplomatic Costs and Military Premises *40*
   Winning *41*
   Credibility *42*

4. Strategy III: Conventional Defense   44
   The Soviet Overland Threat and Proposed U.S. Response *45*
   Phase I: Delaying Action in the North *47*
   Phase II: Delay and Attrition in the Zagros Mountains *56*
   Soviet Readiness and U.S. Warning and Decision Time *61*
   Phase III: Battle of Khuzestan *63*
   Airlifted Assault *89*
   U.S. Carrier Vulnerability *92*
   Summary *97*

5. Conclusions   98
   Asymmetrical Responses *98*
   Symmetrical Response *99*
   Crisis Management *100*
   Organizational Implications *102*
   Analysis and Appeasement *103*

   Appendixes
   A. U.S. Tactical Air Force Requirements for Interdiction in
      Northern Iran *107*
   B. Soviet Logistics Truck Requirements for the Battle of
      Khuzestan *112*
   C. An Adaptive Model of War: Ground and Close Air
      Engagement Equations *117*
   D. Battle of Khuzestan Assumptions, Simulations, and
      Sensitivity Analyses *126*
   E. Critique of Lanchester Theory *146*

   Bibliography   156

   Index   166

   Text Tables
   2-1. Proposed Targets for Attack by U.S. Strategic Air Forces in
        Support of Mediterranean–Middle East Operations, 1949   14
   4-1. U.S. Ground and Close Air Forces, Battle of Khuzestan
        (Baseline RDF)   70
   4-2. Estimated Soviet Ground and Close Air Forces, Battle of
        Khuzestan   71

   Appendix Tables
   A-1. Target Data Inventory for Phase I Air Interdiction: Arteries   107
   A-2. Target Data Inventory for Phase I Air Interdiction: Coverage   108
   A-3. Air Requirements   111
   A-4. Sensitivity to Payload and Accuracy   111
   D-1. Battle of Khuzestan: Numerical Assumptions for Cases 1–4A   127
   D-2. Battle Simulation Results, Case 1: Soviet Direct Drive; United
        States Defends (Baseline RDF)   130
   D-3. Battle Simulation Results, Case 2: Soviet Direct Drive; Soviets
        Defend (Baseline RDF)   132
   D-4. Battle Simulation Results, Case 2A: Soviet Direct Drive;
        Soviets Defend (5-Division RDF with Close Air Enhancement)   134
   D-5. Battle Simulation Results, Case 2B: Soviet Direct Drive;
        Soviets Defend (5⅓-Division RDF with Close Air
        Enhancement)   136

D-6. Battle Simulation Results, Case 3: Soviet Northern Buildup; United States Defends (Baseline RDF) 138

D-7. Battle Simulation Results, Case 4: Soviet Northern Buildup; Soviets Defend (Baseline RDF) 140

D-8. Battle Simulation Results, Case 4A: Soviet Northern Buildup; Soviets Defend (7⅓-Division RDF with Close Air Enhancement) 142

D-9. Sensitivity to Attacker's Equilibrium Attrition Rate 145

D-10. Sensitivity to Defender's Threshold Attrition Rate 145

Text Figures

2-1. Relative Ranks of Low-Yield Strategic and High-Yield Theater Nuclear Strikes, on Input-Based versus Output-Based Escalation Ladders 26

4-1. Iran 46

4-2. Four Basic Contingencies for Battle of Khuzestan 68

4-3. Case 1, Battle of Khuzestan: Soviet Direct Drive; United States Defends (Baseline RDF) 81

4-4. Case 2, Battle of Khuzestan: Soviet Direct Drive; Soviets Defend (Baseline RDF) 82

4-5. Case 3, Battle of Khuzestan: Soviet Northern Buildup; United States Defends (Baseline RDF) 83

4-6. Case 4, Battle of Khuzestan: Soviet Northern Buildup; Soviets Defend (Baseline RDF) 84

4-7. Displacement of the Front in Cases 2 and 3 85

4-8. Velocity of the Front in Cases 2 and 3 85

4-9. Case 2A, Battle of Khuzestan: Soviet Direct Drive; Soviets Defend (5-Division RDF with Close Air Enhancement) 86

4-10. Case 2B, Battle of Khuzestan: Soviet Direct Drive; Soviets Defend (5⅓-Division RDF with Close Air Enhancement) 87

4-11. Case 4A, Battle of Khuzestan: Soviet Northern Buildup; Soviets Defend (7⅓-Division RDF with Close Air Enhancement) 88

Appendix Figure

B-1. Soviet Simultaneous Contingency Penalty Function for Direct-Drive Attack 115

CHAPTER ONE

Introduction

THIS BOOK SEEKS to illuminate general issues of strategy and force planning through the rigorous examination of an important and analytically rich special case: the Persian Gulf. Two questions are of central concern. What is the most credible strategy for the deterrence of large-scale Soviet aggression in the Gulf region? And what force structure is required to carry out that strategy?

In answering them, the study aims to shed new light on enduring problems of strategic choice, escalation control, and deterrent credibility, problems that go far beyond the Persian Gulf. The cluster of particular scenarios examined here also provides a vehicle for the elaboration of new threat-assessment and conventional force-planning methods of general applicability.

Background

The deterrence of Soviet military aggression has been the basis of American national security policy since the Truman administration. The means proffered to secure containment, however, have changed with each administration since. But they have all partaken of two archetypal approaches: the symmetrical and the asymmetrical. One historian has succinctly characterized *symmetrical* response as "reacting to threats to the balance of power at the same location, time, and level of the original provocation," whereas *asymmetrical* response, as the term implies, "involves shifting the location or nature of one's reaction onto terrain better suited to the application of one's strengths against adversary weaknesses."[1]

1. John Lewis Gaddis, "Containment: Its Past and Future," p. 80. Emphasis added. See also Gaddis's *Strategies of Containment*. Full references for works cited herein appear in the Bibliography.

1

The Iranian revolution, the collapse of the shah, and the Soviet invasion of Afghanistan presented the United States with a strategic problem of the first order. Jolted by the alarming convergence of events, President Jimmy Carter threw down the gauntlet, warning in his 1980 State of the Union Address that "an attempt by any outside force to gain control of the Persian Gulf region will be regarded as an assault on the vital interests of the United States of America, and such an assault will be repelled by any means necessary, including military force."[2]

The Carter Doctrine, as this pronouncement came to be known, stopped short of specifying a particular military response, either symmetrical or asymmetrical. To examine the competing strategic options with any rigor—one aim of this book—it is necessary to focus on a specific threat. Without concrete contingencies to plan against, neither the development of strategy nor the derivation of military requirements (force planning) can intelligently proceed.

The Contingency

Uppermost in President Carter's mind was, of course, the Soviet threat, and in particular, the Soviet threat to Iran. As his Central Intelligence Agency director, Admiral Stansfield Turner, put it, "The most demanding need for military force in this region would be to oppose a direct thrust by the Soviets into Iran."[3]

This contingency continues to serve as the principal basis for America's rapid deployment force planning and for NATO's official estimates of the impact on the Central European military balance of a large-scale U.S. deployment to the Persian Gulf. The Soviet threat accounts for the bulk of America's defense spending on Southwest Asia; the case for creating a new unified command (CENTCOM) and for the Reagan administration's plans vastly to expand the force were both couched in Soviet terms.[4]

2. "The State of the Union," January 23, 1980, *Public Papers of the Presidents: Jimmy Carter, 1980–81*, p. 197.

3. Stansfield Turner, "Toward a New Defense Strategy," *New York Times Magazine*, May 10, 1981, p. 16.

4. The Carter administration created the Rapid Deployment Joint Task Force (RDJTF) in 1980 to strengthen America's military posture in the Gulf. On January 1, 1983, the RDJTF was upgraded and converted to a new unified command, the U.S. Central Command (CENTCOM). At that time the force comprised about 220,000

From a force planning and budgeting standpoint, the Soviet threat to Iran is—at the very least—a useful prototype. To be sure, not all threats are "lesser included cases"; palace coups, domestic terrorism, popular revolts, and interstate skirmishes probably do not qualify.[5] Soviet air and land threats to Pakistan and Turkey, on the other hand, or limited Soviet operations in the Gulf area, might well be lesser included cases from a U.S. force structuring viewpoint.

Claims that the Soviet threat to Iran is too low-probability an event to merit serious analysis should be made with caution. Judgments about what is and is not probable in the Persian Gulf are immediately suspect. After all, in 1978 who would have ventured that seven years hence the shah of Iran would be a memory and that, under the Ayatollah Khomeini, Iran would be engaged in a protracted war of attrition against Iraq, or that the Soviets would be bogged down in a guerrilla war in Afghanistan? Occasionally, low-probability events occur.

Moreover, even if strategists felt confident of their judgments of probability, some low-probability events are worth planning against; nuclear war is, of course, the prime example. Indeed, strategic planning is conducted in the *hope* that such probabilities can be held as close to zero as possible. So in the Persian Gulf. The Soviets do maintain substantial ground and air forces north of Iran. Given a collapse of central authority there, competing power centers might well seek superpower support. "Fraternal socialist assistance" might assume far grander proportions should the West seem unprepared or indifferent. Comparing a Soviet takeover of Iran with a conquest of Europe, former Secretary of Defense Harold Brown observed that "the prize would be nearly as great, because control of Persian Gulf oil would make it possible to dominate Western Europe and Japan."[6]

Economic motives could come to the fore were the Soviets to encounter a true energy crisis, as previously projected by the CIA among

---

personnel. That figure, and the Reagan administration's plans for a force totaling 440,000 personnel, are set forth in U.S. Congressional Budget Office, *Rapid Deployment Forces*, p. xv.

5. To say that contingency B is a *lesser included case* of contingency A implies that a force adequate for A is adequate for B; "the dog that can handle the cat can handle the kittens" is the principle involved. A small attack on NATO would be a lesser included case of a large attack, other things being equal.

6. Harold Brown, *Thinking about National Security*, p. 147. If Iran's oil were lost, Saudi oil might remain, but the Soviets would be in a stronger position to interrupt its flow to the West, particularly during a war in Europe.

others.[7] Indeed, such projections led Secretary of Defense Caspar W. Weinberger to state in 1982 that "with the Soviets becoming an energy-importing nation in the next few years, the worry is that they would move down through Iran, Iraq, and Afghanistan and try to seize the oil fields."[8] While this is not an immediate worry, a bleak Soviet energy picture at some point in the future could resurrect the concern, especially if it coincided with great instability, or the emergence of a power vacuum, in Iran. It is certainly hard to imagine a Soviet energy crisis *reducing* the Soviets' temptations under such conditions.[9]

Iran could be implicated in a NATO–Warsaw Pact conflict. In a protracted European war, for example, the Soviets might wish to acquire and control Persian Gulf oil, or deny it to the West.

Finally, it is worth possessing recognized, credible deterrent capabilities even if one's basic concern is political coercion. The Soviets' capacity to coerce is said to rest on perceptions of Soviet military superiority. If, by careful analysis and efficient planning, such impressions can be altered, then the Soviets' capacity to coerce should be diminished as well.

In summary, given the extremely grave consequences that would attend a successful Soviet attack, given the potential threat posed by Soviet forces north of Iran, given the uncertainty surrounding Soviet intentions in the region, and recognizing the economic importance and political instability of the area, it is a contingency that no responsible analyst can ignore. It happens also to be the central planning contingency for the region within the Pentagon and NATO; two administrations have formally committed the United States to prepare adequately against it. Of the numerous Persian Gulf contingencies of interest, *a Soviet invasion for the oil fields of Khuzestan is the threat to be examined in this book.*[10]

7. U.S. Central Intelligence Agency, *The International Energy Situation*, p. 13.

8. Quoted in Richard Halloran, "Weinberger Says Outlay Is Needed," *New York Times*, February 8, 1982.

9. For a sophisticated analysis of the Soviet energy picture, see Ed A. Hewett, *Energy, Economics, and Foreign Policy in the Soviet Union*.

10. Khuzestan province, which borders on the Persian Gulf in southwestern Iran, is the country's principal oil region. In focusing on this specific scenario, I am not denying the existence of many other, perhaps equally important, contingencies—for example, the defense of Saudi Arabia or Kuwait from Iraq or Iran, or limited Soviet attacks on specific isolated objectives such as the strait of Hormuz. Nor am I recommending that the United States straitjacket itself into planning against only this

As suggested at various points, this contingency concerns not just the United States but the Western alliance as a whole. Careful analysis of it may help defuse one of NATO's quiet crises—the "compensation crisis." It is widely recognized that the European NATO allies are, by a variety of meaningful measures, a good deal more dependent on Persian Gulf oil than is the United States. While the United States has never proposed any revision of NATO's formal boundaries to encompass Southwest Asia, it has secured formal alliance consensus—as reflected in a series of NATO Defense Planning Committee communiqués—that, to the extent possible, allied nations should tangibly contribute to the defense of vital interests outside the NATO treaty area; the Persian Gulf is first among these so-called out-of-area concerns. Outright participation in security-related peacetime activities (as by the British and French) is one such possible contribution. Facilitation of American deployments, by granting overflight rights and en route access to facilities (for example, airfields), is another such measure, one whose operational value was highlighted in the American action against Libya in April of 1986. The most basic and politically loaded form of allied support, however, and the one most likely to exacerbate alliance tension, is compensation. The European NATO members are urged to compensate—by adding forces or raising the effectiveness of current forces—in the European theater for a diversion of U.S. forces from the reinforcement of Europe to the Persian Gulf. This, of course, entails further spending, an already divisive and contentious issue. How much spending depends on the measures

---

Soviet scenario. The politico-military situation in the Persian Gulf region is complex and fluid, and this analysis does not claim to be all-encompassing. I do hope that the analytical techniques devised to assess the Soviet threats examined here will prove equally useful in examining the other threats of interest.

One simplifying assumption deserves special note. The Iranians are essentially excluded from the analysis. Their absence lends unrealism to the scenarios examined here, but one should not jump to the conclusion that this automatically biases the assessment in favor of America; on reflection, it probably does not. There are, after all, only three attitudes the Iranians could take, neutrality aside. They could oppose the United States outright and support wholeheartedly the Soviets' absorption of their country. This case poses no analytical problem, since a people that gives itself to the Soviets probably cannot be defended, and the United States probably would not (and probably should not) try. The second possibility is that the Iranians join the United States in defense against the Soviets; this would make CENTCOM's job easier. From this standpoint, the Iranian's absence from the analysis is conservative. Finally, the Iranians could regard any superpower confrontation as a two-front war. But the Soviets would almost surely have the worst of it in this case, since they would have far more of the country to traverse, and their portion would include the worst terrain as well.

required to compensate; the requisite compensatory efforts hinge on the scale and nature of the diversion to the Gulf; the entire issue thus turns on this book's basic question: how much U.S. force is required in the most demanding plausible case? What strategy, and what force structure, will provide the most credible deterrent to large-scale Soviet aggression?

Organization: Three Strategies

Three basic strategies have competed since enunciation of the Carter Doctrine; two are asymmetrical, one symmetrical. They provide the organizational framework of this book.

The first strategy might be called a conventional tripwire–vertical escalation strategy. Here, full conventional (nonnuclear) defense would not be attempted. Rather, a small nonnuclear American force would be quickly emplaced as a signal of U.S. commitment and as a tripwire that, if violated, would ostensibly trigger nuclear employment against targets in the Soviet Union or Iran. The prospect of nuclear reprisal, rather than that of outright conventional denial, would carry the disuasive burden. Chapter 2 examines a range of nuclear employment options available to and considered by the United States in the event that deterrence fails, and assesses the credibility of a strategy relying primarily on the threat of nuclear response.

In so doing, it points out the risks of deploying inadequate conventional forces since their failure would place the United States in a de facto tripwire posture by default. The chapter draws on recently declassified Draft Presidential Memoranda on theater nuclear forces of former Secretary of Defense Robert S. McNamara. Not only is the discussion of historical interest, but the arguments underlying NATO's adoption of the flexible response strategy are shown to apply with force to this contemporary contingency outside the NATO area.

Chapter 3 examines the second asymmetrical strategy that has been considered for the Persian Gulf. Faced with large-scale Soviet aggression, the United States would again escalate—not vertically but horizontally, launching counteroffensives with conventional forces against Soviet targets outside the Persian Gulf theater. Possible targets for horizontal escalation, as this strategy is known, as well as Soviet response options, U.S. force requirements, diplomatic consequences, and other issues are considered in order to assess the credibility of this approach.

The asymmetrical strategies of vertical and horizontal escalation both proceed from the assumption that direct conventional defense (that is, symmetrical response) is beyond America's reach. Is it? Chapter 4 addresses this question.

The prevailing view of American conventional deterrent capabilities is indeed pessimistic. The number of Soviet divisions in the southern USSR exceeds, by a factor of more than three, the number of American divisions currently available to CENTCOM, the unified command responsible for this region. The Soviets enjoy proximity. They share a border with Iran, while the bulk of the U.S. force is thousands of miles away. It is widely assumed in addition that simultaneous contingencies pose far more serious problems for the United States than they do for the Soviets.

As a consequence, many hold that the United States would stand little chance of directly defending against an all-out invasion of Iran. Characteristic of this view, and of the static ("bean-counting") analysis underlying it, are the words of Edward Luttwak: "To consider the military balance in the Persian Gulf, with Iran as the possible theater of war, no computation is even needed: against a maximum of four or five American divisions that could eventually be deployed with great difficulties and greater risk, the Soviet Union could send 20 with great ease."[11] Other prominent analysts have gone so far as to say that Iran "may be inherently indefensible."[12] Shortly after taking office Secretary of Defense Weinberger reportedly warned that the United States was "incapable of stopping a Soviet assault on Western oil supplies,"[13] and later approved plans for a rapid deployment force of 7⅓ ground divisions, almost twice as large as that in existence when, in January of 1983, the Rapid Deployment Joint Task Force was upgraded to a unified command.[14] The conventional military situation, however, has not

11. Edward N. Luttwak, "Delusions of Soviet Weakness," p. 34.

12. Jeffrey Record, "Disneyland Planning for Persian Gulf Oil Defense," *Washington Star*, March 20, 1981.

13. Robert S. Dudney, "The Defense Gap That Worries the President," *U.S. News and World Report*, February 16, 1981, p. 35.

14. The Congressional Budget Office counts 5 U.S. Army divisions and 2 Marine amphibious forces in the planned Reagan force. See CBO, *Rapid Deployment Forces*, p. xv. The additional one-third division is the 6th Combat Brigade Air Cavalry (CBAC), which is also in the force. For fuller elaboration, see chapter 4, note 1.

received the close examination that it deserves. In divisions, the Soviets indeed outnumber CENTCOM, and the larger force is the closer to Iran; those are undeniable facts. But the conclusions drawn from them are unwarranted.

If planned and postured according to the conventional tactics proposed in chapter 4, a U.S. rapid deployment force considerably smaller than that planned by the Reagan administration can present an imposing deterrent to Soviet aggression, while avoiding the risks inherent in either the vertical or horizontal escalation strategies and minimizing the diversion of forces from European defense. This assessment is based on dynamic analyses of the Soviets' attack options in Iran. These analyses are presented in chapter 4; they were conducted using an original adaptive model of war discussed there and set forth in appendix C.

The defensive approach presented in chapter 4 exploits a variety of Soviet vulnerabilities in Iran. These vulnerabilities were of grave concern to the Soviet General Staff in its remarkably detailed World War II *Command Study of Iran*.[15] The same vulnerabilities were pinpointed and thoroughly examined by the U.S. Joint Chiefs of Staff in a long series of American war plans, recently declassified.[16] Fascinating in the light they shed on Soviet and U.S. military thinking, these documents are of immense value to the force planner of today, for they reveal an uncanny agreement among Russian, American, and British military planners concerning key pitfalls for the attacker and opportunities for the defense in Iran and other Southwest Asian areas. The tactical scheme proposed in chapter 4 makes use of these military insights.

Finally, chapter 5 sets forth in detail the study's major findings.

Methodology

The analytical techniques employed to derive the requirements of conventional defense are presented—along with sensitivity analyses—in appendixes A through D. A word about each is in order.

Most analyses of Soviet capabilities are oblivious to logistical constraints, even though historically, logistics has proven to be among

15. Gerold Guensberg, trans., *Soviet Command Study of Iran (Moscow 1941)*.

16. See, for example, Joint Chiefs of Staff, "Decision on J.C.S. 1920/1, Long-Range Plans for War with the USSR—Development of a Joint Outline Plan for Use in the Event of War in 1957," May 6, 1949.

the weaker links in the Soviet military machine. The vulnerability of Soviet land lines of communication (roads and railways) is a logistical factor of potentially great importance, long recognized by U.S. and Soviet military planners. U.S. tactical air requirements for interdiction and delay of Soviet overland rail and road advances through Iran are estimated in appendix A.[17] The equations employed are of general applicability.

Appendix B, also focused on logistics, develops a generalization of the U.S. Army's own truck-requirements equation to assess the Soviets' capacity to sustain high-intensity combat in Iran.

Combat between U.S. and Soviet ground forces in Khuzestan, including close air support, is simulated by use of equations developed in appendix C. The simulation assumptions and results are presented in appendix D, along with several sensitivity analyses. Since warfare is a dynamic process, one in which numerous operational factors interact over time, the prospects for conventional defense cannot accurately be gauged by a mere static comparison of opposing weapon inventories. A dynamic analysis is essential.

One of the pioneers in the development of dynamic methods was Frederick William Lanchester (1868–1946), an English engineer who contributed to such diverse fields as automotive design, fiscal policy, and aerodynamics.[18] He is best remembered for his equations of war, dubbed the Lanchester equations. First set forth in October of 1914, these have a variety of forms, the most renowned of which is the so-called Lanchester square relation.[19]

The Lanchester equations have for decades dominated the dynamic assessment of conventional land balances. The U.S. Army, the Joint Chiefs of Staff, and analytical directorates within the Office of the Secretary of Defense employ Lanchester-based models to assess theater balances and to aid in the selection of weapon systems. Theater-level combat modeling conducted under contract to the Pentagon is also dominated by Lanchester theory and its extensions.[20] Lanchester

17. The equations used are adapted from those developed by me and presented in Joshua M. Epstein, *Measuring Military Power*.

18. James R. Newman, "Commentary on Frederick William Lanchester," pp. 2136–37.

19. For details about the many presentations of Lanchester equations, see appendix E.

20. See U.S. General Accounting Office, *Models, Data, and War*; and Seth Bonder, "Issues Facing Model Developers-I," p. 43.

models are employed by prominent independent defense analysts; they are central to force-planning curricula at major universities and postgraduate service schools, and they form the core of the scholarly literature on conventional war gaming and simulation. Unlike static numerical comparisons, the Lanchester equations recognize some of warfare's operational dimensions. Unfortunately, though directed at the right questions, the Lanchester equations offer a fundamentally implausible representation of combat under all but a very small set of circumstances. The basic deficiencies of Lanchester theory are set forth in appendix E.[21] The alternative equations presented in appendix C were designed to overcome these problems.

My hope is that these methods of analysis will prove valuable to defense planners and to students and teachers of national security policy.

21. The technical critique of Lanchester theory and exposition of my model have been published as a monograph, Joshua M. Epstein, *The Calculus of Conventional War*.

CHAPTER TWO

Strategy I
Vertical Escalation

THREATENING the use of American nuclear weaponry to deter Soviet conventional aggression is an old, and seductive, idea. Based largely on the assumption of overwhelming Soviet conventional superiority in Europe, this was the essence of the Eisenhower-Dulles strategy of massive retaliation articulated in 1954. Notwithstanding NATO's abandonment of massive retaliation in favor of the so-called flexible response doctrine in 1967, and the Soviets' achievement of nuclear parity, the prospect of deterring conventional aggression by threat of nuclear escalation continues to exert a powerful pull on Western leaders.[1]

Tripwire Postures by Default and Design

In the Persian Gulf, the Carter Doctrine, enunciated in January 1980, committed the United States to repel Soviet aggression, but conventional defense was generally assumed to be infeasible. Thus U.S. strategy was seen to consist in "rushing troops to the region as a 'tripwire' force," with "possible use of tactical nuclear weapons as a last resort."[2]

While some official U.S. spokesmen "felt *compelled to* rely on threats

---

1. The evolution of NATO's doctrine from massive retaliation through flexible response is concisely reviewed in David N. Schwartz, "A Historical Perspective," pp. 6–7. The single most comprehensive work on U.S. postwar security policy is John Lewis Gaddis, *Strategies of Containment*.

2. Michael Getler, "Pentagon Trumpets 'Tripwire,' A-Arms," *Washington Post*, February 2, 1980. This is not to say that the Carter administration ever adopted a tripwire strategy officially; neither, however, did the administration assert the existence of any robust conventional alternative.

of nuclear escalation,''[3] other strategists saw the tripwire approach as attractive in its own right. ''What we should strive for is an asset-seizing, deterrent force . . . an alternative to a war-fighting, defensive force.'' Without explicitly adopting a policy of massive retaliation for the Gulf, the proponents of this strategy defined the task as ''linking a minimal defense to America's strategic deterrent.''[4]

Concerning the extent of the force needed to serve as a tripwire, the most articulate advocate of the strategy, Kenneth Waltz, has emphasized that ''the wire must be thick enough so that not a loose band of irregulars but only a national military force can snap it. This then gives the United States the target for retaliation and establishes the conditions under which deterrence prevails.''[5] A tripwire strategy deters ''by physically staking out our claim to the vital resource, by establishing a perimeter, and by saying that if the Soviet Union attacks so hard that we cannot hold, we shall retaliate against appropriate targets.''[6]

But this begs a number of questions, questions that arose in NATO and contributed to the alliance's rejection of a nuclear tripwire strategy. For example, what are the appropriate nuclear targets? Indeed, what nuclear targeting options exist? Is it credible, in light of escalatory and other risks, that the United States would exercise such options were deterrence to fail?

Although they are central in the Persian Gulf context, these questions are in fact quite general. So, accordingly, is the discussion below. In part because they address some of these overarching issues, and in part because they are of historical interest, the formerly top secret Draft Presidential Memoranda (DPMs) on theater nuclear forces developed by Secretary of Defense Robert S. McNamara in the latter 1960s are drawn upon.[7] In citing these Europe-oriented documents, however, no attempt is being made to equate the Persian Gulf with Europe as regards nuclear issues. The collateral damage and military utility of selected nuclear operations may be radically different in the two cases. Whether this warrants heavy reliance on nuclear options in the Gulf is another matter, discussed below.

3. Richard K. Betts, *Surprise Attack*, p. 263. Emphasis added.
4. Kenneth N. Waltz, ''A Strategy for the Rapid Deployment Force,'' p. 63.
5. Ibid., p. 67.
6. Ibid., p. 73.
7. Robert S. McNamara, ''Draft Memorandum for the President on Theater Nuclear Forces,'' October 1965; January 6, 1967; rev., January 11, 1968; and January 15, 1969.

Nuclear Targeting Options and the Romeo Tradition

Targeting options for U.S. nuclear weapons in the event of a large-scale Soviet conventional attack in the Persian Gulf region exhibit remarkable longevity, having been contemplated by American planners since 1949. The Delta-Bravo-Romeo target categories embraced by the Joint Chiefs of Staff (JCS) through the mid-1950s included Soviet nonnuclear forces and conventional military infrastructure. The code word Romeo designated "the *retardation* of Soviet advances into Western Eurasia" specifically.[8] In 1949 the extension of the Romeo mission to encompass Soviet transportation targets north of Iran was proposed. Formerly top secret memoranda from the chief of naval operations (CNO) to the Joint Chiefs concerning the 1950 operation plan Neckpiece explicitly requested that the Strategic Air Command allocate atomic bombs to Russian transportation targets north of Iran with the classic Romeo objective—delay—in mind. "To delay the [Soviet] advance," plans were made "for the attack of vital points on roads, railways, and in harbors" as well as "vital installations at airfields."[9]

Supporting the CNO's targeting proposal, a study was made "of focal points adjacent to the Theater, the bombing of which have an immediate delaying effect on a Soviet advance to the Middle East through its Northern approaches, and on Soviet activities within the Theater."[10] The recommended targets were "main focal points on lines of advance . . . main centers of communications or main communication bottlenecks. Preference has been given to railway targets, as the Soviet forces are certain to make maximum use of all rail facilities." The then top secret list of targets "given in recommended order of priority for attack" is shown in table 2-1.[11]

8. "Delta-Bravo-Romeo" was shorthand for the targeting plan approved by the Joint Chiefs of Staff. "The critical industries fell under Delta, 'the *disruption* of the vital elements of the Soviet war-making capacity.' Bravo called for 'the *blunting* of Soviet capabilities to deliver an atomic offensive against the United States and its allies.' " Romeo is as described above. Declassified JCS document, quoted in Fred Kaplan, *The Wizards of Armageddon*, pp. 41–42.

9. "Memorandum by the Chief of Naval Operations for the Joint Chiefs of Staff on Operation Plan No. ABA 1-49 (Neckpiece)," March 15, 1950, p. 51.

10. "United States Naval Forces: Eastern Atlantic and Mediterranean," appendix to "Note by the Secretaries to the Joint Chiefs of Staff on Targets for Attack by U.S. Strategic Air Forces in Support of Operations in the Mediterranean–Middle East," October 11, 1949, p. 15.

11. Ibid., p. 16.

Table 2-1. *Proposed Targets for Attack by U.S. Strategic Air Forces in Support of Mediterranean–Middle East Operations, 1949*

Priority	Place	Country	Target
1	Tiflis	Caucasia	Main rail and road center
2	Gjorna	Bulgaria	Main rail and road center
	Orekhovitsa	[Bulgaria]	*
3	Rostov	Russia	Rail and road center
	Gudermes	Caucasia	Important rail center
	Baku	Caucasia	Major Caspian port
4	Odessa	Russia	Main embarkation port
5	Belgrade	Yugoslavia	Main rail and road center
	Bucharest	Romania	Main rail and road center
	Cernavoda	Romania	Rail bridge over Danube
6	Plovdiv	Bulgaria	Rail center
	Ingiri	Caucasia	Large rail and road center
7	Constanza	Romania	Embarkation port
	Novorossisk	Caucasia	Embarkation port
	Tuapse	Caucasia	Embarkation port
	Batumi	Caucasia	Embarkation port
8	Jmerinka	Russia	Main rail center
9	Zagreb	Yugoslavia	Main rail and road center
10	Szeged	Hungary	Communications center
	Cop	Russia	Main transshipment station
	Ljubljana	Yugoslavia	Main rail center
	Budapest	Hungary	Main rail and road center

Source: Declassified top secret target list from "United States Naval Forces: Eastern Atlantic and Mediterranean," appendix to "Note by the Secretaries to the Joint Chiefs of Staff on Targets for Attack by U.S. Strategic Air Forces in Support of Operations in the Mediterranean–Middle East," October 11, 1949, p. 17.

* Blank in original.

Interest in nuclear options to thwart Soviet conventional aggression in the Persian Gulf remained strong long after the Soviets had acquired imposing nuclear retaliatory capabilities. Indeed, a Soviet invasion of Iran was among the key scenarios used in deriving U.S. theater nuclear force goals in 1968. The DPM of January 1968 on theater nuclear forces informed President Lyndon Johnson of the following military planning assumptions: "The JCS TANWERE study developed a set of scenarios for planning the tactical nuclear stockpile in 1970. TANWERE's scenarios assume the following: we need nuclear weapons to defeat 129 Warsaw Pact divisions in Europe, plus 94 Chinese and Asian Communist divisions in Korea and Southeast Asia, plus *ten Russian divisions in Iran.*"[12]

12. McNamara, "Draft Memorandum for the President," rev. January 11, 1968, p. 11. Emphasis added.

Despite the fact that Soviet conventional targets had been contemplated for nuclear attack for almost twenty-five years, it was considered momentous when, in 1973, National Security Decision Memorandum (NSDM)-242, "Planning the Employment of Nuclear Weapons," called for "a more flexible nuclear posture," specifically one that "does not preclude U.S. use of nuclear weapons *in response to conventional aggression.*"[13]

Pursuant to NSDM-242, Secretary of State Henry Kissinger, in the spring of 1974, "asked the JCS to devise a limited nuclear option that the President might order in the hypothetical case of a Soviet invasion of Iran." Firmly in the Romeo tradition, "the JCS solution was to fire nearly 200 nuclear weapons at military targets—air bases, bivouacs and so forth—in the southern region of the U.S.S.R. near the Iranian border."[14] Kissinger's displeasure with the scale of this option led the Joint Chiefs to propose as an alternative the use of atomic demolition munitions (ADMs)—nuclear mines—in combination with other nuclear weapons on roads leading into Iran.[15] This use of ADMs was seriously examined during the Carter administration.

A Pentagon analysis of October 1979 offered detailed calculations of the delay that could be imposed on Soviet columns advancing through Iran by the employment of ADMs. "The explosive power of ADM multiplies the speed and efficiency with which delaying forces can create major obstacles." For example, a surface-detonated 30 kiloton ADM, it stated, would displace about 80,000 cubic meters of rock from the side of a gorge or other narrow passage.[16] Based on an analysis of Soviet earthmoving capabilities, the study estimated that "enemy obstacle-reduction capability" equals 3,000 cubic meters a day.[17] Dividing the volume displaced (80,000 cubic meters) by this value for the Soviets' daily obstacle-reduction capacity yields a delay of twenty-seven days. Perhaps not all 80,000 cubic meters would land exactly on the Russians' routes. Nonetheless, adding the secondary rockfall that would be induced by the same surface blast of 30 kilotons, the study estimated "a

13. Quoted in Kaplan, *Wizards*, p. 370. Emphasis added.
14. Ibid., pp. 370–71.
15. Ibid., p. 371.
16. Capt. Henry Leonard and Jeffrey Scott, "Methodology for Estimating Movement Rates of Ground Forces in Mountainous Terrain with and without Defensive Obstacles," p. 3.8.
17. Ibid.

month-long obstacle reduction problem for an invader."[18] Considering
the remarkable speed with which such ADMs can be emplaced and the
very small number of overland invasion routes from the USSR, the study
concluded that "*ADM alone could quickly seal all avenues of approach
into Iran.*"[19]

With President Carter's dramatic 1980 commitment to repel outside
aggression "by any means necessary, including military force," studies
contemplating nuclear options—some already under way—came to the
fore. Notably, though the Carter Doctrine committed the United States
to repel Soviet aggression, conventional defense was almost universally
regarded as infeasible. A spate of revelations concerning a key Pentagon
analysis of the period—the Wolfowitz Report—supported this perception, concluding that "American forces could not stop a Soviet thrust
into northern Iran and that the United States should therefore consider
using 'tactical' nuclear weapons in any conflict there."[20] Reportedly,
the Wolfowitz study contemplated "delivering tactical nuclear warheads
by cruise missiles fired from ships in the Indian Ocean."[21]

That U.S. strategic nuclear options might encompass an Iran scenario
is also evident. While under secretary of defense for research and
engineering, William J. Perry testified that U.S. strategic nuclear targets
included "kasernes, supply depots, marshalling points, conventional air
fields, ammunition storage facilities, tank and vehicle storage yards . . .
command posts, key communications facilities . . . and war supporting
industry [including] railway yards and repair facilities."[22] As the above
history makes clear, there are tactically significant targets of precisely
these sorts north of the Iranian border in the southern military districts
of the Soviet Union. And reportedly "plans for nuclear strikes against
Soviet military facilities near Iran, including military bases and airfields
inside the Soviet Union, have been prepared so as to 'significantly
degrade Soviet capabilities to project military power in the Middle East-
Persian Gulf region for a period of at least 30 days.' "[23]

18. Ibid.
19. Ibid. Emphasis added.
20. Richard Burt, "Study Says a Soviet Move in Iran Might Require U.S. Atom
Arms," *New York Times*, February 2, 1980.
21. Waltz, "Strategy for the Rapid Deployment Force," note 20 on p. 64.
22. U.S. Congress, Senate, Committee on Armed Services, *Department of Defense
Authorization for Appropriations for Fiscal Year 1981*, Hearings, pt. 5: *Research and
Development*, p. 2721.
23. Desmond Ball, *Targeting for Strategic Deterrence*, p. 24.

During the Reagan administration, Admiral Robert Long, while commander in chief of the U.S. Navy's Pacific Fleet (CINCPAC), initiated a major study of Pacific Command's nuclear requirements. The Rapid Deployment Joint Task Force had not yet evolved into a unified command, and the Persian Gulf fell within CINCPAC's area of responsibility. Accordingly, the Long study was to include analyses of CINCPAC's nuclear options in the Persian Gulf under a variety of scenarios, including large-scale Soviet attack. Among the Persian Gulf options considered in the overall Pacific Command study are the use of nuclear weapons against Soviet forces and lines of communication deep in northern Iran; the use of air-delivered nuclear earth-penetrating munitions (not yet developed) to choke off mountain passes where the emplacement of atomic demolition munitions by special forces would be militarily or politically infeasible; the use of nuclear-armed Lance missiles in the Zagros mountains of southern Iran; and U.S. tactical nuclear strikes by manned penetrating bombers, sea-launched cruise missiles, or air-launched cruise missiles extending to support bases, logistics targets, and airfields in the southern Soviet Union and Afghanistan in the late 1980s.[24]

Finally, imposing battlefield and theater nuclear options are inherent in the dual-capable rapid deployment force components, which include maritime theater nuclear forces (such as nuclear-armed attack aircraft launched from carriers), dual-capable U.S. Army and Marine Corps units (such as 155mm and 8-inch nuclear artillery and Harrier aircraft), and nuclear-capable U.S. Air Force units (such as F-15, F-16, and F-111 squadrons). Indeed, few of America's forces are not capable of delivering nuclear weaponry of some sort.

In summary, an impressive array of nuclear options would be available to the United States in the event of large-scale conventional conflict in the Persian Gulf. Virtually all of them—from battlefield use to nuclear strikes on targets in Russia—have been contemplated. They represent the menu of choices that would confront the United States if it adopted a tripwire strategy by design (for example, a Persian Gulf version of massive retaliation) or, perhaps more realistically, if the United States were to deploy inadequate conventional forces. Are any of these nuclear options attractive? Could theater nuclear employment be kept limited?

24. Interviews with members of the Senior Advisory Panel to the Pacific Command Nuclear Requirements Study, August 1984. Various Soviet counterstrike options were also examined.

Even if they were extremely limited (for example, a very small number of low-yield battlefield applications), is there any reason to assume that nuclear exchanges would be of greater benefit to a defender than to an attacker?

Battlefield Nuclear Exchanges: Who Benefits?

There is little evidence that such limited nuclear exchanges would be of particular benefit to the defender. The basic operational difficulty associated with the defensive battlefield use of nuclear weapons was noted in the 1965 DPM on theater nuclear forces. Since forces concentrated for defense against breakthroughs present lucrative targets for nuclear weapons, it was concluded that "the appropriate way to reduce the level of casualties [in] nuclear battle appears to lie in thinning out the density of troops on the battlefield."[25] But forces in a dispersed, so-called nuclear-scared posture, while less vulnerable to nuclear attack, are quite vulnerable to conventional defeat. "Unfortunately, ground divisions deployed in a dispersed posture lack the concentration necessary for conducting a sturdy nonnuclear defense against strong enemy nonnuclear attack. Dispersed too widely to attain the mutual support and massed firepower necessary for nonnuclear defense, they are subject to penetration and forced withdrawal." This, it was stressed, is the "nub of the nuclear transition problem at the engaged battle level."[26]

This dilution in defensive capability is, of course, exacerbated by the outright reduction in conventional firepower that occurs when dual-

25. McNamara, "Draft Memorandum for the President," October 1965, p. 39. This reduction in troop density, McNamara continued, "was attempted in Game II of the Tactical Nuclear-65 study by dispersing defending NATO divisions to a 'nuclear scared' posture, occupying about two and a half times as much area as conventional formations, i.e., frontage of about 50 kilometers and depth of about 50 kilometers. When yields of up to 35 kilotons were employed, the engaged divisions sustained losses of about six percent per day in tactical nuclear conflict and ACE [Allied Command Europe] suffered about 20 percent casualties overall in a 13 day campaign that succeeded in containing the enemy along the forward defense line in Central Europe. . . . Considering that casualty rates in the major battles of the Napoleonic and Civil Wars were over 22 percent and that rates in intensive combat in World Wars I and II came to about 20 percent casualties per day (e.g., the Meuse Argonne Offensive and certain actions in [the] Battle for Normandy), the casualty rates estimated for the Tactical Nuclear-65 game may not be prohibitive." Ibid., pp. 39–40.

26. Ibid., p. 40.

capable platforms (such as tactical aircraft and artillery) are loaded with nuclear weapons and withheld from the conventional battle (precisely when they are needed most).[27]

Not only do these problems bedevil all attempts to integrate nuclear weaponry into battlefield operations, whether in southern Iran or on the north German plain, but—what is less often realized—the same dilemmas make so-called demonstration uses quite risky from the perspective of nonnuclear defense. Specifically, even a completely nondestructive nuclear demonstration shot runs the risk that the Soviets will shoot back. If American forces are concentrated for nonnuclear defense of critical sectors, then they present attractive targets for Soviet nuclear response. If, to reduce this vulnerability, defending U.S. forces disperse and dig in, the Soviets—whose conventional capabilities would be unaffected by a benign demonstration—may respond simply by overrunning the diluted "nuclear-scared" defense conventionally.[28]

At such a point, or as the classic first use, defending U.S. forces could employ low-yield nuclear weapons on enemy force concentrations in hopes of averting battlefield defeat. Pressures to do so would be high.[29]

If a defender enjoys a nuclear monopoly, then nuclear strikes on such attacking concentrations yield, in the narrowest military sense, a tactical edge and can substitute for inferior ground forces (as was hoped in the mid-1950s).[30] If, as would be the case today in the Persian Gulf or NATO, the offense possesses comparable nuclear capabilities, the defensive advantage evaporates, and far from being a substitute for ground troops, nuclear use limited to the exchange (through mutual attrition) of engaged forces would simply favor the side with the stronger reinforcements. This point was made in the 1965 DPM: "Forces of this type kill each other off very quickly. Unless the war terminates as a result, the pros-

27. For insightful discussions of the problems attending the commingling of conventional and theater nuclear forces, see Leon V. Sigal, *Nuclear Forces in Europe*, pp. 162–64; and John D. Steinbruner, "Alliance Security," pp. 198–200.

28. For a discussion of this and other problems associated with demonstration uses of nuclear weapons, see William W. Kaufmann, "Nuclear Deterrence in Central Europe," pp. 36–37.

29. As noted in the 1968 DPM on theater nuclear forces: "The temptation would be high, for example, to attack the enemy's nuclear delivery systems before they could be used to or to destroy his massed ground forces before they could disperse." McNamara, "Draft Memorandum for the President," rev. January 11, 1968, p. 4.

30. See Kaufmann, "Nuclear Deterrence in Central Europe," pp. 33–34; and Morton H. Halperin, *Defense Strategies for the Seventies*, pp. 42–44.

pect is that the battlefield will be left in possession of the side that can get reinforcements there first."[31]

Tactical nuclear weapons, in short, may prove to be manpower-consuming rather than a manpower substitute. On the optimistic assumption of extremely limited exchanges, battlefield nuclear employment seems to offer no particular advantage to a defender facing a comparably equipped offense.

Escalatory Pressures

Whether nuclear employment could be kept limited is, of course, the overriding question; powerful escalatory pressures would be operative. A compact statement on the escalatory operational pressures attending theater use was made in the 1967 DPM on theater nuclear forces:

> The principal question about limited nuclear war is whether it will escalate to general nuclear war. Once the "firebreak" between nonnuclear and nuclear war is breached with the first nuclear weapon, escalatory pressures will rise. Opposing commanders will have strong military incentives to strike opposing nuclear strike forces before they are launched, to attack land forces still concentrated for nonnuclear conflict, to compensate for target acquisition difficulties by directing large yield weapons at likely targets, and to hit logistics concentrations in the rear, rapidly increasing damage to population and industry as the battle proceeds.[32]

Low-Yield Logistical Strikes in Iran

The last of these escalatory factors might not apply to superpower conflict in Iran, where nuclear weaponry could find lucrative targets remote from centers of population or industry. "Some analysts," notes Catherine Kelleher, "have suggested that the low population density and the relatively easy acquisition of isolated military targets in the region augur well for selected nuclear use, particularly in terms of time-critical resistance to a major Soviet ground intervention through Northern Iran."[33]

In particular, the most lucrative targets—and the ones whose low-yield nuclear destruction might entail little collateral damage—are the

31. McNamara, "Draft Memorandum for the President," October 1965, p. 39.
32. McNamara, "Draft Memorandum for the President," January 6, 1967, pp. 4–5.
33. Catherine McArdle Kelleher, "Thresholds and Theologies," p. 161.

transportation choke points of Iran's northern mountains (see chapter 4). However, to extract the tactical benefit (delay), nuclear weapons would have to be used at the very outset of hostilities, crossing the nuclear threshold long before conventional military (not to mention diplomatic) avenues had been exhausted. That could certainly prove to be escalatory.

Admittedly, the existence of remote, lucrative targets in Iran and the prospect of a low level of collateral civilian casualties (and neither U.S. nor Soviet civilians at that) might augur better for escalation control than in Central Europe. But the same factors might bode ill for limitation. Lack of equally strong concern for civilian casualties could foster escalation by relaxing the restraints on collateral damage, inviting operations of ever-widening destructiveness, eventually encompassing opposing forces themselves.

Negligible casualty rates, moreover, could not be guaranteed, even using atomic demolition munitions. As noted in the quasi-historical review of nuclear targeting options above, ADMs are nuclear mines designed to delay an aggressor by creating choke points on his avenues of advance.[34] Low-yield ADMs, detonated in advance of Soviet columns on remote transportation choke points such as narrow mountain passes in Iran, could significantly delay Soviet progress south without subjecting Soviet forces to any *prompt* fatalities. (The critical but separate issue of whether conventional forces could do the same job, avoiding the associated risks, is addressed in chapter 4.) *Delayed* fatalities could not be ruled out, however. Since ADMs are detonated on the ground, they create greater radioactive fallout than airbursts of equivalent yield and leave radioactive craters, hot spots, to which Soviet troops could be subject. Depending on their number, yield, and proximity to the Soviet-Iranian border (near which many lucrative targets are located), such nuclear detonations could subject the southern USSR to substantial fallout and collateral civilian casualties.

Whether the Soviets would be willing to regard the collateral effects as inadvertent is an open question. What the United States foresaw as the most benign form of nuclear employment could be interpreted by the Soviets as a breach of critical salients: violating (with fallout) the Soviet-

---

34. For a brief overview of ADMs, see Thomas B. Cochran, William M. Arkin, and Milton M. Hoenig, *Nuclear Weapons Databook*, vol. 1: *U.S. Nuclear Forces and Capabilities*, p. 60. According to the authors, a special atomic demolition munition (SADM) weighs less than 163 pounds.

Iranian border and violating the salient distinguishing Soviet troops from civilians. The assumption of intentionality where there is none is common in war. During World War I, for example, the British attributed the bombing of a royal palace to official German policy when, in fact, it was accidental.[35] Robert Jervis concludes that "one reason why the restraints on bombing civilians in World War II broke down was that neither side realized that it was not able to bomb accurately enough to hit military targets without doing collateral damage. Each side believed it and the other were bombing accurately."[36] An upward spiral of violence may ensue when each side responds to the other's inadvertent destruction as though it were intentional.[37]

Of course, the clearest and most basic salient that would be crossed by the use of ADMs in the Persian Gulf—even if they killed no one—is the firebreak between nonnuclear and nuclear weaponry. As the 1967 DPM on theater nuclear forces stated: "Despite their advantages, the use of ADMs would risk escalation by violating the demarcation between nuclear and nonnuclear weapons, and the seriousness of such an act would be reduced only slightly by the fact that ADMs are not subject to aiming errors and would be detonated on friendly territory."[38]

The assumption, in short, that low-yield nuclear strikes on remote targets in Iran would not be escalatory rests on the basic fallacy refuted so powerfully by Thomas Schelling a quarter-century ago:

> That small-yield nuclears delivered with "pinpoint" accuracy . . . do not prejudice the issue of limits in war, is an argument based exclusively on an analysis of weapons effects, not on an analysis of the limiting process—of where limits originate in limited war, what makes them stable or unstable, what gives them authority, and what circumstances and modes of behavior are conducive to the finding and mutual recognition of limits.[39]

There can be no assurance that the Soviets would allow an American nuclear challenge—no matter how localized or limited its physical effects—to go unanswered, for political reasons. Once the issue is joined at the meta-military level of national prestige and credibility, of face-

---

35. Robert Jervis, *Perception and Misperception in International Politics*, note 26 on p. 331.
36. Ibid., p. 331.
37. The most comprehensive study of this critical problem is Barry R. Posen, "Inadvertent Nuclear War?" pp. 28–54.
38. McNamara, "Draft Memorandum for the President," January 6, 1967, p. 16.
39. Thomas C. Schelling, *The Strategy of Conflict*, p. 257.

saving, of precedent-setting "submissiveness in the face of American attacks," there is no telling how Soviet leaders would respond. That they would endure U.S. nuclear use and simply back down is far from clear. That their face-saving response would not set off an escalatory spiral is equally unclear. "Because of its competitive character war places a heavy premium on the attainment of an advantage, however fleeting; and this in turn invites imitation. As the belligerents strive to gain a comparative advantage, the conflict undergoes an expansion."[40]

Limited Nuclear Options against Targets in the USSR

If such a sequence of expansions were to take American targeting north of the Soviet-Iranian border, a Soviet nuclear response against a comparable or larger array of targets on U.S. soil (to be symmetrical) would have to be anticipated. Indeed, even if collateral nonmilitary damage in the Soviet Union were nil, a U.S. nuclear attack on the Soviet homeland—no matter how limited or tactically oriented—could provoke large-scale nuclear reprisal.

> It could because the Soviets considered this an intolerable affront and recognized that any failure on their part to respond to the challenge with all-out war would be interpreted as a sign of hopeless weakness, and the United States would become ever more arrogant and intimidating, penetrating Soviet territory whenever it were locally convenient, expecting to use nuclear weapons unilaterally, and knowing that the Soviets having once been pushed to the brink were unwilling to go further. . . . It could also lead to general war because the Soviets responded by reflex, having automatic plans to treat any nuclear attack as all-out war, unable to discriminate a localized attack from a comprehensive one, and thus joining the issue by a process of "automation." [41]

Is it prudent to expect that the Soviets would be able to draw the distinction between "tactical" nuclear employment (which sees the southern USSR as a Romeo target, as an extension of the Southwest Asian theater of conventional war) and "strategic" nuclear employment (against the Russian homeland as such)? Arguably, no.

Moreover, even on the optimistic and debatable assumption that the Soviets would wish merely to reply with a face-saving tit-for-tat response and then negotiate a termination of hostilities, their definition of tit for

40. William W. Kaufmann, "Limited Warfare," p. 112.
41. Thomas C. Schelling, *Arms and Influence*, p. 161.

tat would depend entirely on their (unpredictable) interpretation of the U.S. employment. If they saw it as tactical and directed merely at the unfolding ground and air clash in the Persian Gulf, then Soviet nuclear strikes on American staging areas near the theater, such as Diego Garcia or Guam, might satisfy their definition of tit for tat. If, however, the Soviets take it as axiomatic that any strike against Russia—regardless of its intended effect on conventional operations elsewhere—joins the issue at the level of national survival, then perhaps nothing short of a response on the continental United States (CENTCOM debarkation points, to pick a militarily symmetrical option) would qualify as tit for tat.

In turn, if the U.S. employment is tactically oriented but the Soviets interpret it as strategic, then what they regard as a tit-for-tat response may appear to U.S. command authorities as a clear escalation. *Actions intended to communicate restraint may convince the adversary of precisely its absence, with catastrophic results intended by neither party.*

Strikes against Soviet Forces in Iran

A final tactical use of nuclear weapons contemplated by American planners would be to hit not-yet-engaged Soviet conventional forces moving south in Iran. This would avoid striking the Soviet homeland, but might still be expected to elicit a nuclear response, perhaps against U.S. forces in the Persian Gulf theater: U.S. aircraft carriers would be natural candidates. Once again, what the Soviets might intend as a tit-for-tat response, an American unified commander might see as escalation: "we only hit Soviet conventional forces, but they responded by hitting maritime theater nuclear forces"—which aircraft carriers are— "so now we have to even the score," and so on in a sequence of increasingly destructive nuclear reprisals. American war games suggest some such upward dynamic:

> The U.S. has already run war games in which the U.S. compensated for its weaknesses in land forces by initiating the use of tactical nuclear weapons and in which both sides responded by the large-scale employment of tactical weapons. In one such case, the total yield of the weapons employed on both sides totaled *26 megatons.*[42]

42. Anthony H. Cordesman, *The Gulf and the Search for Strategic Stability*, p. 862. Emphasis added. For a fascinating discussion of whether war games in fact tend to overestimate a conflict's escalatory potential, see Bernard Brodie, *Escalation and the Nuclear Option*, pp. 37–39.

High Tempo, Poor Information, and Escalation Ladder
Misperceptions

The high tempo of modern war, inadequate battlefield situation reporting, and vulnerable (or sluggish) theater communications could exacerbate these problems of escalation control, impelling "a hasty decision in favor of employing nuclear weapons in circumstances which would be more suitably handled without them if the situation were better known."[43] The same configuration of factors may lead to employment packages that are especially jarring and provocative to the adversary. For example, due to *theater* command, control, and communications (C^3) delays or vulnerabilities, U.S. *strategic* nuclear forces may be capable of delivering strikes of greater precision and lower yield more quickly than any theater nuclear forces available to a theater commander at the time. This, in the European context, was the very contention made in the 1965 DPM on theater nuclear forces: "The Polaris and Minuteman systems could probably destroy the threat to Europe faster than MRBMs [medium range ballistic missiles], considering realistically ACE's [Allied Command Europe's] command-control problems and communication delays."[44] The same situation could obtain in a Persian Gulf war, where the American command, control, communications, and intelligence (C^3I) system might be a good deal less robust than in Europe.[45]

Certain strategic nuclear forces might be invoked precisely in order to promptly deliver less damaging, more localized strikes than would be possible with on-call theater nuclear forces. Yet how would such operations be perceived? On an escalation ladder of *outputs* (for example,

43. McNamara, "Draft Memorandum for the President," January 6, 1967, p. 7.
44. McNamara, "Draft Memorandum for the President," October 1965, p. 17.
45. For an overview, see Lt. Gen. Robert C. Kingston, "C^3I and the U.S. Central Command," pp. 23–25. In response to Senate Appropriations Committee questions for the record for fiscal year 1984, the air force stated that "the geography of SWA [Southwest Asia] necessitates the use of HF [high frequency] and satellite systems and precludes the extension of DCS [Defense Communications System] tropospheric scatter or microwave radio systems. The vulnerability and capacity of both HF and satellite systems make it imperative that each be available to back-up the other. Furthermore, the rapid deployment posture requires the use of HF. The best AF [air force] HF stations to support SWA operations are at Clark [Philippines], Incirlik [Turkey], and Croughton [U.K.]. Without these funds, AF operations in SWA will be restricted because of inadequate inter-theater communications capability." U.S. Congress, Senate, Committee on Appropriations, *Department of Defense Appropriations for Fiscal Year 1984,* Hearings, pt. 2, p. 841.

Figure 2-1. *Relative Ranks of Low-Yield Strategic and High-Yield Theater Nuclear Strikes, on Input-Based versus Output-Based Escalation Ladders*

	Package I: a low-yield, time-urgent, localized use of strategic nuclear forces	Package II: a high-yield, delayed, area-destructive use of theater nuclear forces
Input ladder (weapons used)	Higher	Lower
Output ladder (weapons' effects)	Lower	Higher

weapons' effects), this localized use of strategic nuclear forces could rank *lower* than any available alternative theater nuclear employment. On a ladder of *inputs* (for example, weapons used), however, this invocation of central strategic forces could be perceived as an unequivocal case of escalation, as suggested in figure 2-1. Clearly, if the United States has an output ladder and the USSR has an input ladder, American actions taken to show restraint may be interpreted as proof of its absence, with disastrous results.[46]

Ill-Definedness of the Tit-for-Tat Response

In short, the basic *nontechnical* problem of escalation control is the ill-definedness of the tit-for-tat response; neither belligerent knows how the other *defines* escalation. What the United States regards as tit for tat, the Soviets may see as stepping up a rung; even if seeking only termination with honor, the Soviets might respond in ways that they see

46. Another distinct possibility is simply that Soviet strategic early warning sensors would detect U.S. ballistic missile launches (from sea or land), that these would be interpreted as precursors to large-scale nuclear strikes, and that they would set in motion a chain of overreactions leading to escalation on the Soviets' part. Considerations of targeting efficiency could also reduce the attractiveness of such options, from the military planner's perspective; one might not wish to divulge the position of a submarine carrying perhaps 160 warheads just to deliver a package of 10.

as tit for tat but which the United States then sees as stepping up a rung, and so on. There is no objective criterion by which to judge whether a response is tit for tat or more than that—by which to judge, in short, whether it constitutes escalation in the adversary's view. The facile elaboration of escalation ladders simply has no evidentiary basis. Western leaders have no historical record from which to construct the Soviets' internalized escalation ladder, and vice versa. Indeed, no U.S. president or unified commander really knows what his own escalation ladder would be in war; tidy peacetime conceptions of it[47] could be shattered with the first detonation, only to be replaced by something fluid, unfamiliar, and of little use in communicating anything, including the willingness to stop. Surely, the clearest firebreak is at zero.[48]

All of the above risks apply even assuming that the *technical means* of controlling nuclear employment (for example, unauthorized battlefield use) are fully available to each side; they may not be. There may be all sorts of domestic and bureaucratic pressures to escalate as well.[49]

The Price of Success

Nuclear use might work; the Soviets might simply throw in the towel and withdraw their surviving troops. But even a "successful" use of nuclear weapons could have very unfortunate and dangerous side effects for future wars and for international stability.

First, the entire world would be watching. America's "success" would be a graphic example of the military utility of nuclear weapons. Especially after all the grim assessments of the Persian Gulf conventional balance, many governments could conclude that nuclear arms are a feasible, cheap, and desirable substitute for expensive conventional military forces. In sum, a "successful" use could be a positive stimulant to nuclear proliferation. And the United States, having successfully relied on them, would be hard-pressed to argue their superfluity (to potential proliferators).

Second, a demonstration of American willingness to rely on nuclear weapons could reinforce whatever preemptive inclinations the Soviets

47. See Herman Kahn, *On Escalation*, p. 38.
48. The classic discussion of firebreaks, salients, and the limitation of war is Schelling, *Strategy of Conflict*, pp. 257–66.
49. For a discussion of these, see Richard Smoke, *War*, pp. 19–45.

may harbor toward NATO's vulnerable land-based theater nuclear weapons. The Soviets quite naturally might conclude that because Americans used nuclear arms first, to buy mobilization time in Iran, they would use them first to buy mobilization time in Central Europe. In a European crisis, that assumption could be very destabilizing. The European allies themselves, moreover, might well see this as an endorsement of limited nuclear war, certainly among the more divisive issues in alliance politics.

Finally, if a NATO-Pact war were occurring simultaneously in Europe, an American first-use in the Persian Gulf could be interpreted by the Soviets as the "first-use in a global war." A Russian response in Europe (albeit a first-use there) could be more likely than if the onus of "first-use anywhere" rested firmly on the Soviets. Escalation in one theater could weaken the constraints against it in other theaters.

As for the Iranians, collateral nuclear damage to Iran might be far from trivial and could lead to such bitter and enduring animosity toward the United States and its allies as to produce severe economic and other consequences (that is, retaliation against the West). Even "successful" escalation is not without risk, in short. But it is the prospect of an uncontrollable upward spiral that is, of course, most daunting.

Credibility

The United States has paid—in two world wars—an incalculable price for peace in Europe. Since World War II, Americans have run significant risks to make it secure. Cumulatively, trillions of dollars have been invested in Europe's postwar reconstruction and economic development. Today, Western Europe represents one of the largest concentrations of industrial and economic strength in the world. It also represents the largest concentration of political democracy in the industrialized world.

Were Europe to come under Soviet control, the global balance of economic, political, and military power would be revolutionized, and to America's detriment. Democracy, already quite rare, would be eradicated in Western Europe, as it was in Eastern Europe. And in the end, democracy in America could be imperiled as well—not necessarily by war, but by the enduring threat of it. Americans could be denied benefits of trade, and would certainly be denied all allied contributions to the common defense, which—though they should increase—are substantial. The political freedoms America seeks to preserve could vanish in the type of militarized social order that might be necessitated by unremitting long-term arms competition with an adversary controlling, as the Russians would, the preponderance of the world's advanced military-industrial capacity.

America's formal alliance treaty commitment recognizes these interests, while the forward deployment of American ground troops ensures that the United States is *automatically* in conflict should forces of the Warsaw Pact threaten those interests by a military violation of the inter-German border.

Yet even in the case of Europe, where all these political, economic, and military preconditions for deterrence are met in full, persistent questions attend the credibility of the American nuclear guarantee.[50] If it can legitimately be questioned whether a U.S. president would risk trading Washington for Bonn in response to conventional aggression, surely his or her willingness to trade Washington for Tehran under analogous circumstances must be considered highly dubious.[51] Yet a tripwire strategy for the Persian Gulf—whether by default (that is, the deployment of grossly inadequate conventional forces) or design— makes this implicit claim, one severely lacking in credibility.

The Soviets cannot rule out *and should not be permitted to rule out* the possibility of American nuclear use. The presence of that uncertainty and the availability of limited nuclear options enhances deterrence. But if deterrence fails, then for all the reasons above—especially the risk of escalation—the United States must (as in Europe) possess serious alternatives to nuclear response.

---

50. See Sigal, *Nuclear Forces;* and David N. Schwartz, *NATO's Nuclear Dilemmas.*

51. Recent revelations make it even more dubious, particularly viewed against the backdrop of official policy. For example, McNamara revealed in 1983 that "in long private conversations with successive Presidents—Kennedy and Johnson—I recommended, without qualification, that they never initiate, under any circumstances, the use of nuclear weapons. I believe they accepted my recommendation." Robert S. McNamara, "The Military Role of Nuclear Weapons," p. 79. In his Athens speech of May 1962, McNamara had assured the allies: "The United States is also prepared to counter with nuclear weapons any Soviet conventional attack so strong that it cannot be dealt with by conventional means." Declassified text quoted in Schwartz, *NATO's Nuclear Dilemmas,* p. 160.

CHAPTER THREE

Strategy II
Horizontal Escalation

IF ONE ACCEPTS the need for an alternative to nuclear response (vertical escalation), but also believes direct nonnuclear defense to be infeasible, then there is really only one strategic alternative: horizontal (geographical) escalation.[1] In the language of the Republican party platform of 1980, one takes "military action elsewhere at points of Soviet vulnerability—an expression of the classic doctrine of global maneuver."[2]

Would a strategy of horizontal escalation be likely to prove any more credible than the conventional tripwire–vertical escalation strategy discussed above? That is the question which this chapter addresses.

In 1981, shortly after taking office, Reagan administration strategists reportedly issued guidelines to the military "to hit the Soviets at their remote and most vulnerable global outposts in retaliation for any cutoff of Persian Gulf oil." In Secretary of Defense Caspar Weinberger's view, "our deterrent capability in the Persian Gulf is linked with our ability and willingness to shift or widen the war to other areas."[3]

One possibility cited at the time was "to threaten the Soviet brigade in Cuba if Moscow or its surrogates move into the Persian Gulf." Direct conventional defense would certainly be attempted "whatever the odds," but the prospects for symmetrical response were accounted as grim "given the Soviets' inherent geographical advantages in the Persian Gulf region and their superior number of available ground forces."[4]

---

1. Another term sometimes used in place of "horizontal escalation" or "geographical escalation" is "war-widening strategy."

2. *Congressional Record* (July 31, 1980), p. 20631.

3. George C. Wilson, "U.S. May Hit Soviet Outposts in Event of Oil Cutoff: Threat against Cuba Possible," *Washington Post,* July 17, 1981.

4. Ibid.

Much the same language was carried into the administration's first Department of Defense annual report a year later.[5] But in the interim the strategy seemed to have assumed larger proportions: "If Soviet forces were to invade the Persian Gulf region, the United States should have the capability to hit back there or in Cuba, Libya, Vietnam or the Asian land mass of the Soviet Union itself."[6] The list of remote "Soviet" vulnerabilities was longer, and the Soviet homeland itself had emerged as a potential target for horizontal escalation. The procurement of two additional large-deck nuclear aircraft carrier battle groups was advocated, not merely for their capacity to lash back at Soviet weak points, but, on the contrary, for the alleged "capability of a 15-carrier, 600-ship Navy to fight and win in areas of *highest* Soviet capability."[7]

But as ever more challenging horizontal options emerged, the administration reaffirmed its commitment to direct, symmetrical defense: "Whatever the circumstances, we should be prepared to introduce American forces directly into the region should it appear that the security of access to Persian Gulf oil is threatened."[8] Indeed, the Reagan administration embraced horizontal escalation on the assumption that direct defense was infeasible while proceeding nearly to double the

5. For example, "Even if the enemy attacked at only one place, *we* might choose not to restrict ourselves to meeting aggression on its own immediate front. . . . A wartime strategy that confronts the enemy, were he to attack, with the risk of our counteroffensive against his vulnerable points strengthens deterrence and serves the defensive peacetime strategy." U.S. Department of Defense, *Annual Report to the Congress, Fiscal Year 1983*, pp. I-15, I-16. Elsewhere Secretary of Defense Weinberger stated, "For the region of the Persian Gulf, in particular, our strategy is based on the concept that the prospect of combat with the U.S. and other friendly forces, *coupled with the prospect that we might carry the war to other arenas,* is the most effective deterrent to Soviet aggression." Ibid., p. I-14. Emphasis added.

6. Reported by Leslie H. Gelb, "Reagan's Military Budget Puts Emphasis on a Buildup of U.S. Global Power," *New York Times*, February 7, 1982. A May 1984 Rand Corporation report prepared for the Office of the Under Secretary of Defense for Policy also noted such options: "For instance, responding to the intrusion of locally superior Soviet ground forces in Iran by using dominant U.S. naval and air resources to attack Soviet interests elsewhere, say Cuba or Libya, is a familiar concept." Robert Perry, Mark A. Lorell, and Kevin N. Lewis, *Second-Area Operations, A Strategy Option,* p. 10.

7. John Lehman, "America's Growing Need for Seaborne Air Bases," *Wall Street Journal,* March 30, 1982. Emphasis added. This is not to insist that the U.S. Navy's desire for two more carriers derived exclusively from the administration's attraction to horizontal escalation, but the strategic concept and the Navy's offensive proclivities were mutually reinforcing, to say the least.

8. George C. Wilson, "U.S. Defense Paper Cites Gap between Rhetoric, Intentions," *Washington Post,* May 27, 1982.

conventional forces available to the U.S. Central Command.[9] (Whether such an expansion is necessary, even for a strategy of direct conventional defense, is discussed in chapter 4.)

Both direct defense *and* asymmetrical response were apparently embraced; under the latter, not just points of Soviet weakness, but points of extreme Soviet strength as well were contemplated as horizontal targets. This "do everything" quality of the articulated strategy was compounded by the administration's pointed rejection of planning around any specific set of prototypical (or real) contingencies (for example, the one-and-a-half-war or two-and-a-half-war sizing devices)[10] and its exhortations to prepare for "prolonged conventional wars simultaneously in several parts of the globe."[11]

Predictably, when the military was called upon to attach a price tag to the strategy, it was whopping: hundreds of billions—by some estimates $750 billion—beyond the $1.6 trillion Reagan five-year defense plan.[12] The strategy's requirements were reportedly "so grandiose" that the Joint Chiefs of Staff said "carrying them out would require 50 percent more troops, fighter planes and aircraft carriers than now deployed, along with another Marine amphibious force."[13]

It was against that sobering budgetary backdrop that William P. Clark, in his first major speech as national security adviser, announced, "There is not enough money available to eliminate [all] the risks overnight."[14]

9. In 1983, when the U.S. Central Command was formally established, the plan was to expand the rapidly deployable forces available to CENTCOM from 222,000 to 440,000 personnel. Barry M. Blechman and Edward N. Luttwak, eds., *International Security Yearbook 1983/84*, p. 153. The same data are given in U.S. Congressional Budget Office, *Rapid Deployment Forces*, pp. 5, 11–12.

10. For peacetime force-planning and defense-budgeting purposes, it has proven useful to postulate global scenarios in which the United States is faced simultaneously with, for example, one large war involving NATO and one small war involving a third-world contingency ("one-and-a-half wars"), or two large wars and one small war ("two-and-a-half wars"). The Reagan administration rejected this approach as "mistaken" and "mechanistic." Department of Defense, *Annual Report, Fiscal Year 1983*, pp. I-15, I-16. On the one-and-a-half-war and two-and-a-half war concepts as peacetime planning devices, see William W. Kaufmann, "The Defense Budget," in Pechman, ed., *Setting National Priorities: The 1983 Budget*, p. 81.

11. "Flood, and Leak, at the Pentagon," *New York Times*, February 1, 1982; and Richard Halloran, "Needed: A Leader for the Joint Chiefs," *New York Times*, February 1, 1982.

12. The $1.6 trillion is the administration's 1982–86 defense authorization request. Both figures are from Robert W. Komer, "Maritime Strategy vs. Coalition Defense," pp. 1128–29. See also "Flood, and Leak."

13. Wilson, "U.S. Defense Paper."

14. Ibid.

Basic questions remain unresolved, however, about the advisability of a war-widening strategy in principle. And those underlying questions are not addressed merely by admitting cutbacks in the pace of funding; the more basic and enduring issue is whether this course, this entire strategic direction, is advisable at all. Moreover, until that issue is settled, the narrower debate on program priorities can only founder.

Indeed, while the administration has apparently "stepped back" to reexamine the strategy's appeal, none of the actual force structure that was orginally defended in these terms (for example, increasing the offensive striking power of the surface fleet) has been retracted. For that reason and, more basic, because it is an idea of recurrent and enduring strategic interest in any event, it may be constructive to raise some of the unanswered questions about horizontal escalation. Five seem fundamental. First, what is horizontal escalation supposed to do; what is the goal in an operational sense? Second, given some relatively concrete goal, how is the "proper" horizontal target selected? Related to that, in what ways might horizontal escalation affect the probability of vertical escalation by the United States or the Soviet Union? Fourth, what are the risks of "counterhorizontal escalation" by the Soviets? Finally, are there otherwise-avoidable diplomatic costs associated with the strategy? Not only do these questions deserve thought, but attraction to the strategy seems to rest on military premises that are questionable in their own right. Having discussed these issues, the most important question of all—that of credibility—is addressed.

The Question of Wartime Operational Goals

Without some sense of the operational goal of a military action, it is not possible to select its targets. Neither, in turn, is it possible to derive the forces required or to assess the adequacy of those already in being. While "carrying the war to other arenas" and "hitting the Soviets at their vulnerable outposts" may sound clear, such phrases[15] in fact provide little guidance to the military planner, charged with designing a force, or to the public, charged with paying for it.

What, exactly, is the goal of horizontal escalation? Is it to *destroy something* in order to *punish* the Soviets, perhaps holding out the prospect of further punishment unless they comply with American terms,

15. See notes 3 and 5.

whatever those might be? Is it to *take something hostage*, hoping thereby to bargain a return to the prewar status quo or some other political arrangement? Obviously, not both goals can be achieved: one cannot hold hostage that which one has already destroyed. Although it is hard to imagine many Soviet assets whose military acquisition would *compensate* the West for the loss of access to Persian Gulf oil, compensatory acquisition is, in principle, another possible goal, one distinct from punishment or hostage-taking for bargaining purposes.

Perhaps the most intuitively appealing goals for horizontal escalation would be to *inhibit or induce redeployments* of Soviet forces, thereby improving Western prospects for conventional defense in the original contingency. The appeal is natural enough: attacked at point A, one counters at point B in order (1) to fix (tie down) Soviet forces at point B, preventing their use as reinforcements at point A, or (2) to force the Soviets to shift forces from A to B.

In the context of European war, tying down Soviet forces has long been among the U.S. Navy's arguments for opening a second theater by initiating offensive fleet operations against Soviet naval bases in the Western Pacific.[16] And it is true that in a protracted conventional war between NATO and the Warsaw Pact, Soviet ground forces arrayed opposite China might be redeployed to the West as a third or fourth echelon of the Soviet European offensive. Opening up a second theater in the Pacific would allegedly tie down those Soviet forces, improving NATO's chances for conventional defense.

In fact, however, the Soviets' freedom to redeploy to Europe—or to the Persian Gulf—their divisions on the Sino-Soviet border would depend primarily on the posture of the Chinese army, not on that of the U.S. Navy. Admittedly, the Soviets might reinforce their Pacific fleet's air forces with air power normally deployed inland opposite China. But what real role could the corresponding Soviet ground forces play in either the Pacific sea battle or in defending Soviet naval shore facilities? A role significant enough to fix (tie down) more than forty ground divisions? That seems implausible.

Rather than inhibiting Soviet redeployments by fixing Soviet forces, geographical escalation could aim at *inducing* Soviet redeployments.

16. See, for example, CBO, *Navy Budget Issues for Fiscal Year 1980*, p. xviii; U.S. Department of the Navy, "Sea Plan 2000," pp. 15–16; and Peter Samuel, "State Dept., Navy Agree on Opening Pacific Front in Case of War in Europe," *New York City Tribune*, June 23, 1986.

The operational object would be to draw Soviet forces out of the original contingency, improving Western chances for success there. One open question in this regard is simply, when?

The transition, in peacetime, to a predominantly asymmetrical strategy for war would take years to effect. At the end of such a period, horizontal escalation might succeed in forcing Soviet wartime reallocations, but only if, during the transition period, some ceiling on Soviet military growth had been reached. Otherwise, what is to prevent the Soviets from anticipating the strategy by simply adding forces in each theater during the transition period? After all, when the Sino-Soviet split presented them with "a new theater" (that is, their Chinese frontier), the Soviets did not shift many forces. True to Russian form, they essentially built. And unless there is some limit to growth, it may be hard to force Soviet reallocations, at least among theaters in the Soviet Union.

To be sure, there may be military constraints in the Soviet future. But if there are, the Reagan administration has certainly not suggested them by its review of the Soviet military buildup and its projections of continuing growth as Soviet military investment comes to fruition.[17] In short, a reallocative goal for horizontal escalation seems to require a Soviet military growth ceiling, while the Defense Department's projections seem to deny the existence of any such limits.[18]

Target Selection Problems: Soviet Value, U.S. Diversion, and Vertical Escalation

Punishment (destructive retaliation), hostage-taking, compensatory acquisition, fixing Soviet forces, or inducing their redeployment—these may not be the only possible rationales for horizontal escalation. But whatever its operational goal, the compellent effectiveness of the hori-

17. Investment is stressed over spending in the Department of Defense's *Annual Report, Fiscal Year 1983*, pp. II-4 through II-7.

18. Some might argue that this criticism is not fair because it presents horizontal escalation as a strategy toward which the United States is building for the future when in fact, they would claim, horizontal escalation is only an interim strategy until the United States can build up greater conventional defenses in the Gulf. But if horizontal escalation is an interim measure with direct conventional defense the ultimate goal, why is the administration spending so much on carrier battle groups for counteroffensive capabilities far in the future and so much less on programs directly related to Gulf defense (for example, airlift and sealift) today?

zontal action will depend on the value placed by the *Soviets* on its target. The mere fact that a Soviet outpost is vulnerable does not make it valuable, as Secretary Weinberger recognizes: "If [the counteroffensive] is to offset the enemy's attack, it should be launched against territory or assets that are of an importance to him comparable to the ones he is attacking."[19]

In practice, however, it may be difficult to identify a "horizontal target" that is of sufficient value to the Soviets to compel the behavior sought, but at the same time is not of such great value as to stimulate rash and grossly disproportionate (such as nuclear) Soviet responses.

For example, it is an open question whether attacking Soviet fleets in their home waters would be the most efficient way to secure Western sea lines of communication.[20] But even if it otherwise were, such offensive naval operations could well run nuclear risks, and not simply because they would involve hitting the Soviet homeland. Beyond that, in conducting offensive operations against either the Soviet Northern or Pacific fleet, the U.S. Navy might sink Soviet strategic ballistic missile submarines (SSBNs). If American operations were to degrade, even inadvertently and by conventional means, the Soviets' strategic nuclear retaliatory capabilities, the Soviets might escalate. As Barry Posen has written, "a deliberate conventional campaign against Soviet SSBNs could be understood by the Soviets as the beginning of a damage-limiting strategic first-strike. Given the importance of nuclear weapons and nuclear war in Soviet doctrine, *even the appearance* of such a campaign could trigger dire consequences. American leaders may be surprised by the Soviet response, since they seem to believe that so long as nuclear weapons have not been *used* in destroying Soviet strategic forces, the prospect of Soviet escalation is not raised." In fact, that prospect might be raised very sharply.[21]

19. Department of Defense, *Annual Report, Fiscal Year 1983*, p. I-16.

20. See CBO, *Navy Budget Issues for Fiscal Year 1980;* CBO, *The U.S. Sea Control Mission;* and Joshua M. Epstein, *The 1987 Defense Budget*, pp. 41–45. Still among the most concise essays on the factors involved in evaluating offense, defense, and requirements in each case is Arnold M. Kuzmack, "Where Does the Navy Go from Here?" pp. 37–51.

21. Barry R. Posen, "Inadvertent Nuclear War?" pp. 28–54. Emphasis added. The U.S. Navy apparently intends to initiate conventional submarine operations against Soviet strategic ballistic missile submarines at the outset of a NATO–Warsaw Pact conventional war in Central Europe. For unequivocal statements that Soviet ballistic missile submarines would be targets, see Adm. James D. Watkins, "The Maritime

As for targets of too little value, were the Soviets to ultimately acquire control of oil fields in the Persian Gulf, they could certainly afford to buy a new merchant fleet[22] had theirs been swept from the seas in bristling riposte to Gulf aggression. Even Cuba may not be of an importance to the Soviets comparable to the Gulf. Suppose that the Soviets were offered a straight trade: they "give up" Cuba and in return they get Iran's (or Saudi Arabia's) oil. Would Moscow turn it down? What assurance is there that, behind the compulsory fulminations, the Kremlin would not be willing to let Cuba take a "horizontal beating" if it meant Soviet control of Gulf oil? And if the Soviets would accept that trade, how offsetting would horizontal escalation against Cuba be in fact?

Not only may administration strategists have exaggerated Cuba's value to Moscow, but horizontal escalation against Cuba was reportedly envisioned "if Moscow *or its surrogates* move into the Persian Gulf."[23] Are the Iraqis surrogates of the Soviets, and does that mean they have no goals of their own? Would the threat of American retaliation against Cuba (or any other country for that matter) deter them? Would it deter communist elements in Iran, or the Syrians? Even if Moscow wished to bridle any of its surrogates lest the United States respond against "Cuba, Libya, Vietnam, or the . . . Soviet Union itself,"[24] could they do it?

The main point, however, is that even with clear goals for horizontal escalation in mind, the selection of an appropriate target requires knowledge of the Kremlin's valuations. An uncertain affair in peacetime, the problem would be compounded in war when, among other things, values change.[25]

In addition to the problem of Soviet valuation, there is the problem of diverting U.S. resources from an initial contingency to a horizontal one. Although contingency-counting was rejected by the administration, horizontal escalation nonetheless ensures that the United States confronts two contingencies (main plus horizontal) where it might have faced only one (main). And even assuming that a horizontal target of the proper *Soviet* value could be identified, the appropriate action against

Strategy," pp. 9–12. For earlier press reports of this navy objective, see Melissa Healy, "Lehman: We'll Sink Their Subs," p. 18, and "War Game Sends Subs Surging," p. 15.

22. Komer, "Maritime Strategy vs. Coalition Defense," p. 1131.

23. Wilson, "U.S. May Hit Soviet Outposts." Emphasis added.

24. See note 6.

25. This and many other problems of conflict termination are discussed in Fred Charles Iklé, *Every War Must End.*

that target might require a significant commitment of American forces, over and above those allocated to direct defense in the initial contingency.

The obvious question, therefore, is whether the United States would have to divert to horizontal counteroffensives forces that might otherwise have been applied initially or as reinforcements to the main defense, reducing its prospects for success. If so, would not the strategy make it more likely that the United States find itself under pressure either to concede defeat in the main contingency, or to use nuclear weapons there?

On the horizontal front, it should be noted that unless these counteroffensives are to be initiated preemptively (that is, *before* the "provoking" Soviet attack, an option Secretary Weinberger has explicitly rejected),[26] they will probably not achieve tactical surprise, or at least it would be imprudent to design forces on that assumption. And on the prudent assumption that surprise would not be achieved, the horizontal target might enjoy a number of classic warning advantages such as prepared defenses, cover, dispersal, and so forth. These could well exacerbate the diversion problem and, with it, the unpleasant problems of choice between capitulation and vertical (that is, nuclear) escalation. Indeed, in the worst of both worlds, the United States would divert so much force from the Gulf as to come under enormous pressure to use nuclear weapons there, while applying the large resultant counteroffensive force in such a way as to put the Soviets under equal pressure to use nuclear weapons on the horizontal front.[27]

Doubtless such considerations played a role in the services' costing of the strategy: to avoid problems of diversion, one buys much larger forces.[28] But if—as the above-noted $750 billion estimate suggests—the forces necessary to hedge against the diversion problem are too expensive, retaining the strategy may be too risky.

Some argue just the reverse, that "because the development and acquisition of new weapons might be delayed, *more* emphasis would be placed on such flexible tactics as 'geographical escalation.' "[29] Admit-

---

26. Department of Defense, *Annual Report, Fiscal Year 1983*, pp. I-10, I-11.

27. Samuel P. Huntington's proposal for a prompt conventional counteroffensive into Eastern Europe seems to invite this dangerous situation. See Samuel P. Huntington, "The Renewal of Strategy," pp. 1–52.

28. This is just the flip side of the Soviet solution to the problem of confronting a new theater discussed above. To avoid dangerous diversions (in the Soviet case, forced; in the U.S. case, self-imposed), build.

29. Richard Halloran, "Reagan Aides See Pressures to Cut 1984 Military Budget," *New York Times*, July 13, 1982. Emphasis added.

tedly, geographical escalation conjures up attractive images of "regaining the initiative," "turning the tables," and "making the Russians play by our rules." But this ought to suggest a further problem; namely, what if the Russians *do* decide to "play by our rules" and proceed to escalate "counterhorizontally" themselves?

The Risk of Counterhorizontal Escalation

Although the possibility was recognized by some Westerners at the time,[30] Nikita Khrushchev did not choose to play "the Berlin card" in the Cuban missile crisis of 1962. Faced with an American war-widening move against Cuba, his successors might behave rather differently. One might imagine the following scenario: the Soviets invade Iran (initial contingency); American forces attack Cuba or the Soviet brigade there (horizontal escalation); the Soviets attack West Berlin or the U.S. brigade there (counterhorizontal escalation). Then what? The United States would have gotten the Soviets to "play by America's rules." But it is far from clear that the United States would be better off as a result. Is Cuba more valuable to the Soviets than West Berlin is to the Federal Republic? Would European leaderships dutifully fall in behind further American initiatives at this point?

Even assuming that the Soviets could attack the American Berlin brigade "surgically," without killing West German citizens (the legal status of all West Berliners), would the United States allow its forces to be decimated without further response? If West Berlin had been sealed off, then at some point the brigade's survival might require airlift. Would the Soviets allow another Berlin airlift, or would they shoot down Western transports this time? Perhaps the airlift would "fight its way in," suppressing East German air defenses at a time of great tension and high military alert.

Whether or not one finds this particular scenario to be plausible, the point is that forcing the Soviets to play by these U.S. rules may not be in America's interest; move and countermove might quickly bring both

30. In a meeting with President Kennedy during the Cuban missile crisis, Secretary of State Dean Rusk explicitly noted a *New York Times* story reporting that "high Soviet officials were saying, 'we'll trade Cuba for Berlin.' " Excerpts from transcripts of an audiotaped off-the-record meeting on Cuba, October 16, 1962, 11:50 A.M.–12:57 P.M., in Marc Trachtenberg, ed., "Documentation: White House Tapes and Minutes of the Cuban Missile Crisis," p. 172. See also Herman Kahn, *On Escalation*, pp. 86–87.

sides to unforeseen and very unstable situations. And reversing the spiral might be exceedingly difficult.

To provoke—not to say invite—the Soviets to escalate counterhorizontally against countries neutral to the conflict, or to do so oneself, also raises ethical issues. As on so many other topics, Thomas Jefferson had something valuable to say on this moral-strategic question: "War between two nations cannot diminish the rights of the rest of the world remaining at peace. The doctrine that the rights of nations remaining quietly in the exercise of moral and social duties, are to give way to the convenience of those who prefer plundering and murdering one another, is a monstrous doctrine; and ought to yield to the more rational law, that 'the wrong which two nations endeavor to inflict on each other, must not infringe on the rights or conveniences of those remaining at peace.' " As Jefferson put it, "shall two nations turning tigers, break up in one instant the peaceable relations of the whole world? Reason and nature clearly pronounce that the neutral is to go on in the enjoyment of all its rights."[31] Practical considerations may reinforce his eighteenth-century appeal to reason and natural order. In particular, a callous disregard for the fate of neutrals may subvert the devotion of allies, perhaps undermining one's central coalitions (for example, NATO) to the great detriment of one's security.

Diplomatic Costs and Military Premises

Not only crisis management but peacetime diplomacy as well may be compromised by a policy of horizontal escalation. The Soviets, Secretary Weinberger states, "can coerce by threatening—implicitly or explicitly—to apply military force."[32] But might not a strategy of horizontal escalation, *predicated on the assumption that direct defense is infeasible,* facilitate that coercion? That is, in the Persian Gulf, one can only render Soviet threats *more* credible, their local audiences *more* compliant, by suggesting that direct conventional defense is unmanageable, "given the Soviets' inherent geographical advantages in the Persian Gulf region and their superior number of available ground forces."[33]

This, moreover, is a simplistic and misleading characterization of the

31. Thomas Jefferson, *The Living Thoughts of Thomas Jefferson*, pp. 156–57.
32. Department of Defense, *Annual Report, Fiscal Year 1983*, p. I-10.
33. Wilson, "U.S. May Hit Soviet Outposts."

Soviet-American conventional balance in the region. Geographical proximity does not per se constitute Soviet military access, and static prewar "bean-counting" cannot reflect dynamic wartime effectiveness. The latter always depends on operational factors such as terrain, available avenues of advance and their vulnerability, logistics, coordination, reconnaissance, flexibility, leadership, morale, combat technology, and troop skill. That fact is consistently bemoaned on the U.S. side, but is virtually neglected when assessing the Soviet threat. When such factors are accounted for on *both* sides, in a balanced and systematic way, the prevalent assessment proves to be overly pessimistic, a point argued at length in chapter 4.

Furthermore, while there are compelling reasons for the United States to avoid reliance on nuclear employment, the Soviets cannot ignore that possibility. And this, too, contributes to deterrence.

But does the attraction to horizontal escalation derive only from the assumptions, first, that conventional defense is utterly infeasible, and second, that Soviet nuclear developments have stripped the U.S. strategic triad of deterrent value? Perhaps. But it often seems as though the true motivations run deeper—as though the advocates, at bottom, have turned away from the entire concept of limited war.[34]

Winning

General Douglas MacArthur said that "in war, there is no substitute for victory." Neither, of course, is there any substitute for national survival. While at various points proponents of the strategy seem to have adopted MacArthur's heroic dictum without qualification, at other points they seem to be aware of the unheroic fact of nuclear life—"the difficulty that war invites the belligerents to regard the contest as mortal and to continue it until they are reduced to ruins."[35]

More than a decade ago, in an essay entitled "Peace through Escalation?" Fred Iklé—subsequently under secretary of defense for policy in

---

34. In Secretary of the Navy John Lehman's view, the rapid growth of Soviet naval power has "eliminated the option of planning for a regionally limited naval war with the Soviet Union. . . . It will be instantaneously a global naval conflict." Richard Halloran, "Administration Selling Increased Navy Budget as Heart of Military Strategy," *New York Times*, April 11, 1982.

35. William W. Kaufmann, "Limited Warfare," p. 112.

the Reagan administration and presumably an architect of the strategy—
put the enduring dilemma this way:

> If a nation can overwhelm all of the enemy's forces by escalating a war,
> the fighting will of course be brought to an end. . . . Short of inflicting such
> total defeat, successful escalation would have to induce the enemy
> government to accept the proffered peace terms. The trouble is, the greater
> the enemy's effort and costs in fighting a war, the more will he become
> committed to his own conditions for peace. Indeed, inflicting more damage
> on the enemy might cause him to stiffen his peace terms. . . . It is these
> opposed effects of escalation that make it so hard to plan for limited wars
> and to terminate them.[36]

In order, as Secretary Weinberger desires, to "prevent the uncon-
trolled spread of hostilities,"[37] it is critical that the Soviets never see an
advantage in opening new theaters or geographically widening a local
war themselves. In that sense, a strategy of limited war in fact does, and
always has, required "horizontal" capabilities; tacitly, it says "you will
not succeed at the initial point of attack, and we will not be drawn off by
attacks elsewhere; you must fight here, and you cannot win here, so
stop; indeed, don't start."

While multitheater capabilities sufficient to *deny* the Soviets a war-
widening strategy are thus essential to channel and limit conventional
conflict should deterrence fail, it is far from clear that an American policy
of *initiating* such expansions would foster military control or wartime
diplomacy. It might, but having reviewed the risks, another of Iklé's
observations is worth recalling: "It is hard to say whether treason or
adventurism has brought more nations to the graveyard of history. The
record is muddied, because when adventurists have destroyed a nation
they usually blamed 'traitors' for the calamity."[38]

Credibility

If a strategy is to deter aggression, that strategy must be credible. The
United States and its potential adversaries must believe at least two
things about it. First, both sides must believe that, if deterrence fails,
the United States will actually operate its forces in accord with the

36. Iklé, *Every War Must End*, pp. 41–42.
37. Department of Defense, *Annual Report, Fiscal Year 1983*, p. III-101.
38. Iklé, *Every War Must End*, p. 62.

strategy. Second, both must believe that such operations are likely to achieve American wartime goals.

Failure on the second count often results in failure on the first. For example, massive retaliation, America's first great experiment in asymmetrical response, ultimately failed on the second requirement. The American goal was to contain Soviet expansion at military costs acceptable to the United States. But the strategy suggested that the United States would run a high risk of unacceptable damage in response to even the most limited of Soviet encroachments. In the final analysis, not even America believed that it would operate its forces as its strategy prescribed. And so, by that fact, massive retaliation failed on the first count as well.[39] In chapter 2 it was argued that a tripwire–vertical escalation strategy would suffer the same flaw.

Horizontal escalation—the United States' most recent asymmetrical experiment—also fails to meet the basic requirements of credibility. It fails on the first count because it is not even clear what it would mean to operate American forces in accordance with the strategy: it is not clear what its targets would be or, more fundamentally, how one would go about determining them in wartime. Neither is it clear what military actions would be taken against the selected targets.

Horizontal escalation fails to meet the second requirement as well. It clearly runs daunting risks—of nuclear escalation and Soviet counterhorizontal attacks—but the goals of horizontal escalation remain cloudy, in both the broad strategic sense (ultimate victory versus limitation) and in the narrow operational sense (punishment, hostage-taking, and so forth).

"The threat that leaves something to chance," in Schelling's phrase, may be credible. But threats that leave everything to chance most assuredly are not.

With this argument, one arrives at the conclusion that *neither the tripwire–vertical escalation nor the horizontal escalation strategy is credible*. Underlying each was the assumption that a strategy of direct conventional defense was infeasible. Would such a strategy be feasible? What force size would be required if so? Chapter 4 addresses these questions.

---

39. The seminal critique is William W. Kaufmann's "The Requirements of Deterrence."

CHAPTER FOUR

Strategy III
Conventional Defense

THE PREVAILING view of American conventional deterrent capabilities is extremely pessimistic, as noted in chapter 1; there is a general consensus that the United States would stand little chance of directly thwarting an all-out invasion of Iran. For that reason strategies of vertical and horizontal escalation acquire appeal.

The conventional military balance, however, has not received the close examination it deserves. In divisions, the Soviets outnumber the forces available to the U.S. Central Command (CENTCOM), and the larger force is the closer to Iran; those are undeniable facts. But the conclusions drawn from them are unwarranted. If planned and postured according to the strategy proposed here, a rapid deployment force (RDF) considerably smaller than that envisioned by the Reagan administration can present an imposing conventional deterrent to Soviet aggression.[1]

1. In mid-1986 the combat forces available to CENTCOM included 6⅔ U.S. Army and Marine ground divisions plus special operations forces and air and naval units. (Figure derived from U.S. Department of Defense, *Annual Report to the Congress, Fiscal Year 1987*, p. 272; and "United States Central Command," CENTCOM public affairs document.) The planned total is 7⅓ divisions for fiscal 1989. (Figure derived from Barry M. Blechman and Edward N. Luttwak, eds., *International Security Yearbook 1983/84*, p. 153; see also U.S. Congressional Budget Office, *Rapid Deployment Forces*, pp. xv, 11–18.) Neither the Defense Department nor Blechman and Luttwak include the 6th Combat Brigade, Air Cavalry (CBAC), which is correctly included by CENTCOM itself. See "United States Central Command"; and Thomas L. McNaugher, *Arms and Oil*, p. 65. The inclusion of the 6th CBAC raises the Pentagon and Blechman values by a third of a division, yielding the current and planned figures of 6⅔ and 7⅓ divisions.

At various points in this study the term *rapid deployment force (RDF)* is used generically to denote any force designated for the Persian Gulf mission. The current (1986) and planned CENTCOM forces discussed above are RDFs. For purposes of analysis a *baseline RDF* of 4⅔ divisions is defined below (see table 4-1). An RDF of 5 divisions is finally proposed.

Contrary to the prevailing view, moreover, the constraint of simultaneous contingencies may weigh as heavily upon the Soviets as it does on the United States.

The essential features of the proposed strategy are the abandonment of forward defense and the exploitation of warning time. To begin, two issues must be addressed: the Soviet overland threat to Iran and the prospects for Soviet airlifted assaults. Each must be appreciated if Soviet tactics combining them are to be assessed.

The Soviet Overland Threat and Proposed U.S. Response

As a consequence of the terrain (see figure 4-1), a Soviet overland invasion of Iran may be divided into three successive phases.

—Phase I. The advance through northern Iran, over the mountains south to the Tehran line. One might postulate the seizure of Qazvin or Tehran or both as phase I goals. These might then be seen as the main bases of operation for:

—Phase II. The advance south through central Iran for a buildup at Dezful (or some other appropriate area at the southern base of the Zagros Mountains).

—Phase III. The final thrust south to drive the American RDF out of Khuzestan, securing Soviet control of Iran's principal oil and shipping facilities.

This plan closely resembles that set forth in the 1941 *Soviet Command Study of Iran*.[2] There the Soviet General Staff wrote:

> After the capture of Tehran and [Q]azvin, an advance in a straight line on to Hamadan and on to the Persian Gulf (and Iraq) along the Southern leg of the Transiranian Railroad will be possible. Here is where the entire supply of weapons and munitions for Iran [read the RDF] will probably be concentrated. This line leads most directly to the center of Iran's oil industry.[3]

The U.S. objective, given this not-entirely-hypothetical Soviet plan, is to delay and wear down the Soviets' southern advance in such a way that an adequate counterpose can be inserted for the battle of Khuzestan.

2. Gerold Guensberg, trans., *Soviet Command Study of Iran (Moscow 1941)*.
3. Ibid., p. 160.

Figure 4-1. *Iran*

Accordingly, the RDF strategy proposed here falls into three phases corresponding to those of the threat itself.

—Phase I. Delay the Soviet advance into northern Iran while constructing a defense perimeter in Khuzestan.

—Phase II. Delay and wear down the Soviet advance over the Zagros Mountains while building up for the ground war in Khuzestan.

—Phase III. Battle of Khuzestan: engage Soviet forces in a combined-arms conflict including ground, air, and naval units.

Each of these phases will be examined in turn. As will become evident, the defensive plan exploits many of the vulnerabilities stressed in the Soviets' own *Command Study*, and recognized in the once top secret postwar plans of the U.S. and British Chiefs of Staff.

Phase I: Delaying Action in the North

There are three axes from the Soviet Union into Iran by land: from the Caspian Sea directly, and across the Soviet borders to the east and west of the Caspian. All three axes suffer a number of common problems.

Soviet Vulnerabilities

First, the transportation system along each axis is very limited: altogether there are only about a dozen surface arteries from the Soviet Union to Tehran.[4] Second, each artery (rail or road) must pass over formidable mountain ranges, notably the Qareh Dagh in the northwest, the Elburz south of the Caspian Sea, and the Golul Dagh in the northeast. Third, each artery is punctuated by so-called choke points. These are points at which (a) destruction or blockage of the artery is feasible; (b) bypassing a blockage or obstacle is not feasible; and (c) clearing a blockage or otherwise restoring the route is time-consuming.

The Soviets were, and doubtless are, well aware of these vulnerabilities and especially, as the *Command Study* emphasized, of each route's vulnerability to air interdiction. As for the axis east of the Caspian Sea, consider their commentary on the road (of which there remains essentially one) from Ashkhabad, in the USSR, to Mashhad, in northeast Iran. In reference to the Dash Arasy gorge, through which that road must pass, the Soviets wrote: "At kilometer-25 the gorge narrows at some places down to 3 or 4 m. The walls of rock on both sides reach heights

---

4. This and all subsequent statements concerning the number, length, or condition of surface arteries in the various sectors of Iran are derived primarily from Sahab Geographic and Drafting Institute, "Road Map of Iran." A careful attempt has been made to compare the Soviets' 1941 discussion with the current transportation system. The match remains very close in the sectors of interest. While certain arteries have doubtless been upgraded for commercial use, this need not entail any reduction in vulnerability to military attack. Lightweight construction materials, for example, may be efficient from the point of view of economic growth, while representing no enhancement in hardness or reduction in susceptibility to structural attacks. Moreover, even where arteries have been upgraded in the latter respect since 1941, so have conventional munitions grown in effectiveness. In the view of experts, the net effect of these developments has not been to reduce the vulnerability of the Iranian transportation system significantly. Indeed, some feel that it is more vulnerable (to contemporary ordnance) than it was in 1941.

of 200 and 300 m. The gorge can be easily destroyed which would seriously impede traffic.'' In general, the Soviets stressed that "the road—along its entire stretch—is easily attackable from the air. Mountain sides and the narrow width of the plain (15–20 km) provide cover and allow divebomber attacks with ease."[5]

In each of the successive mountain chains of the Khorassan region in northeast Iran, the Soviets enumerated "narrow gorges which can be easily blocked."[6] Roads remain scarce and vulnerable, as they were in 1941. For these reasons, it is difficult not to concur in the Soviets' own view that the mountain range of the northeast "constitutes a mighty frontier protection which makes very difficult an invasion from the north into the Khorassan interior."[7]

Looking westward, to the Caspian Sea axis, the Soviets wrote of the Elburz Mountains that "they simplify considerably the defense of the important central areas of Iran against an enemy who has landed along the southern shores of the Caspian Sea."[8] Why? Because, of the roughly five roads over the Elburz to Tehran or Qazvin, all must cross bridges over precipitous faults thousands of meters in the mountains, or pass through narrow gorges. For example, from the coastal city of Now Shahr, southeast of the main port of Bandar-e Anzali, the meticulous Soviet planners noted that "the more deeply the path penetrates the gorge (up to kilometer-20) the more difficult becomes the traffic. A dynamiting of the rocks or the destruction of the road or the bridges would greatly slow down the movement of troops. . . . By-passing the road in the event of destruction is nearly impossible. The traffic can only be resumed after the road has been repaired."[9] So concerned were the Soviets that the few available arteries would be closed off, that they took an inventory of all draught animals (horses, donkeys, mules, and camels) in each of twenty-three Iranian regions, anticipating that air interdiction might force them to advance over the pack animal tracks that lace this craggy terrain.[10] The Soviet planner cannot but be haunted by Clausewitz's description of mountain warfare:

5. Guensberg, trans., *Soviet Command Study*, pp. 218–19, 220.
6. Ibid., p. 220.
7. Ibid., pp. 20–21.
8. Ibid., p. 164.
9. Ibid., p. 176.
10. Their totals were 329,530 horses, 1,126,345 donkeys, 44,415 mules, and 236,000 camels. Ibid., p. 100.

A column toils at snail's pace up a mountain through narrow gorges; gunners and teamsters yell and swear as they flog their weary beasts along the rocky tracks; each broken-down wagon has to be removed at the cost of indescribable effort while behind it the rest of the column stops, grumbles, and curses. At such a moment, each man secretly thinks that in this situation a few hundred of the enemy would suffice to cause a total rout. Here one can see the origin of the expression used by historians who speak of a gorge so narrow that a handful of men could hold off an army.[11]

There is one railroad from the Caspian to Tehran, the trans-Iranian railroad. It is the only railroad from Tehran south to Dezful (a buildup area for Soviet phase III combat in Khuzestan). It traverses the rugged terrain described above, first in the Elburz Mountains and again south in the Zagros Mountains. Of its passage over the Elburz, the Soviets wrote that the line "can be easily attacked from the air." Even in the lowlands near Tehran, they cautioned that "the entire section is observable from the air and it can be easily attacked."[12]

On another continent five years later, American planners independently made a top secret estimate of the same section of the trans-Iranian railroad. As though by telepathy, their assessments matched the Soviets'. Of its passage from the Caspian Sea over the Elburz Mountains to Tehran, the U.S. Joint Intelligence Staff stated: "This is the only Iranian railroad reaching the Caspian Sea. It is standard gauge. The line is extremely susceptible to sabotage, since at one point, in a horizontal distance of 22 miles, there are 69 tunnels totaling nearly 12 miles in length. In order to eliminate gradients, 11 spiral tunnels have been driven in one short distance. The bridges are also extremely vulnerable, one of them consisting of a single span of 181 feet."[13] Expanding on this intelligence staff estimate, the U.S. Joint War Plans Committee, in then top secret studies later that year, noted that "additional tunnels, bridges, [and] badly disintegrated rock along much of the mountainside and the fact that the whole region is subject to heavy rainfall and severe earthquakes make this line extremely vulnerable." The committee also pointed out that it would "be necessary to transship wherever the Iranian

11. Carl von Clausewitz, *On War*, p. 417.
12. Guensberg, trans., *Soviet Command Study*, p. 201.
13. U.S. Joint Intelligence Staff, "Overland Lines of Communication," appendix A to "Service Members, Joint Intelligence Staff: Intelligence Estimate of Specific Areas in Southern Europe, the Middle and Near East, and Northern Africa (Overland Lines of Communication)," October 24, 1946, p. 87.

standard gauge joins the Soviet gauge'' (a Soviet bottleneck enforced, ironically, by Stalin to impede Nazi invasion of Russia from the south during World War II).[14]

Finally, in the northwest, in the Iranian Azerbaijan provinces, the same vulnerabilities prevail. There is a single road from Jolfa (just across the Soviet border in Iran) to the first main city, Tabriz. Of that crucial artery, the detailed *Soviet Command Study* records: "At kilometer-22 from Dzhulfa [Jolfa] begins the Daradis gorge which is 7 km long. The advance of troops through this small and narrow pass can be most difficult. The movement of troops can be made even more difficult if the enemy employs roadblocks or attacks from the air."[15]

As if stalking the Soviet surveyors, the U.S. Joint War Plans Committee again echoed their Russian counterparts: "The road net leading south from Dzhulfa at the Soviet frontier is limited by the capacity of the road through the Ruwandiz Gorge. This road . . . passes through a very narrow gorge and over a number of steel bridges. It . . . could be sabotaged at the bridges and at points where the road is cut through overhanging rocks."[16] Again, bypass is virtually impossible. The shoulders of the gorge are walls of boulder. Detonations creating rockslides would severely hamper troop movement and could be cleared only with extensive military engineering efforts.

In summary, the once top secret assessment of the Joint War Plans Committee still applies to the first phase of the Soviet overland threat to Iran: "In the case of the three-pronged drive south from the Caucasus-Caspian . . . the roads and railroads within this area are extremely vulnerable."[17] Indeed, the entire series of then top secret Joint Chiefs of Staff planning documents concerned with global war in the late 1950s assert that "Soviet operations in the mountainous and desert areas of the Near and Middle East would be tremendously complicated because of the inadequacy of suitable railroads, roads, the shortages of truck transportation and the extreme vulnerability of the numerous bridges and tunnels through the area." Specifically, in Iran "avenues of invasion

14. U.S. Joint War Plans Committee, "Overland Lines of Communication," annex D to appendix to "Joint War Plans Committee Strategic Study of the Area between the Alps and the Himalayas, Short Title 'Caldron,' " November 2, 1946, p. 86.

15. Guensberg, trans., *Soviet Command Study*, p. 127.

16. Joint War Plans Committee, "Overland Lines of Communication," November 2, 1946, p. 87.

17. Ibid., p. 122.

. . . are tenuous and incapable of supporting sizeable military forces, particularly if subjected to interdiction."[18]

The first phase of the defensive plan proposed here is to delay the advance of Soviet units by choking off this transportation system. This mission could be accomplished with nuclear weapons or with conventional forces.

As noted in chapter 2, "ADM [atomic demolition munitions] alone could quickly seal all avenues of approach into Iran."[19] It is far from clear, however, that nuclear employment is necessary, despite claims to the contrary. Those claims generally fail to draw a critical distinction. They begin by noting that the American rapid deployment force is, among other things, designed to *protect* the West's "oil lifeline"; this is located in *southern* Iran. In the same breath, however, recourse to nuclear weapons is deemed necessary, for lack of other means, to *blunt* a Soviet violation of *northern* Iran.[20] The prevailing assumption that the use of nuclear weapons is necessary therefore rests critically upon the premise that a forward defense of the northern Iranian border is required to prevent Soviet control of Khuzestan's oil riches. But why should it be? The oil lies roughly a thousand kilometers and two formidable mountain chains south of the "inviolable" border.

If, by a series of conventional delaying operations, enough time can be bought to permit the emplacement of an adequate American defense

18. U.S. Joint Chiefs of Staff, "Decision on J.C.S. 1920/1, Long-Range Plans for War with the USSR—Development of a Joint Outline Plan for Use in the Event of War in 1957," May 6, 1949, pp. 112, 162. For virtually identical language, see the formerly top secret U.S. Joint Logistics Plans Committee, "Directive—Comments on Logistical Aspects of Dropshot," October 19, 1948, p. 73.

19. Capt. Henry Leonard and Jeffrey Scott, "Methodology for Estimating Movement Rates of Ground Forces in Mountainous Terrain with and without Defensive Obstacles," p. 3.8.

20. For example, the *New York Times* related that "a Defense Department report on the military situation in the Persian Gulf region has concluded that American forces could not stop a Soviet thrust into northern Iran and that the United States should therefore consider using 'tactical' nuclear weapons in any conflict there." Richard Burt, "Study Says a Soviet Move in Iran Might Require U.S. Atom Arms," *New York Times*, February 2, 1980; the Pentagon study referred to was the Wolfowitz Report, discussed in chapter 2. The *Washington Post* similarly reported that "President Carter established the far-flung, multiservice Rapid Deployment Force to protect our oil lifeline. Yet top military hands warn that it . . . could never be a match for the Soviet juggernaut across the Iranian border." Jack Anderson, "Frightening Facts on the Persian Gulf," *Washington Post*, February 3, 1981. Whether the current or planned RDF could in fact prevent a Soviet violation of the Soviet-Iranian border is a question outside the scope of this book, as noted in the Introduction.

force there, Soviet control of Khuzestan could be denied. In the final analysis, the RDF's problem is time. To be sure, nuclear weapons would buy more time, and more quickly, for a Western buildup in the south than would conventional munitions. But if enough time can be bought conventionally, that, for a host of reasons, is surely the approach to be preferred. And it *is* a feasible approach. The first step is to delay the Soviets' advance through northern Iran.

To do this the forces initially available to CENTCOM at present are impressive and include more than 6⅔ U.S. Army and Marine divisions; 10 U.S. Air Force, Marine, and carrier-based Navy tactical air wings; 2 squadrons of strategic bombers configured for conventional bombing; 3 carrier battle groups and 1 surface action group; 3,500 unconventional warfare and special operations forces; and various reconnaissance and command and control elements.[21]

While the regional basing currently available to CENTCOM may be inadequate to accommodate so large an air arm, that fact does not warrant fatalism about this first delay phase. Its limited goal, recall, is to bound the Soviets' rate of advance sufficiently to ensure enough time for the United States to mount an adequate combined-arms defense in Khuzestan. As will become evident, if the interdiction campaign were to ensure a month in transit from the Soviets' bases to the point at which the second delay phase is conducted (in the Zagros), that should be adequate (as always, on the assumption that warning time is exploited).

The on-road distances involved are all on the order of 1,000 kilometers at least. To ask that the RDF's phase I delaying operation yield a month in transit is therefore merely to require that it limit the Soviets' overall (repair plus movement) rate to no more than roughly 33⅓ kilometers a day. But that would be a remarkable pace by historical standards. It would exceed that achieved by Hitler's armies in their blitz of Flanders in 1940 (31 kilometers a day) and in Operation Barbarossa the following year (29 kilometers a day). The Normandy Breakout of 1944 saw a rate of 28 kilometers a day, while 13 kilometers a day was logged by the North Koreans in their offensive of 1950. The Israelis' victories on the West Bank and the Golan Heights in 1967 were achieved under advance rates of 27 and 18 kilometers a day respectively.[22] Notwithstanding the

21. For the 6⅔-ground-division figure, see note 1. For the other forces, see McNaugher, *Arms and Oil*, p. 55; and Department of Defense, *Annual Report to the Congress, Fiscal Year 1987*, p. 272. The figure for special operations forces is from "United States Central Command."

22. Col. T. N. Dupuy, *Numbers, Predictions and War*, p. 16.

myriad differences between each of these campaigns and the Soviet advance as posited here, 33⅓ kilometers a day is a spirited clip. And in none of these historical cases was the cited rate sustained over so great a distance as that facing a Soviet "drive for oil."

In short, the Soviets would be operating in truly forbidding terrain, over northern Iran's limited and vulnerable transportation system—a system so constricted that at its narrowest points, the mere disabling of lead elements would bring whole columns to a standstill; it is a network dotted with severe choke points. Under such conditions, to hold the Soviets down to one of the highest advance rates in history must be seen as a modest goal. And although more ambitious goals may fall within its grasp should the RDF's regional basing expand, current resources should be capable of holding a Soviet advance to that rate or lower. Indeed, an array of options presents itself. In their own formerly top secret analysis, U.S. war planners noted as possibilities "sabotage by raiding parties," "demolitions by retreating Allied forces," and "damage by Allied air action."[23]

As stressed in chapter 3, it is folly to purchase conventional forces in the hope of avoiding nuclear war and then to apply conventional force in ways that are likely to precipitate nuclear war; sensitivity to problems of escalation control must be made a central feature of conventional operations planning. The question of how to conduct this northern interdiction operation offers an interesting perspective.

While seeking to avoid unnecessary risks of escalation by one's adversary, it is equally important to avoid imposing escalatory pressures upon oneself. Casualties are, of course, to be minimized on humane grounds. But they should be minimized for this less immediate reason as well. As one's casualties mount, so may the pressure to prosecute the war to an extent or in a manner not called for by its original, limited, objectives. That is, if the human "sunk costs" quickly come to outstrip the original objectives, since the former cannot be reclaimed, the latter may be raised to ensure that death was not in vain. Ill-considered expansions of war goals and an ever-increasing commitment of troops may follow.

Although the risk of Soviet escalation is clearly associated with a nuclear defense, these considerations counsel against use of airlifted ground troops and in favor of air power as the conventional instrument in phase I. First, transport of airborne (dropped) troops into the northern

23. Joint War Plans Committee, "Overland Lines of Communication," November 2, 1946, p. 122.

mountains of Iran would be quite vulnerable to Soviet-based fighters. Moreover, whereas in the south the Soviets would have serious trouble sustaining large ground forces, in the north, close to their border, they would not. Third, even assuming that a sufficiently large contingent of U.S. troops could be securely delivered, are they to be recovered or left to fend for themselves? To pick them up would require the use of vulnerable aircraft; to resupply them for a sustained defense would be equally demanding. To lose them or the forces engaged in either their recovery or resupply could be self-escalatory.[24] For these reasons the use of conventional tactical air forces is indicated.

The preferred solution would be to operate tactical fighter-bombers from airbases in eastern Turkey. Given such access (and adequate stockages, support infrastructure, ground support, and so forth) the RDF's two wings of F-111s could create four to six serious choke points (each assumed to result from the accurate delivery of six appropriately tailored air-to-ground munitions) on each of the major surface arteries (rail and road) from the USSR south to Tehran, in one day of high-intensity flying. This target system is fully elaborated, and the interdiction calculation performed, in appendix A. As is also demonstrated there, the less stringent is one's demand for time urgency, the less demanding the interdiction operation becomes. And there is no compelling military reason, if the United States exploits warning time, either to strike every lucrative choke point in a single day or to conduct the operation solely with tactical air. In one of the more innovative moves of recent years, twenty-eight B-52Hs (in North Dakota) "have been organized into a quick-response outfit called the Strategic Projection Force, or Spif." Designed specifically for conventional bombing operations in the Gulf region, Spif's "war plans call for the eight-engined bombers to strike at night at low level."[25]

Although feasible from the continental United States, such conventional B-52 operations could also be staged from bases in Guam, Australia, Clark Field in the Philippines, and elsewhere. Diego Garcia is

---

24. The classic method of dealing with the vulnerability of air-dropped forces would be to press an advance north, expanding one's perimeter until the airborne forces were within it. Aside from being totally inconsistent with all of America's expressed aims in Iran, this tactic—essentially an occupation—would subject the United States to the same geographic vulnerabilities upon whose exploitation its strategy should be based.

25. George C. Wilson, " 'Anytime Anywhere': A New Conventional Role for B52 Bombers," *Washington Post*, March 31, 1981.

presumably capable of accommodating the B-52s.[26] It can be hoped, as former SAC Commander General Richard H. Ellis has noted, that "sending B-52s to the trouble spot in the first hours of a crisis might be enough to freeze the Soviet military. Bombs might not have to be dropped at all, as long as the will and ability to do so were demonstrated."[27]

If deterrence fails, however, the RDF could initially create the northernmost tier of choke points, working south only as reconnaissance dictates, relying primarily on the bombers, and phasing in air from the Khuzestan perimeter as it becomes available. This "tiered interdiction" could effectively deny Soviet engineering units any opportunity to restore routes before their main columns arrive. Aircraft from the two carriers on station in the region could, from the Gulf of Oman, be used to provide escort for the bombers or, if they were aerially refueled, to conduct a portion of the interdiction operation. The carriers' classic mission, however, would be to provide tactical air cover (power projection) for the Marine beachhead in Khuzestan, cover that could be augmented by offshore support (if necessary) from smaller surface combatants inside the Persian Gulf. As the Marine perimeter expands and establishes its air defense, the carriers can be withdrawn while, from within the perimeter, U.S. Air Force or Marine aircraft take over the continuing air interdiction campaign from the bombers. The latter could then be withheld as an intrawar deterrent or could strike targets in central Iran, Afghanistan, or elsewhere. With the establishment of a perimeter air defense, carrier air, arrayed from the Gulf of Oman to the Arabian Sea, could be flexibly employed in a variety of ways, including fleet defense, power projection, and sea-line-of-communication (SLOC) protection. With warning, the RDF's third carrier could supplement aerial refueling and air defense of the two on-station carriers, used in any of the above capacities.

This particular scheme is not the only one possible. The range of tactical combinations and employment schedules is wide. It is one of many alternatives to carrier operations, however brief, inside the Persian Gulf. Although further regional basing—particularly Turkish, Israeli,

---

26. I conclude this because all the military construction funding that was requested for Diego Garcia has been appropriated; no further request has been made. Any upgrading for purposes of accommodating B-52s would, presumably, have been funded under these military construction appropriations.

27. Wilson, " 'Anytime Anywhere.' "

Omani, or Saudi—would simplify it, the RDF's northern interdiction campaign is feasible and, while limited in scope, it would form an effective spearhead to an imposing deterrent posture.

Phase II: Delay and Attrition in the Zagros Mountains

Phase II of the proposed RDF strategy is conducted in the Zagros Mountains from within the southern perimeter by highly mobile special forces. The tactics are similar to those used by the Finns in the Soviet-Finnish Winter War, in which ambush and hit-and-run tactics figured prominently. Termed *motti* tactics, their employment by the vastly outnumbered defenders thoroughly frustrated the Soviets' continuing attempts to penetrate the waist of Finland.

The Soviets' overland passage through the Zagros would be as difficult as in the north; there are again few arteries. In every case, choke points abound, and they may be selected to maximize defensive opportunity. Of the countless gorges through the parallel chains which are the Zagros, the Soviets wrote, "with the use of obstacles or roadblocks these can be turned into excellent defensive positions."[28]

The same promising defensive approach was recognized by American and British planners preparing for a potential Soviet military attack on Iran as one of several "possible Soviet moves in the light of the Korean situation." In combined U.S.-U.K. planning pursuant to National Security Council document NSC 73/4 (adopted August 25, 1950),[29] the British acquired principal responsibility "for the planning of the destruction of critical road and rail lines of communication in Iran, including the Trans-Iranian railroad and neutralization of Iranian oil installations."[30] Shortly thereafter, on October 2, 1950, the British Chiefs of Staff forwarded to their American counterparts a report setting forth the British plan of operations in detail. From formerly top secret JCS studies

28. Guensberg, trans., *Soviet Command Study*, p. 190.
29. U.S. National Security Council, "NSC 73/4: Note by the Executive Secretary to the National Security Council on the Position and Actions of the United States with Respect to Possible Further Soviet Moves in the Light of the Korean Situation," August 25, 1950, pp. 375–89. The section on the division of labor between the United States and United Kingdom "in the event of overt attack by organized USSR military forces against . . . Iran" is on pp. 386–87.
30. U.S. Joint Strategic Plans Committee, "Brief of Joint Outline Emergency War Plan (Short Title: Offtackle)," May 26, 1949, p. 48.

and U.S.-U.K. correspondence a relatively clear operational scheme can be reconstructed.

"British forces will be deployed for screening operations along the Sulamania-Zagros Mountains. . . . Forces withdrawing in the face of Soviet pressure will impose the maximum delay upon the Soviet forces by executing planned demolitions."[31] U.S. planners stressed that "this task is one in which small forces in the Middle East prior to the arrival of Soviet forces could seriously reduce the Soviet capability to build up and develop the area. . . . The road and rail lines leading from the USSR through Iran . . . contain a great many bridges and tunnels. Destruction of the tunnels and bridges could seriously delay Soviet overland movement into the Middle East and could limit the size of build-up that could be made until all damage was repaired."[32] Hence U.S. top secret guidance sought quickly to complete "preparations of combined plans with the British for D-Day destruction of LOC's [lines of communication] from the U.S.S.R. to the Persian Gulf."[33] If successfully executed "the capability to maintain control of the area could be extended well into the second phase,"[34] which spanned the period D + 3 to D + 12 *months*.

Moreover, as formerly top secret U.S.-U.K. correspondence reveals, it was precisely this operational scheme that was to guide the postwar modernization of the Iranian armed forces. The formula adopted in all U.S.-U.K. military-to-military correspondence was that with appropriate equipment and adequate training in ground attack methods, the Iranian air force would "strengthen the ability of the ground force [in] carrying out delaying tactics."[35] The Iranian army's delaying tactics would rely heavily on demolitions of the sort discussed above. The British Chiefs of Staff suggested, in addition, that "a force to be stationed in the Hamadan area should be equipped with tanks in order to enable it to attack the flank of the Russian advance."[36]

Defensive tactics recognized as excellent by U.S., British, and Soviet

31. Ibid., pp. 46, 48.

32. Joint Strategic Plans Group, "Crankshaft," May 11, 1948, p. 104.

33. Joint Strategic Plans Group, "Proposed Guidance for an Alternative Plan to 'Bushwacker,' " March 8, 1948, p. 15.

34. Joint Strategic Plans Committee, "Brief of Joint Outline Emergency War Plan," May 26, 1949, p. 45.

35. For one of many such papers, approved by Generals Vandenberg and Bradley, see Maj. Gen. Ray T. Maddocks, "Memorandum for the Chief of Staff, U.S. Army: Joint U.S.-British Policy with Respect to Iran," July 13, 1948. Quotation is from p. 2.

36. Formerly top secret letter from Capt. R. D. Coleridge, "Assistance to Persia," July 8, 1948.

planners in the 1940s and 1950s look just as good today. The RDF would have two objectives in phase II: delay and attrition. Both can be made quite severe with surprising economy, as noted by Pentagon planners in 1979. As for attrition, the 1979 study previously cited estimating movement rates of ground forces in mountainous terrain concludes that

> the mission of light forces in the delay phase of the defense should be to inflict losses on the invader without becoming decisively engaged. Airmobile infantry forces employed in small-unit (company or even platoon) ambushes can seriously harass heavier enemy forces for very short periods without risking severe losses or entrapment. . . . Our forces could choose the time and place of the ambush, and enjoy, briefly, the advantage of surprise.[37]

Indeed, "gaming of a five-minute engagement between a U.S. light infantry company and the point of a Soviet mechanized column . . . indicates that the U.S. unit would incur minor losses while practically wiping out the opposing force."[38] Finally, and consistent with the Soviets' own observations:

> The use of a small expedient obstacle such as a point minefield would make the engagement even more lopsided, as it would provide the ambush force with stationary targets from the onset of the fighting. . . . Ideally, the ambush force would be positioned only a short time before the enemy column came into range. It would be withdrawn immediately after the ambush. Given adequate helicopter transportation and ammunition, a light infantry company could conduct three or four such ambushes per day for a period of time. . . . A battalion of 3 companies could impose practically constant attrition and harassment on enemy columns.[39]

It is difficult to say precisely how severe the attrition exacted by these measures would be. There seems little doubt, however, that they could significantly reduce the force that the RDF would face in Khuzestan, and the same campaign affords the United States still more time to expand its force there.

In addition to the delay imposed by the phase I air interdiction campaign, one can use the study's "planning guideline of two days' delay per engineer platoon day of effort" to gauge the extent of further delay imposed in phase II on Soviet troops in the Zagros.[40] Bearing in

---

37. Leonard and Scott, "Methodology for Estimating Movement Rates," p. 4.1.
38. Ibid.
39. Ibid., pp. 4.1, 4.3.
40. Ibid., p. 4.5. This planning factor is given in connection with Zagros operations specifically.

mind that a platoon is 1/81st of a division, the economies available are quickly evident.[41]

Only two roads pass over the Zagros directly onto Dezful. The trans-Iranian railroad is a third avenue, assuming (favorably to the Soviets) it has survived the air campaign in the north. The two additional roads that descend on Dezful from the city of Kermanshah in the west bring the total to roughly five arteries. From the above planning factor, it follows that a force of six platoons could, with two weeks of effort, close each of those approaches for thirty-four days.[42]

Despite these prospects for very lucrative operations by special demolition teams, some analysts advocate the deployment of two entire U.S. Army divisions and smaller Ranger units "along the northern rim of the Zagros Mountains"[43] out of concern for a limited Soviet attack to control northern Iran. First, it is not clear why the Russians would prefer (to the status quo) a partition in which the U.S. "gets" the oil-rich south and the Soviets "get" the north. But, even supposing they would, this proposal is problematic. The deployment of two divisions along the northern rim of the Zagros would do little, if anything, to prevent Soviet control from the Russian border south to Tehran, since Tehran is many miles north of the Zagros's northern rim. If, on the other hand, the goal is simply "to complicate a Soviet advance"[44] in the north, it has been shown that U.S. airpower (not to mention U.S. or Iranian special teams) alone can do that. A more serious objection is that if the United States deploys two of its available divisions north of the Zagros in the expectation of a limited Soviet operation, and then an all-out Soviet invasion for Khuzestan unfolds, the United States would be in much worse shape than if all American divisions had been withheld for the main defense in the south, and the earlier delaying and ambush operations had been left to special forces and tactical air.

The units deployed north would have been denied the benefits of a second barrier zone in which to wear down and delay the Soviet overland advance, namely, the Zagros passes and choke points. Also, U.S. forces

41. A standard U.S. division structure is three platoons per company; three companies per battalion; three battalions per brigade; and three brigades per division.

42. Needless to say, the planning factor is a linear approximation of a more complicated relationship. However, even if it overestimates the effectiveness of such tactics by a significant margin, the effort involved in imposing the same delay would remain modest. Some of the demolition responsibilities could also be assumed by tactical air.

43. McNaugher, *Arms and Oil*, p. 70.

44. Ibid.

lodged along the Zagros's northern rim would be within range of Soviet tactical fighter-bombers based in the USSR. In addition, this approach would increase logistical burdens on the U.S. forces (while relieving Soviet logistical burdens considerably): the Soviets could sustain far more forces north of the Zagros than in Khuzestan, whereas the United States could sustain far fewer. Moreover, the Iranian central plain north of the Zagros would afford the Soviets far better basing for close air support than the Zagros themselves would offer the United States (thus eroding for the units in question one of America's major advantages, close air). Perhaps more serious, withdrawal (retrograde) of sizable U.S. forces from engaged Soviet forces *in such terrain* would be extremely dangerous. Soviet mines or mortar launched into roads south of retreating U.S. ground troops would trap American combatants in "killing zones" between the choke points or mines to the south and advancing Russians to the north.

For force-planning purposes one cannot dismiss the threat of a Soviet drive for the south. In the event of such aggression, this north-of-the-Zagros approach—of doubtful benefit against the limited aggression it purports to address—is seriously flawed. It would sacrifice a number of significant defensive advantages, and exacerbate U.S. logistical— truck and intratheater lift—burdens considerably, all the while subjecting U.S. units to precisely those vulnerabilities that an imaginative defender would exploit, as the Soviets are very well aware. Small and stealthy special operations forces, conducting demolitions, ambush, and laser-designation for U.S. tactical fighter-bombers, are indicated north of the Zagros, *not* divisional units, much less entire divisions of any kind.

There is one other, deeper, reason to reject staging multidivisional engagements north of the Zagros; it was touched on above. The longer the United States defers a pitched ground battle involving large-scale casualties, the more time is available for a negotiated cessation of hostilities. Where *equally effective* conventional force options are available, the least-escalatory one should be chosen. Aside from being of questionable value (there are alternatives) against the limited Soviet attack it claims to address, the staging of multidivisional engagements north of the Zagros would violate this rule of thumb for escalation control.

Time is the name of the game in phases I and II. Under reasonable assumptions, the phase I air interdiction operation should ensure thirty days of mobilization and deployment time for the battle of Khuzestan.

Motti-like tactics by special forces in phase II should raise the Soviets' time in transit (movement plus repair time) to Dezful in northern Khuzestan by roughly another month. As far as the Soviet overland advance is concerned, then, sixty days does not seem overly optimistic as an estimate of the time the Soviets would require to emerge at the base of the Zagros. Is that all the time the RDF would have for mobilization and deployment for a final pitched battle in Khuzestan? It seems unlikely that it is. The RDF would have warning time as well. The question is, how much?

Soviet Readiness and U.S. Warning and Decision Time

The 1968 Soviet invasion of Czechoslovakia was preceded by a three-month buildup of which Western intelligence was aware. The invasion of Afghanistan was also preceded by three months of warning.[45]

Soviet divisions have three degrees of combat readiness: category 1, between three-quarters and full troop strength, with complete equipment; category 2, between half and three-quarters strength, complete with fighting vehicles; and category 3, cadre (some 20 percent) strength, possibly complete with older fighting vehicles (some obsolescent).[46] Of the divisions stationed in peacetime in the southern military districts of the Soviet Union (North Caucasus, Transcaucasus, and Turkestan), one or two are accounted as category 1, and two or three qualify as category 2. The rest are rated category 3 divisions.[47] To ready these forces for combat, the Soviets would have to call up manpower and train or refresh much of it. Petroleum, oil, lubricants, spares, water, ammunition, and other supplies would have to be marshaled and loaded. The shipment of combat equipment into the area would be required, while backlogged maintenance and, in some cases, final assembly of equipment would be performed. If the mobilization for Poland was any indication, a great many trucks would be impressed from diverse quarters.

All this activity takes time, and much of it would be visible to the West. Reports do indicate that following the invasion of Afghanistan the readiness of these forces increased somewhat.[48] However, all indica-

---

45. See Jiri Valenta, "From Prague to Kabul," pp. 114–41.
46. International Institute for Strategic Studies, *The Military Balance, 1985–1986*, pp. 22–23.
47. Ibid., p. 28.
48. William W. Kaufmann, "Defense Policy," p. 305.

tions are that category 3 levels predominate, while even category 1 would credit the Soviets with as little as 75 percent of their full wartime manpower.

The standard category ranking of forces is, moreover, a static indicator. The "readiness" of forces depends on the missions facing them. One should not think of forces as "ready," but as "ready *for*" something; something specific.

In Czechoslovakia, resistance was essentially passive, while in Afghanistan, though tenacious, it has lacked the sophisticated air force or the ground firepower that today's Soviet planner must anticipate in combat with U.S. forces in Iran. Thus even granting some increase in "static readiness" to the Soviet units of interest, one must assume that the Soviet planner recognizes the vast difference between the resistance of the Czechs and Afghans and that for which his forces must be ready in Iran. For all these reasons, it is perfectly plausible that warning time would stay in the neighborhood of the usual three months. But to be conservative this analysis will assume only one month of warning. The entire mobilization and deployment time available to the main ground force of the RDF would thus appear to be ninety days.

Warning time	1 month
Phase I delay (air interdiction in northern Iran)	1 month
Phase II delay (special forces in the Zagros)	1 month
Total mobilization and deployment time	3 months

It must be stressed that warning time, in this military sense, and decision time among political figures are radically different entities. A great deal can be done with warning time: it can be used to broadcast one's cognizance of developments, to enhance the credibility of one's deterrent commitments, and to ready one's forces.[49] The availability of warning time, however, does not ensure that it will be used. Among the most important peacetime goals for the United States is to ensure that it *is* used, through procedural agreements with U.S. intelligence services and forces, and through diplomatic understandings with countries in the region. Time bought with warning is cheaper than time bought with force. Indeed, if it is used to communicate one's military readiness and

49. For example, load cargo, fuel up for the lift, predeploy certain materiel, increase reconnaissance densities, move further Marine units into position, marshal allied commercial shipping, stand down and perform backlogged maintenance, and increase NATO alerts.

political determination to the enemy, warning time may, by deterrence, avoid the conflict. If war should come, however, the Soviets would have little basis for confidence.

Phase III: Battle of Khuzestan

There are three basic issues concerning the ground balance. First, in the time available for RDF mobilization and deployment—warning time plus time purchased by phases I and II—what is a conservative estimate of the U.S. buildup in Khuzestan? Second, how many divisions could the Soviets support south of the Zagros? And finally, what confidence could the Soviets have of defeating the deployed U.S. force in battle?

U.S. Buildup Estimates and Simultaneous-Contingency Problems

As to the first question, a range of estimates has appeared regarding the size of the RDF that could be brought to bear in sixty days. There is a well-founded consensus, however, that in addition to a Marine contingent of 1⅓ Marine amphibious forces (each a Marine division), 3⅓ U.S. Army divisions and their initial support increments could be deployed to Khuzestan in roughly that time.[50] Since ninety, rather than sixty, days of mobilization and deployment time would likely be available to all but the very spearhead of the force, the estimate of 4⅔ divisions may be unduly conservative. A force considerably larger than this might be brought to bear if more equipment and stocks were pre-positioned in or near the region, particularly if warning time were exploited in a pre-arranged commitment of allied commercial shipping to the RDF's sea line of communication.[51] This valuable allied contribution would be a clear signal of their involvement without being a commitment of allied troops to combat.

It is true that, at present, the figure of 4⅔ divisions assumes use of the full U.S. fleet of C-5 strategic transports, the only U.S. aircraft capable

50. This force is roughly equivalent to the baseline RDF defined below (see table 4-1). On deployability, see, for example, Sir John Hackett, "Protecting Oil Supplies," p. 14; and U.S. Congressional Budget Office, *U.S. Airlift Forces*, pp. 23, 55. Relevant force weights, airlift planning factors, and computational methods are provided in that study and in CBO, *U.S. Projection Forces*.

51. For a discussion of pre-positioning equipment in the CENTCOM area, see McNaugher, *Arms and Oil*, pp. 55–56, 66–69.

of lifting outsized cargo.[52] This commitment represents a compromise in the U.S. ability to reinforce other theaters simultaneously. Completion of CENTCOM's maritime pre-positioning programs and the scheduled deployment of fifty C-5Bs will relieve the constraint on lifting outsized cargo. These and the planned sealift program should by fiscal 1988 make possible the delivery of 5 U.S. Army and Marine divisions five weeks after deployment.[53] Procurement of more SL-7 fast sealift ships would further loosen these logistical constraints. Eight SL-7s alone would allow the movement of "a mechanized infantry division from the East Coast to the Persian Gulf in about three weeks."[54] Commitment of U.S., Japanese, and European commercial air and shipping to logistical support would add a further measure of confidence to the sustainability of combat operations.

Since a Soviet attack on Iran would raise the specter of nuclear war, the Strategic Air Command would probably rank high in the pecking order for tanker support. Although this is not a crippling constraint, either through procurement of additional long-range tankers, or by other measures, it is one that must be addressed.

Finally, third parties, such as North Korea, could take a superpower conflict in Iran as the occasion to settle vendettas of their own. Were such contingencies to coincide with wars in Central Europe and Iran, current U.S. strategic mobility and active duty forces might well be stretched far too thin for comfort. That problem, however, is not irremediable.[55]

The United States faces challenges in the area of simultaneity. But so do the Soviets. The only Soviet aircraft with outsized capabilities are the Antonov-22 and Antonov-124, of which there are reported to be fifty-five and three, respectively.[56] And in reference to a statement by Defense Secretary Weinberger, the *New York Times* has reported that

52. Jeffrey Record, *The Rapid Deployment Force and U.S. Military Intervention in the Persian Gulf*, p. 50.

53. McNaugher, *Arms and Oil*, p. 68.

54. Rapid Deployment Joint Task Force Headquarters, "Fact Sheet," January 1981, p. 7.

55. The effect on the conventional balance in Europe of various RDF deployments are estimated in CBO, *Rapid Deployment Forces*, pp. 19–29, where a number of compensatory measures are noted.

56. IISS, *Military Balance, 1985–1986*, p. 24. The introduction of the Antonov-124 strategic transport will increase the Soviets' capabilities for outsized lift but is unlikely to make a big difference in the immediate future. See Joshua M. Epstein, remarks on "Improving Soviet Airlift," pp. 58–59.

"the airlift capacity of the Soviet Union was said to be unable to cope with two large operations at one time."[57]

Thus while the lift to Iran would initially tie up the American C-5 fleet, any comparable lift on the Soviets' part would similarly strain their outsized-airlift capacity.[58] Moreover, Iran would be the Soviets' *fourth* contingency, after China, NATO, and Afghanistan—one which could severely hamper their capability elsewhere.[59]

Soviet Force Estimates: Attack Options and Logistical Constraints

The Soviet force with which the RDF would have to contend, more than a thousand kilometers south of the Russian border, depends also on factors other than simultaneity constraints, factors that have not been widely appreciated. The mode of Soviet attack is one issue; logistical constraints on Soviet operations in the Persian Gulf theater are another.

Two basic Soviet attack options are of central concern. The first option is a buildup north of the Iranian border in the Soviet Union itself, followed by a direct drive for Khuzestan. The second attack option is to take northern Iran first, stop, and build up for a later (and significantly larger) drive on Khuzestan.

As to option one, a direct-drive attack from the USSR, while the peacetime deployment of 24 divisions in the southern Soviet Union has been publicized, the pertinent questions have not been raised. Over what duration of conflict could the Soviets *support* a field force of a given size? To provide a force with the consumables required to sustain combat at the distances facing the Soviets is a major logistical challenge, and one they have never faced before. Indeed, they have addressed far less challenging logistical problems with something less than virtuosity.

For example, in the invasion of Czechoslovakia, the Soviets met little resistance. "No bridges were destroyed, no road blocks erected, and no minefields were planted in the invaders' path. Under such conditions, there was no reason to expect anything other than a brilliant performance by the Soviet Army." Yet "short of organic transport, the armored and

---

57. Richard Halloran, "U.S. Is Weighing Aid to China if Russians Act against Poland," *New York Times*, April 5, 1981.

58. The vulnerability of Soviet airlift is discussed below.

59. The logistical penalties imposed on Soviet operations outside the Persian Gulf theater by large-scale operations in that theater are explicitly accounted for below.

mechanized divisions were left without many basic supplies on the third day of occupation. Under actual combat conditions, they would have lacked many essential items after the first 24 hours."[60]

Although the Soviets appear to have expanded their organic transport somewhat, logistics remains among the weakest links in the Soviet military machine. Assuming the Soviets choose to make a direct-drive attack for Khuzestan, the average on-road distance from USSR bases to the line of engagement in southern Iran is roughly 1,200 kilometers. The Soviet ground force that could be sustained (with ammunition, spare parts, petroleum, oil, and lubricants) at full lethality in high-intensity combat at this distance from the USSR without serious penalty to Soviet strength elsewhere (for example, in the European USSR, the Far East, or Afghanistan) is estimated in appendix B to be 7¼ divisions. Beyond that level, the requirement in logistics trucks alone grows at so disproportionate a rate that to sustain the full 24-division "threat"[61] could dictate a drawdown (from outside the theater) on the order of 55 category 1 divisions' worth of trucks.[62] This would exceed the supply available from *the sum of* Soviet forces deployed opposite China and in Afghanistan; indeed, since those forces are not all category 1, a 24-division force in Khuzestan would, in fact, denude an even greater number of divisions.

The calculation underlying these assertions is presented in appendix B. It is quite conservative. It assumes no attrition of Soviet trucks even though such attrition would probably occur in phase I and would almost certainly occur in phase II. The calculation also assumes that no Soviet trucks suffer mechanical breakdown. Furthermore, it leaves out of account all limitations on road capacity, a factor that alone could limit the Soviet force to the same low level.[63] In calculating the Soviets'

60. Leo Heiman, "Soviet Invasion Weaknesses," pp. 39, 43.

61. Includes the 24 tank and motorized rifle divisions of the Transcaucasus, Northern Caucasus, and Turkestan military districts. IISS, *Military Balance, 1983–1984*, p. 16.

62. This calculation is offered in appendix B.

63. Some Pentagon analysts claim as few as 6 Soviet divisions could be sustained in high-intensity combat in Khuzestan. Interviews. As an alternative to appendix B, and as yet another indication of how such estimates may be arrived at, the following calculation is offered. Iran's total road network is 66,800 kilometers, of which 30,800 kilometers are paved roads and 36,000 kilometers are gravel and crushed stone roads. Mark Heller, ed., *The Middle East Military Balance, 1983*, p. 92. Logisticians classify roads as type 1 (cement/bituminous), type 2 (stone/gravel), and type 3 (earth). The types vary in the extent of truck movement they can sustain. For example, during the dry season, a "fair" type 1 road (4.6 to 5.4 meters wide, with shoulders of 1 meter or less) through mountainous terrain can sustain 3,091 three-ton trucks a day. In the same

combat tonnage requirement, such necessities as food and water were excluded, again to be conservative, as were logistical requirements of tactical air units not organic to ground divisions.

Giving the Soviets the benefit of some rather serious doubts, then, this study assumes that a 7¼-division combat force could be supported for a battle of Khuzestan in a direct-drive attack from the USSR.

The Soviets' second major attack option would be to take northern Iran first, moving south over the Elburz Mountains to Tehran, then stop and build up for a later and significantly larger drive on Khuzestan. The Soviet ground force that could be sustained at full lethality, under the above conservative logistics assumptions, at this much shorter distance (about 800 on-road kilometers) from major Soviet supply points is estimated in appendix B at 10⅞ divisions—roughly 50 percent larger than in the direct-drive attack from Russia. Clearly, this increase in Soviet force size would come at a cost in surprise.

Assessing the Balance

It is necessary to gauge the adequacy of American rapid deployment forces against each of these two basic Soviet attacks. The critical question in each case is whether the U.S. force can establish a defense in the south *before* Soviet forces arrive. If it can, then against either attack the RDF would enjoy a number of classic defensive advantages.

The defense, for example, may enjoy the advantage of operation from prepared, or even fortified, positions, while an attacker must come out into the open to advance, exposing himself to fire. If the attacker is not to increase his vulnerability further by halting, he must locate the more concealed target and fire on it while in motion; but motion generally reduces accuracy. If need be, the defender may conduct retrogrades

---

terrain and environmental conditions, a "fair" type 2 road (4.6 to 5.2 meters wide, with shoulders of 0.91 meter or less) can sustain 1,030 three-ton trucks a day. Leonard and Scott, "Methodology for Estimating Movement Rates," tables 2.1, 2.2, on pp. 2.7, 2.8. Figuring the Iranian road net to be almost equally divided between type 1 and type 2 roads, as suggested above, one would estimate two type 1 roads (at 3,091 three-ton trucks a day) and three type 2 roads (at 1,030 three-ton trucks a day) over the Zagros Mountains, for a capacity of 9,272 three-ton trucks a day. With half arriving and half returning, the delivering flow is 4,636 three-ton trucks a day, or 13,908 tons. At the same daily divisional consumption rate used in appendix B (1,675 tons/division/day), 8.30 Soviet divisions could be sustained. If one of the three type 2 roads could be kept out of commission, the sustainable Soviet force drops, on these assumptions, to 7.38 divisions.

Figure 4-2. *Four Basic Contingencies for Battle of Khuzestan*

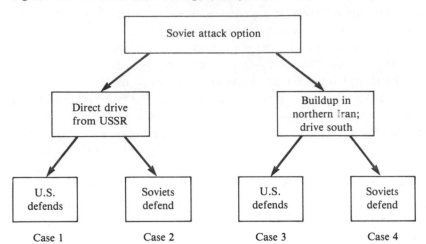

over lines of communication that shorten as his withdrawal proceeds. The attacker, by contrast, must pull his supply lines behind him, extending them as he proceeds over roads, bridges, and areas that have been destroyed, obstructed, or hastily booby-trapped (for example, mined) by his receding prey.

Where such defensive advantages apply, military commanders who do not mismanage their resources should be able to extract favorable exchange ratios (that is, better than 1:1). Or, to revise Nathan Bedford Forrest's familiar adage, "If you get there firstest, you may not need the mostest."

Of course, if the Soviets are able to outrace U.S. forces into position and establish their sustainable force as the defender in Khuzestan, the same defensive advantages would redound to them. They—this study assumes—would impose an equally high exchange rate (discussed below) on the RDF as it tried to overcome their numerical edge.

Hence there are four basic contingencies to consider, depending on which of their two main attack options the Soviets implement and (in each case) whether it is U.S. or Soviet forces who get into position first and establish themselves as the defender in Khuzestan. The possibilities are depicted in figure 4-2.

No amount of bean counting—the enumeration of static prewar inventories—will yield reasoned judgments about a force's wartime adequacy. In order to assess the adequacy of U.S. forces in the above four cases, it is necessary to conduct conservative dynamic simulations of U.S.-Soviet combat.[64]

Three basic ingredients are required to do this: (1) The prebattle *inputs* must be accounted *under some common measure* of potential lethality (so apples are not compared with oranges); (2) an explicit criterion of wartime effectiveness, a requisite *output*, must be specified; and (3) equations *relating inputs to outputs*, bounding the interaction of forces in time (that is, dynamics) are needed. Each of these ingredients deserves some explanation before the simulation results are presented and discussed.

The Inputs

The ground and close air support forces—the prebattle inputs—confronting one another in these cases are shown in tables 4-1 and 4-2. As the benchmark for the analysis a baseline rapid deployment force is defined in table 4-1. (Experts will recognize this as a slightly enhanced version of the force existing when the U.S. Central Command was established in January of 1983. At 4⅔ divisions plus corps-level assets, it is a good deal smaller than the 7⅓-division force planned by the Defense Department for the 1990s.)

For purposes of dynamic analysis, Soviet and American ground forces need to be expressed in common units of lethality. This study employs a method of scoring developed and used by the U.S. Army. In the so-called Weapon Effectiveness Indices/Weighted Unit Values, or WEI/WUV, system the lethality of a force is gauged by a weighted aggregation of the strength of its components. By a combination of test range and other data, the components—weapons such as small arms, tanks, antitank missiles, and artillery—are assigned effectiveness indices (WEIs). These are then weighted and summed to obtain the unit's weighted value (WUV). The WUV score of a standard U.S. armored division works out to 47,490.[65] This, by definition, is the WUV score of one armored division equivalent, or ADE, and can be used to convert ADEs to WUVs and vice versa.[66]

64. For a detailed argument to this effect, see the preface to Joshua M. Epstein, *Measuring Military Power*.

65. For the entire computation, see William P. Mako, *U.S. Ground Forces and the Defense of Central Europe*, p. 114.

66. For further details of the computational procedure, see U.S. Department of the Army, Concepts Analysis Agency, War Gaming Directorate, *Final Report: Weapon Effectiveness Indices/Weighted Unit Values (WEI/WUV)*, vol. 1: *Executive Summary*.

Table 4-1. *U.S. Ground and Close Air Forces, Battle of Khuzestan (Baseline RDF)*

	Ground forces[b]			Close air forces[c]		
Units[a]	U.S. Army and Marine divisional units	Armored division equivalents	Weighted unit value	Rotary-wing aircraft	Fixed-wing aircraft	Total
24th Mechanized Division	1	0.94	44,641	30 AH-1s	. . .	30
82d Airborne Division	1	0.69	32,768	27 AH-1s	. . .	27
101st Airmobile Division	1	0.77	36,567	27 AH-1s	. . .	27
1⅓ Marine amphibious forces	1⅓	1.33[d]	63,162	32 AH-1s	50 A-4s, AV-8As, AV-8Bs, AV-8Cs	82
6th Combat Brigade (Air Cavalry)	⅓	0.39	18,521	153 AH-1s	. . .	153
Corps-level assets	. . .	0.17	8,073	. . .	. . .	. . .
354th Tactical Fighter Wing	. . .	. . .	. . .	. . .	72 A-10s	72
Total	4⅔	4.29	203,732	269	122	391

a. From Rapid Deployment Joint Task Force Headquarters, Public Affairs Office, "Fact Sheet," August 1982, cited in U.S. Congressional Budget Office, *Rapid Deployment Forces*, p. 2; and "United States Central Command," CENTCOM public affairs document.

b. ADE scores for U.S. mechanized, airborne, and airmobile divisions, corps assets, and air cavalry are from William P. Mako, *U.S. Ground Forces and the Defense of Central Europe*, p. 109. For all Soviet and American units, WUV scores were obtained by multiplying the ADE estimate by the WUV score per ADE of 47,490. Mako, *U.S. Ground Forces*, p. 114. Any discrepancies between WUV scores thus obtained and WUV scores obtained by direct aggregation of WEIs are due to rounding.

c. The AH-1 figure for the 24th Mechanized Division is courtesy of the Force Development Directorate, Office of the Deputy Chief of Staff for Operations and Plans, Department of the Army, October 1984. The 82d and 101st airborne divisions each have an air cavalry squadron of 27 AH-1 Cobras. U.S. Department of the Army, *U.S. Army Armor Reference Data*, vol. 1: *The Army Division*, pp. 191, 209. Marine rotary and fixed-wing figures are from U.S. Department of Defense, *Annual Report to the Congress, Fiscal Year 1983*, p. III-39. The 6th CBAC has 153 AH-1 Cobras. Department of the Army, *U.S. Army Armor Reference Data*, vol. 2: *Non-Divisional Organizations*, p. 405.

d. Assumes that a Marine amphibious force is worth 1.0 ADE. Each Marine amphibious force comprises three Marine amphibious brigades (MABs).

Table 4-2. *Estimated Soviet Ground and Close Air Forces,*
Battle of Khuzestan

	Ground forces			Close air forces[a]		
Attack mode	Sustainable Soviet divisions[b]	Armored division equivalents[c]	Weighted unit value	Rotary-wing aircraft	Fixed-wing aircraft	Total
Direct drive from USSR	7.25	4.64	220,354	128	222	350
Buildup in northern Iran; drive south	10.88	6.96	330,530	128	222	350

a. The fixed-wing figure accounts all fighter-bomber assets from the Turkestan and Transcaucasus Air Armies as close air. This study assumes three regiments per air army and 37 aircraft per regiment, for a total of 222 for two air armies. Department of the Army, Intelligence and Threat Analysis Center, *Soviet Army Operations,* p. 5-32. The same source gives one helicopter regiment per army. The rotary-wing close air figure counts 64 Mi-24 Hinds per regiment, for a total of 128. David C. Isby, *Weapons and Tactics of the Soviet Army,* p. 326.

b. Number of Soviet divisions that could be sustained in Khuzestan from main buildup points in either the USSR (assuming a direct-drive attack) or northern Iran (assuming a take-northern-Iran-first attack) as calculated in appendix B.

c. Assumes 0.64 ADE per Soviet division. Mako, *U.S. Ground Forces,* p. 111.

This is not the only possible measure of ground force lethality, nor is it free of all bias.[67] Indeed, the WEI/WUV scoring generally considers only the assets of the division and, in leaving combat support and nondivisional (for example, corps) assets out of account, it attributes disproportionate weight to the Soviet division's front end, or "teeth." Not only should the United States be able to position corps assets in the region, but the proposed RDF's second delay phase (in the Zagros) has, as one of its primary functions, the attrition of precisely those Soviet "teeth" that weigh so heavily on the WEI/WUV scale. This study

67. Firepower scores are an alternative, computable using divisional tables of organization and equipment (TO&E) and firepower scores for divisional units. U.S. and Soviet TO&Es may be obtained, respectively, from U.S. Department of the Army, *Staff Officers' Field Manual*; and U.S. Department of the Army, *Soviet Army Operations.* For U.S. and Soviet unit firepower scores, see U.S. Department of the Army, *Maneuver Control.* Another alternative is to modify the armored division equivalents, using different category weights or weapons effectiveness indices. The data required are given in Mako, *U.S. Ground Forces.* NATO (including U.S.) and Warsaw Pact forces are scored in Soviet motorized rifle division equivalents in Klaus Arnhold, *Zur Problematik Eines Vergleichs der Konventionellen Landstreitkräfte von NATO und Warschauer Pakt in Europa.* Yet further scorings are set forth in Andrew Hamilton, "Redressing the Conventional Balance," pp. 111–36. These approaches will, of course, suffer problems common to all such aggregations. For a discussion of them, see J. A. Stockfisch, *Models, Data, and War.*

corrects partially for the usual omission of nondivisional assets by including an estimate for corps.[68]

However, by assigning to Soviet divisions their full prewar lethality, this scoring implicitly brings all the Soviets' phase II casualties "back from the dead" to fight again in Khuzestan. The scoring procedure itself is, if anything, biased in favor of the Soviets and the employment of the pre-attrition Soviet scores seems conservative as well. So while this measure suffers inherent problems common to any aggregation across diverse systems, it is hard to see its use as biasing the analysis against the Soviets. In addition to being suitably conservative, the use of ADEs and WUVs does render U.S. and Soviet units commensurable, an improvement essential to any rigorous analysis.

Output: A Criterion of Sufficiency

Having normalized U.S. and Soviet ground forces to some common standard (in this case, armored division equivalents and weighted unit values), one wishes to arrive at a reasoned judgment about the *wartime material adequacy* of one's force; have commanders been given the material wherewithal to succeed? This is the force planner's question; it should be distinguished from other questions with which it is often confused.

For instance, to arrive at a conservative judgment about material adequacy is *not* necessarily to predict "who will win" should deterrence fail. That obviously depends, among other things, on the amount of human suffering and of economic and social dislocation that society in general and its leaders in particular are willing to endure to achieve given aims. If, due to such political considerations (or other factors not manipulable through force planning), authorities choose to forgo the option of employing the full conventional force available, they may succumb regardless of that force's potential lethality.[69] The fact that Czechoslovakia capitulated in 1938 does not prove that Czech force planners were derelict in their duties. Vietnam is another good example. As Barry R. Posen has written: "The U.S. armed forces were not destroyed on the battlefields of South Vietnam. By virtue of the pain inflicted and the costs incurred on those battlefields, the will of the

68. William P. Mako estimates corps assets at 0.17 ADEs in his *U.S. Ground Forces*, p. 109.

69. See Barry R. Posen, *The Sources of Military Doctrine*, p. 61.

government and people of the United States was destroyed."[70] The planner's or budgeter's problem is not, therefore, to predict outcomes literally. Rather, it is to arrive at, and to defend, in as explicit and plausible a way as possible, his or her judgment that *if* authorities decide to use available force, and *if* military commanders are relatively adept in its application, then sufficient force has (or has not) been provided to achieve postulated wartime objectives.

For peacetime force-planning purposes, the wartime objective—the success criterion—is taken to be *the attrition of the adversary's force.* Just as many will be quick to scold explicit analysts for attempting to "predict outcomes," so they may expect undue reproach for being enamored of "attrition war," when, to be sure, the name of the game is to break the adversary's will, undermine his cohesion, and destroy his capacity for acute and timely tactical decisionmaking. Presumably, a certain amount of attrition must be exacted before any of these deeper effects are evident. The problem, of course, is that no one knows what level (or distribution) of attrition will produce them. As a conservative peacetime planner, therefore, one assumes the objective to be total, or near total, attrition.

If, by strokes of tactical brilliance or by dint of superior morale or "maneuver warfare," the United States is able to secure its battlefield aims without enduring or exacting much attrition, that's fine. Then the conservative planner will simply have budgeted the commander with more than he needs by assuming no such tactical brilliance or other extraordinary advantage in his or her assessments.

Relating Inputs to Outputs

To gauge whether material inputs are adequate to achieve the specified output, the force planner can use equations that capture, in a conservative and plausible way, the relationships among dominant variables. Some of these variables are straightforward. For example, every ground engagement in history has had a duration; each party to such engagement has experienced losses; the ratio of their respective losses is the engagement's exchange ratio. While they may not have been tabulated, these numbers certainly exist for every war that has ever occurred. Similar fundamental statements apply to the contribution of tactical airpower

70. Ibid.

on the battlefield (close air support). There is always a time span of operations, always an average sortie rate per day, always an average attrition rate per sortie, and always some average number of ground combatants killed per sortie.

The equations developed in appendix C capture the basic dynamic relationships among such dominant variables, and the numbers assigned to those variables are, on balance, conservative, as a few examples may illustrate.

CONSERVATIVE PERFORMANCE NUMBERS. Clausewitz believed that *"the defensive form of warfare is intrinsically stronger than the offensive."*[71] As noted above, defenders have historically enjoyed a number of tactical advantages; operation from prepared, or even fortified, positions, and relative concealment, are among them. Where such advantages apply, many claim on the basis of military experience that a competent defender should be able to hold even if attacker-to-defender lethality ratios reach 3:1. In the words of a May 1984 NATO Military Committee document, "classical military wisdom suggests that a 3:1 ratio in favour of the offense at the point of attack is necessary to assure a reasonable chance of success."[72] According to the U.S. Army's 1976 version of its *Operations* field manual, FM 100-5, "as a rule of thumb, [defending generals] should seek not to be outweighed more than 3:1 in terms of combat power. With very heavy air and field artillery support on favorable terrain, it may be possible to defend at a numerical disadvantage of something like 5:1 for short periods of time."[73] Similarly, on the Soviet side, the European Security Study report notes that "the minimum numerical superiority ratio sought by the Pact is about 3 to 1 in both ground and air operations. Doctrinally, however, the ratios to be achieved in local conflict situations are to be higher."[74] Indeed, according to the Pentagon, the Soviets' large military inventories in part "reflect the offensive nature of Soviet military doctrine and strategy in that attacking forces are believed to require at least a 5:1 force ratio in anticipation of high losses inherent in offensive operations."[75]

Although a range of alternative assumptions can be entertained in

71. Elsewhere he calls defense *"the stronger form of waging war."* Clausewitz, *On War*, pp. 358–59. Emphasis in original.

72. Karsten Voigt, rapporteur, "Draft Interim Report of the Sub-Committee on Conventional Defence in Europe," p. 8.

73. Department of the Army, *Operations*, p. 5-3.

74. Donald R. Cotter, "Potential Future Roles for Conventional and Nuclear Forces in Defense of Western Europe," p. 214.

75. Department of Defense, *Soviet Military Power*, 5th ed., p. 63.

sensitivity analyses, this study's simulations assume a ground-to-ground exchange ratio of 1.5:1 for the defender, *whoever that might be*. (In cases 1 and 3 it is the United States; in cases 2 and 4, the Soviets.) Few American planners would deny the Soviets the ability to extract such a ratio if offered all the defensive opportunities suggested above. And neither do I; I insist, however, upon the proposed RDF's enjoying the same (quite modest) advantage given the same opportunities in time and space. This value, moreover, is well within the range of historical plausibility[76] and is a great deal lower than values considered plausible by a number of U.S. and NATO planners.[77] Close air sortie rates, attrition rates, and effectiveness per sortie are also quite conservative, as indicated in appendix table D-1, where all the numerical assumptions are set forth.

Numerical estimates in hand, one arrives at the matter of equations.

CONSERVATIVE AND PLAUSIBLE EQUATIONS. Like all applications of mathematics to the physical world, the equations used for the simulations here (see appendix C) are an idealization. They do not purport to be realistic in a depictive sense; innumerable factors are intentionally left out of account. For force-planning purposes, however, it is not necessary to attain depictive precision. So long as the equations— simple as they may be—capture the dominant dynamics and do not build in assumptions biased against the adversary, they can suffice as a conservative gauge of material adequacy.[78]

76. According to Barry Posen, "The Israeli 7th armored brigade in 1973 . . . successfully defended 20 km of front on the Golan Heights with less than one-quarter of an ADE, no major reserves (other than the brigade's organic reserve), and virtually no CAS [close air support]. This brigade was outnumbered 4:1 or worse." Barry R. Posen, "Measuring the European Conventional Balance," note 41 on p. 75. Overall, Posen estimates the 1973 Arab-Israeli tank exchange rate (that is, Arab tanks killed per Israeli tank killed) to be 3:1. The Syrian-Israeli rate specifically he estimates to be 4.5:1. Ibid., table 4, p. 81. James Dunnigan, citing attacking-tank-to-defending-antitank exchange ratios of World War II, estimates that even with defenders outnumbered by 2–3:1 (as the Israelis were in the cases above), offense-defense exchange rates of 4–6:1 are to be anticipated on the modern battlefield. James F. Dunnigan, *How to Make War*, p. 40. Summarizing B. H. Liddell Hart, Posen notes that Hart "observed that the level of quantitative superiority that the attacker must enjoy if he is to achieve a successful breakthrough has been rising. Citing U.S. and British experience in World War II, he noted that superiorities between 3:1 and 5:1 were required, with some attacks failing at ratios of 10:1." Posen, "Measuring the European Conventional Balance," note 38 on p. 74.

77. NATO planners interviewed in spring 1984 considered 2.75 to be a reasonable exchange ratio to expect from a prepared defender operating with modern weaponry.

78. For a further discussion of this methodological point, see Epstein, *Measuring Military Power*, preface, chap. 5, and app. D.

So, for example, various qualitative factors are not represented in these equations. The issue, however, is whether, in any of these less tangible and perhaps decisive qualitative areas, the Soviets would enjoy a relative advantage.

The least tangible, *morale*, is by far the most difficult to assess. But descriptions of the Allied resupply of Russia through the Persian Corridor during World War II may suggest the type of fatigue these routes would exact: "Mile after mile of washboard roads took toll on men as well as vehicles. As an anonymous military scribe put it, vibration 'shook the trucks to pieces . . . and pounded the men's kidneys to jelly.' "[79]

Though an open question, such physical stress, when compounded by the trauma of surprise ambush day and night in the Zagros, would hardly seem to contribute to the élan of Soviet troops.

Even were such punishment to galvanize the steely invaders, the Soviets would not enjoy the advantage of *mobility*, canalized as their descent would be into a very few corridors onto Dezful. The RDF would not be so channeled, operating from the relatively open lowlands south of the Zagros. Moreover, insofar as Soviet *training* consists in refining the advance in broad echelons, that training and that tactic are wholly inappropriate to this terrain.

As for relative *sustainability*, in Khuzestan it is the RDF that could avail itself of a shorter and more secure line of communication, certainly for the first few weeks, after which time the RDF's reliance on long-distance sealift would grow. While there is debate concerning the interdiction which that sea line of communication might suffer, it is hard to see it as being any *more* vulnerable than Soviet lines, strung out as they would be over hundreds of miles of vulnerable terrain.

On this point, the U.S. Joint Strategic Plans Group went even further in their formerly top secret analysis. "Supply and support of Allied operations in this area can be effected over sea lines of communication least critically threatened by Soviet operations." By contrast, "Soviet offensive forces will be limited by their dependence on long overland lines of communication readily harassed by guerrilla or commando type operations and ideally suited to interdiction by Allied air."[80] Nor would

79. T. H. Vail Motter, *United States Army in World War II, The Middle East Theater*, p. 327. More historical information on aid to Russia through the Persian Gulf may be found in Richard M. Leighton and Robert W. Coakley, *United States Army in World War II, The War Department*.

80. Joint Strategic Plans Group, "Proposed Guidance for an Alternative Plan to 'Bushwacker,' " March 8, 1948, p. 130. The same analysis stressed that "the Persian

the Soviets be likely to enjoy any advantage in the aerial resupply of forces, a point discussed below.

More important, perhaps, than questions of morale, mobility, training, or sustainability is that of *coordination*. In particular, the prebattle Soviet WUV estimates used here (table 4-2) are predicated on the assumption that all the Soviet divisions emerge from the Zagros at the same time and instantaneously constitute themselves as a fighting force. If they come through two or three divisions at a time, they can be taken on piecemeal and, by the lethality measures adopted here, would be grossly outweighed by the RDF proposed below. Indeed, at anything less than a simultaneous arrival, the Soviet forces would be unlikely to achieve parity with the proposed RDF. Earlier American planners went so far as to say that "no potentially disputed area in Afro-Eurasia is better suited to successful and early isolation of the 'battle field' by tactical air and/or subversive and guerrilla operations than the Persian Gulf area." This is one important basis for their overall assessment that "the physiography of the Persian Gulf area is suitable for defensive operations by inferior forces."[81]

The coordination problem was not lost on the thorough Soviet planners, who wrote: "As a result of the mountainous terrain structure and because of the few roads, the combat engagements will be carried out mostly with mixed units which, at times, must operate completely independently. For this reason, the coordination of individual separate columns . . . is of exceptional importance."[82]

To recognize the problem is one thing. To solve it is another. And there is no neat way for the Soviets to circumvent it. Concentration (reducing the number of advance axes) in the interest of simultaneous arrival merely raises the value of each choke point while reducing their number, thus simplifying the RDF's delaying operations. On the other hand, dispersion (raising the number of advance axes), though forcing the United States to spread its resources over a greater (but still very small) number of choke points, exacerbates the coordination problem, possibly reducing the land threat with which the RDF would ultimately contend in Khuzestan. Neither alternative should be especially attractive to the Soviets.

Of course, the simulated Soviets are never confronted with the choice,

---

Gulf area presents great logistic and physiographical limitations to large scale Soviet build-up." Ibid., p. 13.

81. Ibid., pp. 13, 130.

82. Guensberg, trans., *Soviet Command Study*, pp. 240–41.

since they are assumed to constitute themselves instantaneously as a field fighting force (including units from beyond the graves of phase II).

In addition to being suitably conservative, a planner's equations must relate inputs (prebattle force structures) to outputs (performance in the execution of wartime missions) in a *plausible* way, explicitly representing—to the extent possible—the dominant variables and their interaction over time. For reasons spelled out in appendix E, the traditional Lanchester equations and their contemporary extensions fail the test of plausibility.[83] The adaptive model of war presented in appendix C and used here to simulate U.S.-Soviet conflict in Khuzestan was developed to overcome the basic shortcomings of Lanchester theory.[84]

While allowing one to calculate requirements, my equations reflect the defensive—and also offensive—feedback to which Lanchester theory is oblivious. For example, they capture both the effect of defensive attrition rates on defensive withdrawal rates (that is, the velocity of the battlefront) *and* the effect of defensive withdrawal on defensive attrition. Unlike Lanchester equations, they permit the trading of space for time, and they do so without claiming linearly increasing returns to the force ratio, an unsubstantiated assumption implicit in the most widely used form of Lanchester's equations, the so-called Lanchester square rela-

83. The technical critique of Lanchester theory and exposition of my model have been published as a monograph, Joshua M. Epstein, *The Calculus of Conventional War*.

84. In so doing, they overcome biases inherent in the Lanchester square equations and their contemporary extensions. The question of relative bias is important, though elusive when the models being compared do not use the same independent variables. (For example, my model dispenses with the Lanchester coefficients, while Lanchester does not use the threshold attrition rates defined in appendix C). While any conclusion is possible given the right numerical assumptions, the Lanchester square equations exhibit three structural biases. First, they favor the numerically larger force since, in the stalemate (N^2) condition, the numerical force ratio is squared while the effectiveness ratio is not. Second, the Lanchester equations (and all other models in which attrition is unaffected by withdrawal) are either inconsistent (in positing withdrawal without attrition-benefit), or systematically favor the offense, as spelled out in appendix E at note 6. Third, since there is no feedback from withdrawal *to* attrition, the sacrifice of territory does not prolong the war: there is no trading space for time. Hence no strategy will emerge as militarily preferable to forward defense. Although it could not have been Lanchester's intent, when applied to the conventional balance in Central Europe these structural biases support the conventional wisdom: they favor the numerically larger force (the Warsaw Pact); they presuppose offensive advantage (or are inconsistent when applied to cases where substantial movement is possible), and they support (that is, will recommend no alternative to) a Western strategy of forward defense, NATO's doctrine. For an application of my alternative equations to NATO, see Joshua M. Epstein, *The 1987 Defense Budget*.

tion. Full details of my model appear in appendix C. Here a brief overview is offered.

AN ADAPTIVE MODEL OF WAR. The attacker makes an opening "bid" on the pace of war, the rate at which his own forces are consumed (he can, of course, set his rate at zero by not attacking). He may want to press the attack at an extremely high pace, and be willing to suffer extremely high attrition rates, if—for operational, strategic, or political reasons—a quick decision is paramount.[85] Via a casualty-exchange ratio (defenders killed per attacker killed) this imposes an attrition rate on the defender. The latter may elect to hold his position and accept this attacker-dictated rate, or he may choose to reduce his (and in turn the attacker's) attrition rate by withdrawing at a certain speed.

Operational, strategic, or political factors may preclude a defender's trading space for time. However, given its tactical advantages, so eloquently described by Clausewitz, a plausible model should permit it.[86]

The adaptive model of war offered in appendix C does so and also yields a more realistic picture of movement on the ground. Rather than the smooth velocity curves generated by traditional (no-feedback) methods, these equations generate a jagged sequence of velocities reflecting the alternation of action and inaction so characteristic of real war.[87] (This

85. As an operational matter, a quick decision can circumvent flexibility or sustainability problems that could prove telling in a prolonged war. Strategically, the attacker may seek a decision before the defense has a chance to mobilize superior industry, superior reinforcements, or superior allies. An attacker with unreliable allies of his own may seek a quick win lest they begin to defect. An attacker may also choose to press the attack at a ferocious pace to secure a decision before the defender's nuclear options can be executed. Many would impute all these motives to the Soviets in Europe today. A classic strategy of states facing enemies on multiple fronts has been to win quickly through offensive actions on one front and then switch forces to the second.

Political factors may also impel attackers to endure exceedingly high attrition rates in hopes of securing a rapid decision. For example, the war powers resolution basically gives U.S. forces sixty days to succeed before Congress intervenes; one can imagine a military planner feeling that high attrition at the outset, if it leads to a rapid decision, is preferable to low attrition, a prolonged contest, and congressional involvement. (I thank Richard Betts for this observation.) Israel may feel compelled to suffer high rates of attrition to impose its terms on adversaries before superpowers intervene to impose other ones on Israel. Also, it may be necessary to suffer high attrition in order to push enemies back, ensuring that war is fought in someone else's territory, perhaps undermining the enemy's domestic political support as well.

86. Clausewitz, "Retreat to the Interior of the Country," On War, bk. 6, chap. 25, pp. 469–79.

87. See figure 4-8 and the simulations offered in appendix D.

rhythm held great fascination for Clausewitz, who wrote of it at some length.)[88] This analysis also explicitly includes the direct battlefield contribution of each side's fixed-wing and helicopter close air support forces (see tables 4-1 and 4-2). This is an important but often neglected aspect of the dynamic balance. The model's close air terms calculate the daily reduction in each side's ground force that results from the adversary's close air operations, while keeping track of the ongoing attrition to which the U.S. and Soviet planes are subject. (The velocity and cumulative displacement of the front as well as other data for each of the cases examined below are presented in appendix D.) If this study's assumptions are deemed not sufficiently conservative, the reader is invited to apply different values in the appendixes.

Simulation Results: Battle of Khuzestan

Using the adaptive model, and assumptions of the sorts discussed above—*all* of which are explicitly set forth in the appendixes—the following results obtain for the four basic contingencies depicted in figure 4-2. (The simulation data plotted in the curves below are given in tables D-2 through D-8 of appendix D.)

CASE 1. SOVIET DIRECT DRIVE; UNITED STATES DEFENDS. As shown in figure 4-3, while initial conditions apparently favor the USSR in a direct-drive attack, moderately favorable exchange ratios deriving from U.S. defensive advantages in concealment, target acquisition, and close air support outweigh and reverse Soviet advantages in a relatively brief war of high intensity. In short, the baseline RDF (see table 4-1) should prove sufficient if it is able to prepare its defense in advance of Soviet columns. If the United States acts in a timely fashion, using the warning time afforded by Soviet mobilization, this is an entirely plausible outcome.

CASE 2. SOVIET DIRECT DRIVE; SOVIETS DEFEND. What, however, is the penalty if the United States fails to use warning time and the Soviets are able to outrace the RDF to Khuzestan and seize defensive positions? Matters are very different. The Soviets' input advantage is not reversed; it is magnified as conflict proceeds. This is illustrated in figure 4-4.

88. Clausewitz, *On War*. See "The Suspension of Action in War," bk. 3, chap. 16, pp. 216–19, and especially "Tension and Rest: The Dynamic Law in War," bk. 3, chap. 18, pp. 221–22.

Figure 4-3. *Case 1, Battle of Khuzestan: Soviet Direct Drive;*
United States Defends (Baseline RDF)

Ground lethality surviving on *t*th day (WUVs)

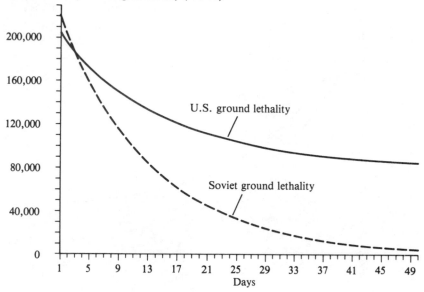

Days

Sources: Appendix tables D-1 and D-2.

CASE 3. SOVIET NORTHERN BUILDUP; UNITED STATES DEFENDS. Figure 4-5 depicts the case in which Soviet forces consolidate in the north and, in so doing, concede southern defensive preparations to the United States. Remarkably, even a 50 percent increase in the Soviets' sustainable force (see table 4-2) is insufficient to outweigh the defensive advantages assumed above. The comparison of this result with the previous case has important implications for crisis stability, as is discussed below in chapter 5.

CASE 4. SOVIET NORTHERN BUILDUP; SOVIETS DEFEND. If, however, the United States fails to exploit the time afforded by the Soviets' northern buildup, and with the north as a base the Soviets are permitted to establish defensive preparations in the south, the situation would verge on the hopeless, as figure 4-6 illustrates. Recourse to nuclear or horizontal escalation would be the only alternatives to a conventional rebuff of truly disastrous proportions.

The total (cumulative) displacement of the front in the two relevant cases is summarized in figure 4-7. (Displacement is the result of defensive

Figure 4-4. *Case 2, Battle of Khuzestan: Soviet Direct Drive;*
Soviets Defend (Baseline RDF)

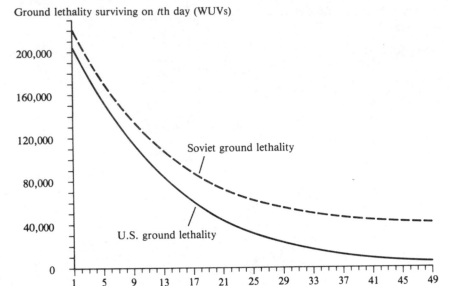

Ground lethality surviving on *t*th day (WUVs)

Soviet ground lethality

U.S. ground lethality

Days

Sources: Appendix tables D-1 and D-3.

withdrawal; in case 2 the USSR and in case 3 the United States
withdraws, while in cases 1 and 4, no movement takes place.) The
velocity of the front in cases 2 and 3 is plotted in figure 4-8.

It is clear that the adequacy of the baseline RDF will vary enormously
depending on the Soviets' mode of attack and the timeliness of the U.S.
response.

The short story, however, is simple enough: *if the baseline RDF gets*
there first (cases 1 and 3), it should fare adequately against either mode
of Soviet attack. If the United States gets beaten to the punch (cases 2
and 4), it loses.

The United States can hedge against case 2 (Soviet direct drive;
Soviets defend) by a modest expansion over the baseline RDF, combined
with a more efficient close air operation. Specifically, the addition of 1
Marine amphibious brigade and additional close air forces,[89] for a total
of 5 divisions plus air, would suffice, *given* an increase in the readiness
of close air (from 0.7 to 0.8) and in the close air sortie rate (from 1.5 to

89. See note s under case 2A of appendix table D-1.

Figure 4-5. *Case 3, Battle of Khuzestan: Soviet Northern Buildup; United States Defends (Baseline RDF)*

Ground lethality surviving on *t*th day (WUVs)

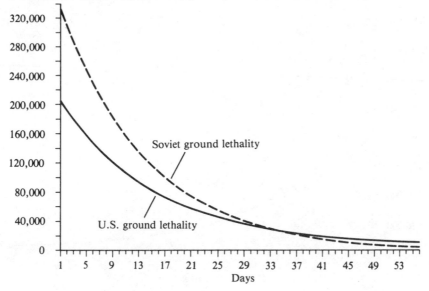

Sources: Appendix tables D-1 and D-6.

2.0 a day), as shown in case 2A (see figure 4-9). Neither of these close air improvements would be at all extraordinary.[90]

Those who—despite the evidence—hold such levels of close air

90. On the contrary, a strong case can be made that the lower values were unduly conservative to begin with. Regarding readiness, a 1984 Rand report, *Concepts of Operations and USAF Planning for Southwest Asia,* gives operationally ready (OR) rates of 80 percent to the A-7, F-4, and F-111. For these aircraft the U.S. Air Force's mission-capability (MC) rates are, respectively, 72.7, 65.9, and 61.4 percent. The corresponding ratios of OR to MC are 1.10 (A-7), 1.21 (F-4), and 1.30 (F-111). Applying the lowest of these ratios (1.10) to the A-10's mission-capability rate of 76.1 yields an operationally ready rate of 83.71; applying the same ratio to the AH-1's mission-capability rate of 73.0 yields an operationally ready rate of 80.30. As an estimate of operational readiness, 80 percent is not wildly optimistic. As for sortie rates, if—as the same Rand study assumes—the A-7 and F-4 can be counted on for two sorties a day, surely one can expect as much from the more sturdy A-10, the Marine AV-8B, and the AH-1 (whose sorties are comparatively brief). See Christopher J. Bowie, *Concepts of Operations and USAF Planning for Southwest Asia,* p. 37; Department of Defense, *Annual Report to the Congress, Fiscal Year 1984,* p. 287; and U.S. Department of the Air Force, Comptroller of the Air Force, *United States Air Force Summary, 1984,* pp. D-34 through D-36.

Figure 4-6. *Case 4, Battle of Khuzestan: Soviet Northern Buildup;*
Soviets Defend (Baseline RDF)

Ground lethality surviving on *t*th day (WUVs)

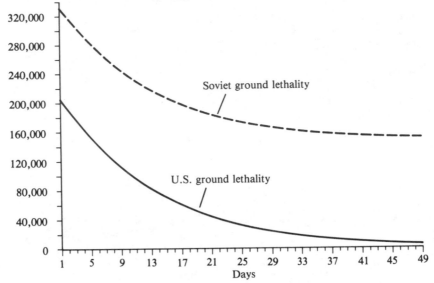

Sources: Appendix tables D-1 and D-7.

effectiveness to be unattainable may achieve a comparably favorable
outcome for the United States by opting for a 5⅓-division RDF (case
2B). Its performance is simulated in figure 4-10 below. It assumes the
same low close air sortie rate (1.5) and low readiness rate (0.7) as case 1
does, but compensates by adding a second Marine amphibious brigade
and additional close air.[91]

In no event is the planned 7⅓-division RDF required, however. While
so large a force is not necessary in cases 1, 2, or 3, it is not nearly large
enough to hedge against case 4, as shown in case 4A (see figure 4-11),
where 7⅓ U.S. divisions are assumed.

If the United States is going to respond with the glacial sluggishness
depicted in simulation 4A, then not even the Reagan administration's
force of 7⅓ divisions will save the day; a more timely response is
imperative. Over the four basic contingencies examined here, any U.S.

91. See note t under case 2B of appendix table D-1.

Figure 4-7. *Displacement of the Front in Cases 2 and 3*

Cumulative km

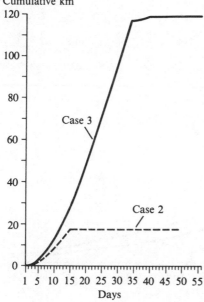

Days

Figure 4-8. *Velocity of the Front in Cases 2 and 3*

Km per day

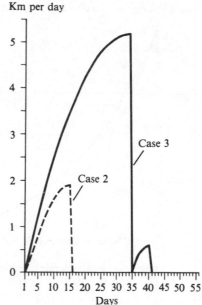

Days

Sources: Appendix tables D-3 and D-6. Plots are of unrounded values.

Sources: Appendix tables D-3 and D-6, Defender's withdrawal rate columns. Plots are of unrounded values.

response timely enough to make 7⅓ divisions effective is timely enough to make 5 divisions sufficient.[92]

As noted above, against either mode of Soviet attack (direct drive or

92. Beyond the inclusion of an additional Marine amphibious brigade, the main difference between the 5-division force recommended here (which includes U.S. Army light divisions and Marine units) and the force of 7⅓ divisions envisioned by the Pentagon is the inclusion in the latter of 2 more army light divisions and their close air power. See notes g and u under case 4A of appendix table D-1 for my detailed assumptions concerning the ground lethality and close air forces of 2 army light divisions.

Based strictly on their utility in the Persian Gulf, therefore, the case for these light divisions is weak. Their utility in a NATO–Warsaw Pact war in Central Europe is also open to serious question. See McNaugher, *Arms and Oil*, note 30 on p. 69. One alternative is to disband 2 army light divisions, retaining and reorganizing their personnel as 2 independent brigades outfitted with tanks (such as M60A3s) and other stockpiled heavy equipment appropriate for armored warfare in Europe. In the event of war, these brigades could be "rounded out" with existing National Guard or Reserve forces to form an additional division equivalent for NATO. See Epstein, *1987 Defense Budget*, p. 28.

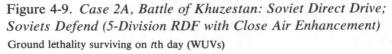

Figure 4-9. *Case 2A, Battle of Khuzestan: Soviet Direct Drive;*
Soviets Defend (5-Division RDF with Close Air Enhancement)

Ground lethality surviving on *t*th day (WUVs)

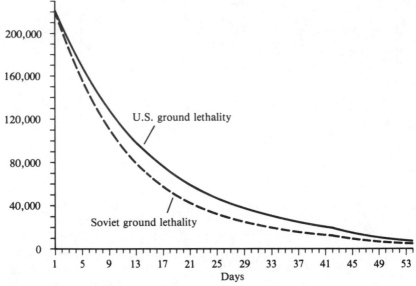

Sources: Appendix tables D-1 and D-4.

northern Iran buildup), the United States does far better as the defender
than as the attacker. Although today's numbers are different, formerly
top secret analyses by the Joint Chiefs of Staff are in striking agreement
with this general point that a defensive strategy (*holding* the area against
an aggressor) is easier than an offensive strategy (*retaking* the area after
the Soviets have occupied it).

> The most desirable course of action would be to hold the oil-bearing
> areas since it would obviate the necessity for their recapture and the 3⅓
> divisions and 3 fighter groups required would be considerably less than
> would be required to retake them either immediately or subsequently.
> Immediate retaking of the oil areas as far north as the Iranian areas at
> the head of the Gulf would require a total of approximately 5 divisions
> and 5 fighter groups.

Also consistent with my analysis, they continued: "The greater the
delay in retaking the oil areas, the more time would be available to the
Soviets for consolidation of their positions and consequently subsequent

Figure 4-10. *Case 2B, Battle of Khuzestan: Soviet Direct Drive; Soviets Defend (5⅓-Division RDF with Close Air Enhancement)*

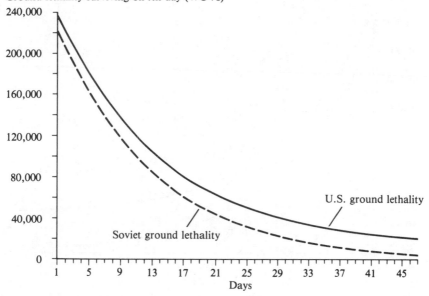

Ground lethality surviving on *t*th day (WUVs)

Sources: Appendix tables D-1 and D-5.

retaking would be even more costly to the Allies."[93] So resounding an affirmation of the advantages of defense is quite rare in postwar military annals.

A Drive from Afghanistan?

It should be noted that a Soviet overland drive from Afghanistan, which would be extremely difficult in its own right, would exacerbate the Soviets' coordination problems if attempted as the eastern axis of a grand envelopment. The distances to Khuzestan from Afghanistan are considerably greater than those from the Soviet Union. This alone would make a simultaneous arrival difficult. In addition, there are no surfaced roads directly across the intervening desert of the Khorassan. There,

93. JCS, "Decision of J.C.S. 1920/1," May 6, 1949, p. 186. Lest there arise any confusion about the relevance of these observations, the Joint Chiefs noted that "the forces for holding . . . would be sufficient . . . to protect the oil areas from Soviet airborne attacks and overland advances *through Iran*." Emphasis added. Ibid., p. 187.

Figure 4-11. *Case 4A, Battle of Khuzestan: Soviet Northern Buildup;
Soviets Defend (7⅓-Division RDF with Close Air Enhancement)*

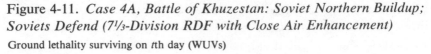

Ground lethality surviving on *t*th day (WUVs)

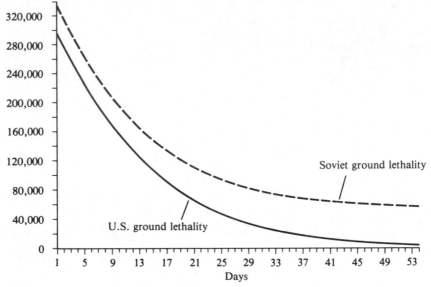

Sources: Appendix tables D-1 and D-8.

the Soviets tell us, "during the summer the temperature is so high that
the inhabitans [*sic*] of the cities withdraw to the so-called 'Sirisamin'
(cellar) and along the caravan routes, the caravans usually do not
continue travel during the day."[94]

Water sources are confined to a few oases. In addition to sending up
clouds of dust to advertise its position, a summer blitz across this terrain
would ensure a very high mechanical breakdown rate. Roads south of
the desert either terminate in the difficult Zagros or traverse them. On
the other hand, the "end run" above the Khorassan (which reduces to a
single road along the base of the Golul Dagh Mountains) would force a
crossing of the Zagros from the north, over the same limited and
vulnerable system of roads already glutted by the advance from the
Soviet Union. To pull any significant force from Afghanistan would
require a reinforcement of Soviet efforts there, thus entailing a drawdown
from other theaters.

While summer is surely the worst time in the Khorassan, winter finds

94. Guensberg, trans., *Soviet Command Study*, p. 42.

the mountain passes of northern Iran snowed in. In the spring thaw, lowlands, particularly those of the Caspian basin, are transformed into a swampy morass, precluding off-road traffic.[95] Finally, fall, though probably the best season in general, is the rainy season in the northwest region, opposite which the bulk of Soviet forces are deployed. During that time, the main rivers of the Azerbaijan become unfordable torrents, making indispensable what few bridges exist. In any season, an attempt to coordinate the simultaneous advance of forces along all of these axes would be, in short, a logistician's nightmare.

IN SUMMARY, if the United States can demonstrate the capacity to use warning and deploy forces in a timely way, a 5-division ground complement should make a purely overland advance appear exceedingly risky to the Soviets. Thus one may expect them to consider airlifted assault. Airlift, however, would face vulnerabilities just as severe.

Airlifted Assault

The Soviets have developed a considerable airlifted power projection capability, as demonstrated in the October War, Angola, Ethiopia, and Afghanistan. However, none of these lifts was opposed by anything even remotely resembling the kind of airpower the Soviets would face in Iran. Their problem is not one of lift capability per se; rather it is fighter escort for the lift. Without the protection provided by that escort, the Soviets' chances for an airborne insertion and aerial resupply of forces would be slim. If the United States exploited warning, the Soviets' prospects would be slight indeed.

Recognizing the importance of fighter escort, it is important to note that, despite strides since Khrushchev's ouster, the Soviets remain outclassed in the air-to-air combat arena.

First, the United States retains the technological edge.[96] While the

95. In fact, the main port of Bandar-e Anzali (formerly Bandar-e Pahlavi) is situated in an area called the "Gilan," meaning "swampy (muddy) place." Ibid., p. 161.

96. Gen. Charles A. Gabriel, U.S. Air Force chief of staff, reportedly declared that the Soviets are ten years from having planes to match U.S. F-15 and F-16 fighters. George C. Wilson, "Air Force Chief Denies Soviets Ahead in Space," *Washington Post*, June 18, 1986. See also U.S. Organization of the Joint Chiefs of Staff, *United States Military Posture for FY 1987*, p. 16. Of the twenty basic technology areas listed by the JCS, the Soviets are listed as superior in none.

very sophistication of U.S. systems has created serious problems in areas of ground support, notably those of sortie generation and sustainability, it is far from clear that the Soviets have avoided the same problems. There is every reason to believe, in fact, that while Soviet air systems are by some measures simpler than those of the United States, the Soviet ground support (maintenance, logistics) system is so much less efficient than the American that, in the net, the Soviets find their advanced systems no more supportable than the United States finds its own to be. In turn, it can be argued that, because of the inefficiency of their ground support environment, the Soviets face equally severe problems in sortie generation and sustainability.[97]

Second, U.S. pilot skill exceeds that of the Soviets. Soviet pilot training is far more routine and is far less realistic than American.[98] Furthermore, the U.S. pilot flies roughly twice as much as his Soviet counterpart.[99] American nonflying hours are spent, in part, on highly sophisticated simulators, of which the Soviets are reported to possess nothing comparable. U.S. training, moreover, has built on a great deal of air-to-air combat experience gained since World War II, in Korea and in Vietnam, far more than the Soviets. Finally, the United States can learn from the winners in Middle East air combat, while the Soviets must glean their insights from the losers.

Given these advantages—more realistic training, and more of it, plus the benefits of far more combat experience—it is difficult to imagine the United States enjoying anything less than a significant margin in pilot skill, the importance of which cannot be overemphasized. Essentially alone it accounted for the exchange ratios (enemy planes lost for each friendly plane lost) of 12.5:1 recorded in Indochina (MiG-21s versus F-4s). And when combined with a technological advantage, it goes a long way toward explaining the extraordinarily high exchange rates logged by the Israelis in 1967, 1973, and 1982 (20:1, 40:1, and more than 80:1).[100]

97. Epstein, *Measuring Military Power*.

98. Ibid. The Soviet military literature is full of high-ranking commentary attesting both to the routinized character of Soviet pilot training and to its adverse effect on flexibility. Characteristic examples are Gen.-Lt. G. Pavlov, "Inexhaustible Reserve"; Gen.-Col. Anatoliy Ustinovich Konstantinov, "Thorough Knowledge of Affairs"; and Gen.-Col. Aleksandr Ivanovich Babayev, "Flight and the Combat Maneuver."

99. Robert P. Berman, *Soviet Air Power in Transition*, p. 57.

100. The Vietnam and 1967 and 1973 Middle East data are given in Steven J. Rosen, "What the Next Arab-Israeli War Might Look Like," p. 160. The 80:1 figure slightly underrates Israeli performance in Lebanon. "In all, in the course of the first week's

Thus even if this conflict presented a classic air-to-air combat situation, the Soviets would have little basis for confidence that they would enjoy air superiority. That being the case, under the highly nonclassic conditions of Iran, the RDF would enjoy a number of pronounced advantages.

For one, the exchange ratios of the Korean and Vietnam conflicts, as well as the remarkable Israeli ratios, were kills of *fighters* by other fighters. In opposing a Soviet airlift, however, U.S. pilots would be attempting to shoot down Soviet *transports*—sluggish, easily acquired on radar, and highly vulnerable targets. The situation, then, is highly preferential to the defense. Khuzestan, moreover, is simply out of range of virtually all Soviet tactical fighters flying from bases either in Afghanistan or the Soviet Union.[101] A direct airlift to Khuzestan, for these reasons, would be vulnerable in the extreme.

Much of central Iran is also out of range for all but late-model Soviet fighters (whose adaptability to the local basing system must be considered an open question).

Even where central Iran is within range of those aircraft, it may be well out of range of Soviet ground control.[102] Under Soviet ground-controlled intercept (GCI), target acquisition, vectoring, and other critical intercept instructions are transmitted from stations on the ground. If not actually out of range of Soviet-based GCI, then Soviet fighter operations in much of central Iran and all of southern Iran could be at ranges where the GCI link is highly susceptible to jamming by, for example, carrier-based EA-6B (four per carrier) electronic warfare aircraft. However rigidly the Soviet pilot is trained to fight under ground control, he is virtually untrained to fight without it.[103]

---

fighting in the war, a total of 86 Syrian planes, all first line, of the MiG-21, MiG-23 and Sukhoi-22 types, were shot down without the loss of one Israeli plane." Chaim Herzog, *The Arab-Israeli Wars*, p. 348. See also Peter deLeon, *The Peacetime Evaluation of the Pilot Skill Factor in Air-to-Air Combat*.

101. The possibility of re-equipping the longer-range Su-24 ground-attack aircraft for air-to-air combat is unpromising. First, it is an open question whether rudimentary Afghan bases could accommodate the system. But more important, the Su-24 pilot, rigidly drilled in his ground-attack mission, cannot easily be converted to a master of air-to-air combat, even if his aircraft could be so adapted. Similarly, air-to-air pilots are unlikely ever to have flown the Su-24 and would be ill prepared to substitute for its usual operators.

102. Soviet problems in maintaining the integrity of the ground-control data link as range increases are discussed in Col. V. A. Uryzhnikov, "In a Complex Situation." For further discussion, see Epstein, *Measuring Military Power*, chap. 4.

103. See Epstein, *Measuring Military Power*; and U.S. Department of the Air Force, *Soviet Aerospace Handbook*, p. 45.

The Soviets' problem is how to transport the GCI south of the northern mountains. An overland passage, because of all the vulnerabilities discussed above, would not be promising and would certainly be slow. So if the GCI is to be established with any dispatch, it must be airlifted in. To airlift it in, however, fighter escort would be essential. But the escort cannot be run effectively until the GCI is in place! There is the rub.

Even if airlanded in central Iran, the GCI radars and other components would be highly vulnerable to low-altitude attack by U.S. aircraft, especially if the strikes were conducted under cover of darkness using forward-looking infrared (FLIR) technology. And while Soviet airborne reconnaissance of low-level attack is progressing, it is generally agreed that, even in daylight, Soviet fighters do not possess a sophisticated look-down/shoot-down capability.[104] These factors support the assessment of General David C. Jones, who as chairman of the Joint Chiefs of Staff, in June of 1980, "told the Senate Armed Services Committee that 'a few AWACS' (Airborne Warning and Control Aircraft) 'and a few fighters could just devastate an airborne operation,' if the Soviet Armed Forces sought to seize oil fields in the Persian Gulf region."[105]

It is implicit in such assessments that warning time is exploited and that the decision to use force be taken. Otherwise, the West's significant advantages could erode and its promising defensive avenues quickly close.

U.S. Carrier Vulnerability

Finally, in a Soviet invasion of Iran, the worst-case scenario would posit the simultaneous initiation of airlifted and overland assaults, coordinated with a massed Soviet bomber attack on U.S. carriers. In discussing that threat, certain points should be stressed.

First, the strategy proposed here has four basic elements: two delay phases against the overland threat, the interdiction of Soviet airlift, and a buildup and combined-arms defense in Khuzestan. This, not the carriers per se, is what the Soviets must overcome. After all, even to sink the carriers would not, in and of itself, transport a single Russian to Khuzestan. Nor would it guarantee that the United States would be

104. Department of the Air Force, *Soviet Aerospace Handbook*, p. 66; and Epstein, *Measuring Military Power*, p. 113.
105. Quoted in John M. Collins, *U.S.-Soviet Military Balance*, note on p. 394.

incapable of carrying out its own strategy. If the carriers can survive and perform effectively long enough to ensure that the four basic operations are executed, they will have accomplished their war mission.

Just as carrier interdiction is not, per se, the Soviets' war goal, so carrier survival is not, per se, the RDF's goal; that is to deny Soviet control of Khuzestan. And if American interests in the area are vital, then the United States should be willing to run the risk that carriers will be lost. The carriers, after all, were bought to fight. And while their vulnerability can and should be minimized, in a fight, they may be destroyed.

The carriers are at their most vulnerable only in the initial period, when the northern tier of Iranian choke points is being struck and the Marine perimeter in Khuzestan is being established. But even in that period, as noted above, the carriers can be employed in a way that avoids their passage into the Persian Gulf, leaves them substantial resources for air defense, and allows for their timely and rapid withdrawal to the Arabian Sea area. And while all is not lost even if the carriers are lost, there is no particular reason that they should be.[106]

The Soviet Bomber Threat

Of the two Soviet bomber forces, Long-Range Aviation (LRA) and Naval Aviation, the former is deployed to the European Soviet Union (two air armies) and to the Far East (one air army).[107] A significant diversion of Long-Range Aviation's bomber resources to a Gulf campaign would clearly represent a sacrifice in the Soviets' capacity to execute either the NATO or Sino-Soviet contingency at the same time, not to mention those strategic nuclear missions for which LRA might be withheld. Particularly in the European theater, the presence of LRA and of Naval Aviation's Northern and Baltic fleet bomber forces would be critical, if the Soviets are credibly to threaten the execution of their short-war doctrine, or the achievement of their vaunted preemption there.

Accordingly, unless it is assumed that the Soviets are willing to free

106. Of course, should the carriers be destroyed by nuclear means, a U.S. nuclear response on the northern transportation system would still deny the Soviets their posited objective, as would the clearly more provocative nuclear response on division bases, rail lines, air fields, supply dumps, or other conventional military facilities in the southern USSR.

107. IISS, *Military Balance, 1981–1982*, p. 11.

U.S. forces otherwise earmarked to cope with those Soviet threats to Europe, one's attention should first be directed to the Pacific and Black Sea fleets of Naval Aviation. However, were the entire Pacific Fleet force reallocated to the Gulf, the Soviets would have to forgo maritime strike operations in defense of critical facilities in the Vladivostok area. Similarly, a full redeployment of the Black Sea Fleet would free U.S. forces in the Eastern Mediterranean from the threat of bomber attack. Even if such wholesale redeployments were attempted, one may doubt the basing capacity of the southern Soviet Union to accommodate them. Finally, the *total* Backfire inventory of Naval Aviation's *four* fleets is reported to be roughly 100 bombers.[108] Thus even on the questionable assumption that a sizable portion of *two* (Black Sea and Pacific) fleet bomber forces were allocated to this mission, the number of Backfire bombers involved could be even more limited.

As for warning of such an attack, the Soviets would need a certain amount of time to ready their forces. They might succeed in doing so under cover of deception. But if, as postulated, the bomber attack is to take place simultaneously with the overland drive, it must wait until the Soviet ground forces are mobilized. And of that activity, the United States would have warning. It would certainly be odd for the Soviets to maximize surprise in the bomber attack by launching it a month before the ground forces were ready to exploit it. In short, the United States would have warning time in which to ready its resistance.

"Layered" Carrier Defenses

Although there are uncertainties, when the above factors are taken into account, the bomber threat facing the carriers' multiple defensive "layers" does not seem unmanageable. Assets for the so-called outer air battle, in the words of former Chief of Naval Operations Admiral Thomas B. Hayward,

> consist primarily of the E-2B/C airborne early warning aircraft used to detect and track incoming aircraft and missiles, the F-14 variable-geometry fighter which is capable of launching and tracking as many as six AIM-54A long-range PHOENIX air intercept missiles, and the F-4 fighter aircraft capable of launching the AIM-7 SPARROW all-aspect air intercept missile.[109]

108. IISS, *Military Balance, 1985–1986*, p. 25.

109. U.S. Congress, House, Committee on Appropriations, *Department of Defense Appropriations for 1980*, Hearings, pt. 2, p. 266.

The F-4 and A-7 are being replaced by the F/A-18. Former Secretary of the Navy W. Graham Claytor testified, moreover, that the F-14 "can go out and shoot down the Russians' Backfire out of range of its ability to launch a missile."[110]

Soviet bombers surviving that first layer, while remaining susceptible to further counterair (air-to-air) resistance and jamming, would pass into the second ring of carrier defenses. Again, the usual discussions present an image of carriers operating alone. But the carrier, albeit a prima donna, is a social animal whose coterie of guided missile escorts is designed to provide it with a tough area defense.[111]

Finally, the Soviet bombers would encounter the carrier battle group's so-called self-defense. Here, the U.S. Navy looks "at two types of 'kills'—the 'hard kill' in which we destroy the inbound missile and the 'soft kill' in which we deceive the missile so that it misses the target."[112]

In addition, it should be borne in mind that the closer a Soviet bomber gets to the carriers, the thinner becomes its fighter escort. And over a broad perimeter around the carriers, it would be likely to lack any fighter protection. Essentially the same serious vulnerability would then prevail as in the case of Soviet airlift.

If a Soviet bomber survives to launch its missiles, and the carrier battle group's layered defenses fail to intercept or deceive them, there still remains the question of accuracy. One may assume hit probabilities greater than 50 percent if one chooses, but it would be irresponsible not to raise those assumed on the RDF's side correspondingly. And to do so would allow the RDF's northern interdiction campaign (phase I) to be conducted more quickly.

Moreover, even a hit is not necessarily a kill. Carriers can be rather durable entities.

> During training exercises in 1969, the nuclear carrier ENTERPRISE endured explosions of nine major caliber bombs (equivalent in explosive weight to 6 anti-ship cruise missiles) on the flight deck. All essential ship systems remained operable, effective damage control contained the effects of the fire, and the ship could have resumed flight operations within hours.[113]

The carrier's defense against ship- and submarine-launched cruise

110. Ibid., p. 277.
111. Ibid., p. 266.
112. Ibid.
113. Ibid., p. 268.

missiles is likewise one layered in depth, terminating in "rings of long and medium range surface-to-air missiles (SAM), close-in SAMs, and aircraft."[114] The carrier-based F-14 is reported to have demonstrated a capacity to engage six such targets.[115] The tactical antisubmarine warfare system of the carrier task force is organized along similar lines and might be visualized as an inverted, underwater variation on its anti-air-warfare rings.

These capabilities give the carrier battle group a more-than-fighting chance in the Gulf region, an area in which the limited Soviet surface fleet would lack comparable defensive avenues and logistical support, that is, underway replenishment.[116]

Destruction of the carriers would in itself be a formidable task. Moreover, to frustrate the larger four-point RDF strategy proposed here, the Soviets would have to destroy them *very* quickly. If the United States uses its warning time to ready the carriers' imposing defenses, it is hard to imagine great Soviet confidence of success even if the Russian bombers are focused on their destruction. And that allocation is questionable.

Diversion of Soviet Bombers

For the Soviets to focus their full bomber threat on the RDF's carriers would leave them virtually no resources with which to harass the proposed Marine landing in Khuzestan. As noted above, the preponderance of Soviet *tactical* air effectively lacks either the range to attack the Khuzestan landing or the capacity to operate from the crude Afghan bases that might be within range.[117]

Diego Garcia, which the United States already controls, is presumed capable of accommodating B-52s.[118] Given its importance as a maritime

114. Ibid., p. 282.

115. Ibid., p. 264.

116. Indeed, a Washington official has stated that "even if they move in the Minsk [V/STOL carrier], it would be no contest." "Soviet Naval Presence Doubles in Indian Ocean, Lacks Support," p. 60.

117. If one is to assume that from Afghanistan, the Soviet Bear bomber can penetrate the F-14 net to attack U.S. carriers in the Persian Gulf or Gulf of Oman, then the U.S. B-52H should certainly be assumed capable of penetrating the Soviet MiG-21 (or MiG-23) net to attack Afghan bases. Spif's B-52H night–low altitude mission is specifically designed to exploit the weakness of Soviet look-down/shoot-down capabilities. See Wilson, " 'Anytime Anywhere.' "

118. See note 26.

staging area generally, Diego Garcia would be yet another target to which the Soviets might be forced to divert bombers.

In short, the Soviets face a target system considerably more complicated than the two carriers. And this contributes to the carriers' already substantial survivability by forcing some dispersion of Soviet bomber resources.

If, during the warning time that should be available, the RDF's third carrier were brought on line, the force's interdiction and landing operations might be conducted even more rapidly. In that case, the Soviets would have (a) yet more targets to destroy, (b) an even denser air defense to overcome in doing so, and (c) even less time in which to accomplish the task.

Summary

While facing a redundant, flexible, and in fact rather dispersed resistance, the Soviets possess only two viable modes of advance—airlifted and overland—into Iran. In capitalizing on the Soviets' recognized vulnerabilities, the proposed RDF's essential missions are to delay the overland advance (phases I and II) and to interdict Soviet airlift, while building up for and executing a combined-arms defense in Khuzestan (phase III). If the Soviet goal is control of Iran's oil region, this tactical scheme, rather than a forward defense, is appropriate. And *if warning time is exploited,* U.S. forces should be able to execute the plan conventionally. In the pitched battle of Khuzestan, that is, the Soviet force which could be supported without penalizing the USSR's capacity to handle simultaneous contingencies would be unlikely to enjoy any meaningful superiority over a 5-division RDF assembled under the same strategic constraint.[119] And if the deep problem of Soviet coordination were exploited, it is questionable whether the Soviet force would even achieve parity with that RDF.

119. Indeed, if deployment is sufficiently timely, the baseline RDF of 4⅔ divisions (see table 4-1) should be adequate against either mode of Soviet attack, as demonstrated in cases 1 and 3 above. Beyond providing greater confidence of success in the event of timely response, the 5-division force recommended here provides a hedge against the situation in which the U.S. response to a Soviet direct-drive attack is insufficiently timely (case 2). The adequacy of the 5-division force with augmented close air support in that event was demonstrated in case 2A. (For detailed assumptions, see appendix table D-1.)

CHAPTER FIVE

Conclusions

THE IRANIAN revolution and the Soviet invasion of Afghanistan presented the United States with a strategic problem of the first order. Guided by a conviction that symmetrical response (that is, direct conventional defense) was essentially infeasible, the search for a strategy of containment in the Persian Gulf led the United States to entertain asymmetrical responses of two distinct kinds: vertical and horizontal escalation. Neither can provide the basis for a credible deterrent to Soviet aggression.

Asymmetrical Responses

If the West had ever overcome its "nuclear addiction" of the 1950s, it certainly had a relapse when Soviet troops invaded Afghanistan. As in Europe, however, it is extremely doubtful that the tactical use of nuclear weaponry in the Gulf—even if limited to a small number of extremely localized applications—would be of net advantage to the United States. And it is highly questionable whether, once over the threshold, the use of such weapons could be so limited in any event. Escalatory pressures would be exceedingly high on both sides. The availability of remote and tactically lucrative targets in the Persian Gulf, moreover, could do as much to stimulate escalation as to restrain it.

While the presence of nuclear options enhances deterrence, a primary reliance on them would undermine its credibility. The Soviets must not be permitted to rule out the possibility of American nuclear use. But if deterrence fails, then for all the reasons set forth in chapter 2—and especially the risk of escalation—the United States must, as in Europe, possess powerful conventional alternatives to nuclear response. The internal rationale (as revealed in once top secret Draft Presidential

98

Memoranda) for reducing NATO's reliance on such options in favor of flexible response applies with great force to superpower contingencies outside Europe today.

If one accepts this logic but also believes symmetrical response to be infeasible, then there is only one alternative: horizontal escalation, a second type of asymmetrical strategy. Entertained by the Carter administration, this idea was elevated to the level of official defense policy only in the Reagan administration. Despite the surface appeal of the approach, a number of critical issues have never been addressed. What Soviet behavior (capitulation? redeployment of forces? negotiation?) is the horizontal counteroffensive supposed to elicit? How does one determine a horizontal target to be of sufficient value to the Soviets to compel the behavior sought, but not of such great value as to provoke rash and wildly disproportionate (especially nuclear) reactions? Would an effective horizontal action divert so much American force from direct defense as to leave the United States under pressure to use nuclear weapons in the main contingency? (In the worst of all outcomes, both sides could face such incentives.) What opportunities would the Soviets have for counterhorizontal escalation (against Berlin, for example)? Were such Soviet options exploited, how confinable, controllable, would the war be? How much would horizontal escalation cost? In light of the strategy's grave risks and uncertainties, the case for its credibility is very weak indeed.

The attraction to strategies of asymmetrical—vertical or horizontal—response rests on the assumption that symmetrical response is not feasible. In fact, it is feasible.

Symmetrical Response

The Soviets possess only two viable modes of advance into Iran: airlifted and overland. In exploiting the Soviets' numerous vulnerabilities, a U.S. rapid deployment force has four essential missions: to delay, in two successive phases, the overland advance and to interdict Soviet airlift, while building up for and executing a combined-arms defense in Khuzestan. This strategy, rather than any form of asymmetrical response, is appropriate. And if warning time is exploited, an RDF of 5 divisions should be able to execute the plan conventionally. Specifically, the 5-division force (whose ground and close air makeup and assumed performance parameters are detailed under case 2A of appendix table D-1) succeeds as the *defender* against either mode of Soviet attack (direct drive or northern Iran buildup).[1] It also succeeds as the *attacker* following a Soviet preemptive direct-drive attack (case 2A of chapter 4). The only case in which the recommended 5-division force fails is when the Soviets, having first consolidated northern Iran as a base of operations, are permitted to entrench themselves as the prepared defenders in Khuzestan. But in that case not even the large 7⅓-division RDF envisioned by the Pentagon would stand a significant chance of driving the Soviets out (as shown in case 4A of chapter 4). In pitched battle against such Soviet defenses, the United States would likely face the dread choice between conventional defeat and escalation (vertical or horizontal). Meanwhile, the larger RDF incurs a larger diversion of conventional forces from NATO's European theater,[2] exacerbating alliance tensions associated with burden sharing.

In summary, if it gets there in time, a 5-division RDF should present an imposing deterrent to Soviet aggression. If it gets there too late, then not even a much larger RDF is likely to succeed. Thus rather than increasing the U.S. force's *size*, the highest priority should be to increase its *speed*.

The United States could efficiently meet its requirements by discarding its plans to expand the current RDF (CENTCOM) to 7⅓ divisions, holding the force to 5 divisions, and ensuring that it deploys in time to execute the plan elaborated above.

Crisis Management

As noted in the previous chapter's simulations, the Soviets actually do *better* outracing the United States into defensive positions with a force of 7¼ divisions (case 2) than they do with a force fully 50 percent larger that arrives too late to defend (case 3). Because the same operational pressures to "get there firstest" would be working on both the Soviets and the United States in a crisis, a superpower mobilization

1. This follows from the adequacy of the smaller (and less capable) baseline RDF of 4⅔ divisions (see table 4-1), whose successful performance as the defender against either mode of Soviet attack is demonstrated in cases 1 and 3 of chapter 4.

2. On the diversion, see U.S. Congressional Budget Office, *Rapid Deployment Forces*, pp. 19–27.

race in the Gulf would be ripe for escalatory miscalculation on both sides. Without putting too much emphasis on it—since the adversaries, the battlefield, and a host of other circumstances differ greatly—the analogy to 1914 is instructive. The perception of preemptive advantage certainly contributed to the outbreak of World War I.[3] Peacetime diplomacy should explicitly recognize and seek to reduce this crisis instability, communicating clearly the interpretation (if not the specific response) that will likely be assigned to Soviet actions short of—but preparatory to—war.

Regionally, any RDF is clearly better off with more military basing than it is with less. And there is no reason for the United States to abandon its efforts to negotiate suitable arrangements in the event of crisis. In doing so, however, the United States can afford to bargain from a position of strength, eschewing entanglements with regimes less worthy of American political support than military relationships may suggest; regimes whose stability (as Iran should have taught) may be far more tenuous than Americans might wish to believe; regimes which, in the final analysis, may acquire political interests quite inimical to those of the United States and to those of its proven ally, Israel.

It is understandable that European NATO allies would wish *to consult* before the United States deployed forces outside the NATO treaty area. It is also understandable that they would like the diversion of forces from the reinforcement of Europe to the Persian Gulf to be minimal. Unfortunately, these goals—to consult *and* have a minimal diversion—conflict rather seriously. The simulations in chapter 4 clearly show that a relatively small force (that is, the proposed 5-division RDF), entailing a modest diversion, is adequate only if it is *fast*. But it cannot be fast if its deployment requires that the North Atlantic Council convene and consult beforehand. If formal consultation is to take place, precious time will be lost, the deployment will not be fast, and an RDF even larger than 7⅓ divisions would, for that reason, be required. If so, the diversion from NATO could be very significant. Formal alliance consultation and minimal diversion are mutually exclusive.

A solution would seem to lie in the direction of *informal bilateral* agreements on such necessities as overflight rights and en route access

3. See Stephen Van Evera, "The Cult of the Offensive and the Origins of the First World War," pp. 58–107. The analogy to Liège is particularly appealing given the enormous advantage accruing to the prepared defender, and the vulnerability of road and rail lines in Iran.

that can facilitate the deployment. These arrangements could be settled long before a crisis; procedures could be put in place that would meet European definitions of consultation without endangering the RDF's conformity to its demanding deployment schedule, permitting the proposed force to be effective. The smaller diversion made possible by speed might—to a significant extent—be compensated for in Europe by a variety of relatively inexpensive means: enhancing the effectiveness of current NATO forces;[4] making more effective military use of NATO civilian assets;[5] and expeditiously proceeding with NATO's Long-Term Defense Program.[6]

Organizational Implications

Beginning in the 1940s and continuing through the 1950s, the Soviet General Staff, the U.S. Joint Chiefs of Staff, and the British Chiefs of Staff all examined in great operational detail the prospects for a Soviet invasion of Iran. Given the extreme secrecy of their work, it is truly remarkable that Soviet and Western planners should have arrived at such strikingly similar conclusions. Each of these professional military staffs—the three major planning organs of the postwar world—concluded in the strongest possible terms that Iran's forbidding terrain, the long distances from Russia to Khuzestan, the limited and vulnerable transportation system, and other factors combined to create imposing vulnerabilities for a Soviet invasion. Professional—then highly classified—opinion also converged on the most appropriate means by which to exploit those vulnerabilities and on the basic feasibility of doing so.

Given Western reliance on a militarily well-heeled shah, conventional force planning for this contingency fell by the wayside. With the fall of the shah, the Soviet invasion of Afghanistan, and the enunciation of the Carter Doctrine, it suddenly acquired renewed urgency. Although the fear of a Soviet invasion was resurrected, the plans for dealing with it were not. Why?

4. For NATO air forces, increases in airbase survivability, readiness, and sortie rates would fall into this category, for example.

5. NATO's vast commercial shipping capacity could be exploited more fully than it is. The British employed commercial shipping (for instance, the *Queen Elizabeth II*) with great success in the Falklands.

6. See U.S. Congress, House, Committee on Government Operations, *The Implementation of the NATO Long-Term Defense Program (LTDP)*.

Why, when each of the major planning organizations had studied the problem, when each had discovered independently the identical Soviet vulnerabilities, and had arrived (as if by telepathy) at the same tactics to exploit them, was this contingency proclaimed with such unbounded pessimism? Rather than dusting off the old—but solid—plans and updating them, it took the United States almost five years to arrive at the same basic solution the Joint Chiefs had outlined in 1949, entertaining some rather bizarre, and diplomatically damaging, strategic concepts in the interim. Tripwire nuclear deterrents and the threat of horizontal escalation were among them.

One answer is that military authorities were well aware of the highly relevant old plans and suppressed them, seeing the whole contingency as a way of justifying increased defense expenditures and creating new bureaucratic empires (which has occurred with the establishment of CENTCOM). This reading would be in keeping with the postulates of organization theory, generally speaking. Another answer is simply that the existing plans were forgotten, so that planners on the Joint Staff had to "reinvent the wheel." This reading is consistent with an impressive body of congressional testimony and blue-ribbon studies of the structure of the Joint Chiefs of Staff organization. As a consequence of service promotion patterns and the rapid rotation of officers through the Joint Staff, there is little institutional memory. There appears to be no institutionalized mechanism whereby elderly plans are regularly reviewed, resurrected, updated, and made accessible should circumstances warrant, as they most certainly did in this case. Some such mechanism—an operational-planning memory—should be created.

Analysis and Appeasement

The risks of underrating an adversary's strength are obvious. But there are also risks of overrating it. One of the forgotten "lessons of Munich" is that an overassessment of German confidence contributed to the policy of appeasement.[7] If we want political authorities to act and avoid surprise despite warning, we must convince them that resistance

7. The interested reader might begin with the Nuremberg testimony of the German generals themselves. See William L. Shirer, *The Rise and Fall of the Third Reich*, pp. 423–25.

stands some chance of success; nothing undermines timely decision-making more than a conviction that action is doomed to fail.

To argue the feasibility of a conventional defense is not to deny that the proposed RDF would have work ahead of it. It would, particularly in the areas of logistics, training, command and control, and in further detailed planning for the employment of its forces, some of which must be tailored very precisely to the tactics contemplated here. However, while stressing that the RDF would face challenges, the situation does not warrant the kind of pessimism that has been heaped upon it.

No one has found a way to predict with *certainty* the outcome of any given conflict. But the invasion of Iran would be an exceedingly *low-confidence* affair for the Soviets—a fact that I believe they have known for roughly forty years. Indeed, it can be argued that they now regard it as far less attractive even than their 1941 *Command Study* portrayed it as being. While, to be sure, Soviet military capabilities have evolved significantly since that time, so have those of the United States and, more important, so have the Soviets' military commitments and deterrent needs. Certainly to cover three contingencies simultaneously would strain the United States. But beyond China, NATO, and Afghanistan, an invasion of Iran would be the Soviets' fourth contingency. And it is one which, as has been shown, could severely hamper their capability elsewhere.

The Soviets face the grave threat that the military cost of a move on Iran would vastly outweigh its potential benefits—indeed, the risk that all such benefits would be decisively denied. It can only be assumed, therefore, that the Soviets would prefer to secure their ends in the Gulf by other means, by coercive measures short of direct intervention. All those measures find their underpinning, finally, in the appearance of crushing Soviet military power and in the perception that the Soviets are prepared to use it to get what they want, and are confident of doing so with success. The fundamental question, and it is a political one, is this: by overdrawing the direct Soviet threat to Iran—or to any country— does the United States not aid the Soviets in their diplomacy of coercion?

By presenting the United States as if it alone suffers simultaneous-contingency problems, and by presenting the Soviets as if they enjoyed some sort of clear superiority in the Gulf, we do. In the final analysis that is not "getting tough" with the Soviets. One gets tough with an adversary by credibly threatening to exploit his military vulnerabilities, not by refusing to admit that any exist, as is the general practice among so-called hard-liners. Such talk, however, is not hard on the Soviets. On the contrary, the rhetoric of an invincible Soviet threat, while alienating those whose cooperation we seek or exposing them to the coercion we fear, merely discredits the larger cause it purports to champion—management of the global East-West competition and deterrence of war. These are feasible goals. In the case of the Gulf, forces exist which can and should be postured to communicate that fact. While they are not invincible, the Soviets are attentive. They will get the message.

U.S. Tactical Air Force Requirements for Interdiction in Northern Iran

THIS APPENDIX presents in detail the target system to be struck in the first phase of the defensive plan proposed in chapter 4. The force of aircraft required to cover the target system is derived using the mathematical model of interdiction operations developed below. The equations are of general applicability.

The arteries to be struck and the coverage requirements per artery are elaborated in tables A-1 and A-2.

Table A-1. *Target Data Inventory for Phase I Air Interdiction: Arteries*

Artery	Number
Roads	
From Nakhichevan and Astara to Tabriz	2
From Tabriz to Qazvin	2
Over the Elburz Mts. to Qazvin or Tehran	6
From Bandar-e Torkman to Tehran	1
Rail	
Trans-Iranian railroad	1
Total	12

Sources: U.S. Central Intelligence Agency, "Map of Iran"; and Sahab Geographic and Drafting Institute, "Road Map of Iran." According to Stephen Canby and Edward Luttwak, the number is less than a dozen: "Across the 1,000 miles of the Iranian-USSR border as the crow flies, there are only ten transborder routes suitable for vehicular passage (including the Herat route from Afghanistan)." Stephen L. Canby and Edward N. Luttwak, *The Control of Arms Transfers and Perceived Security Needs,* p. 113.

Table A-2. *Target Data Inventory for Phase I Air Interdiction: Coverage*

Artery class	Number	×	Choke points specified per artery	×	DGZs[a] per choke point	=	DGZs
Roads	11		4		6		264
Rail	1		6		6		36
Total DGZs	. . .		. . .		. . .		300

a. A DGZ, or designated ground zero, is simply a specified detonation point. As the term is used here, the creation of a choke point is assumed, on average, to require the accurate delivery of six munitions. The munitions may differ from target to target, however. For example, bridge destruction and the setting up of rockslides are somewhat different matters. And there are uncertainties in each case. In setting up rockslides, a high-explosive munition employed against a sandstone wall will merely pulverize it, dusting the road one hopes to obstruct, while a munition of low yield, used with the intent of dislodging sandstone, may have no effect if the wall turns out to be marble. In short, very precise geological and positional data are required to tailor the attack to the terrain. In the case of heavily reinforced bridges, relatively heavy precision-guided ordnance (2,000-lb. MK-84 or 3,000-lb. M-118) is envisioned. According to a recent Rand Corporation report, "GBU-15s would prove most effective against such high-value targets as bridges, tunnels, and landslide areas. . . . The GBU-15 is a television-guided cruciform wing glide bomb that carries a 2,000 lb warhead. It can be launched from both low and high altitudes and its high accuracy would make it very effective against bridges, tunnels, and other point targets." Christopher J. Bowie, *Concepts of Operations and USAF Planning for Southwest Asia*, p. 37. Against softer targets, perhaps rail lines, somewhat lighter precision-guided munitions, or PGMs (1,000-lb. MK-83), may be appropriate. In the same use, the GBU-15 module with a dispenser munition (SUU-54) replacing the MK-84 warhead might also be appropriate, as could various fuel-air explosives. Either of these latter could be effective in the harassment of Soviet repair operations. In general, the GBU-15 modular glide bomb affords the RDF considerable flexibility in munitions guidance. Forward-looking infrared (FLIR) low-altitude night approaches combined with the GBU-15 infrared imaging guidance/MK-84 package would be difficult to counter in bridge interdiction, for example. While the Walleye II (850 lbs.) was designed for the above mission, it could be suitable in setting up rockslides, as could standard 750-lb. bombs.

I do not tailor the munitions to the targets here. On the reasonable assumption that munitions are so tailored, the further assumption that, when averaged, the accurate delivery of six will suffice to create a choke point is conservative and is consistent with U.S. operational experience using precision-guided bombs against bridges in Vietnam. See Maj. A. J. C. Lavalle, ed., *The Tale of Two Bridges and the Battle for the Skies over North Vietnam*.

Interdiction Model: Variables, Values, and Equations

To estimate the force required to execute the interdiction campaign summarized in table A-2 (300 accurately delivered munitions), a model is developed. The variables involved, the numerical values assumed, and the equations employed are presented below.

	Variable	*Assumed value*
r	Operational readiness rate of the weapon system, in this case the F-111	0.80[a]

a. Christopher J. Bowie, *Concepts of Operations and USAF Planning for Southwest Asia*, p. 37.

m	Mean number of ground attack munitions carried per aircraft	4.00[b]
P_K	Mean probability that each such munition is accurately delivered on its DGZ	0.45[c]
n	Mean number of Soviet air defense shots to which each attack aircraft is exposed per sortie	2.00[d]
P_d	Mean kill probability for each such Soviet shot	0.10[d]
s	Mean sortie rate (sorties/plane/day)	2.00[e]
d	Total days allotted for the operation (300 accurate deliveries in expected value)	See below
$E(d)$	Expected number of munitions accurately delivered at the end of d days	300
t	Sortie counter	. . .
$F(0)$	Number of aircraft required initially to conduct, without reinforcement, the specified operation ($E(d) = 300$)	To be solved for

b. Ibid., four GBU-15s per F-111 sortie.

c. Despite projections of extremely high accuracy, and despite peacetime "lab" accuracies in the 90 percent range, actual wartime experience indicates that precision-guided (laser and electro-optical) munitions (PGMs) achieved hit frequencies of between 0.41 and 0.55 when used in 1973 against bridges in North Vietnam (Operation Linebacker). The figures 0.41 and 0.55 are computed from data given in Maj. A. J. C. Lavalle, ed., *The Tale of Two Bridges and the Battle for the Skies over North Vietnam*, p. 90. The lower figure counts only confirmed hits, the higher figure counts probable hits as well. The assumption of 0.45 is clearly quite conservative by these lights. See Joshua M. Epstein, *Measuring Military Power*, pp. 148–49, for a further discussion of the gap between peacetime expectations and wartime performance in this area.

d. The assumed values for n and P_d taken together imply an attrition rate per sortie of $1 - (1 - P_d)^n = 1 - (0.9)^2 = 0.19$, or 19 percent. The highest per sortie attrition rate suffered by the Israelis in the Yom Kippur War was on the Golan, 1.5 percent (A-4s). Overall, the Israelis suffered 0.8 percent attrition per sortie. Over North Vietnam, from 1965 to 1973, the U.S. Navy value was 0.1 percent, and overall, for the same period, in Southeast Asia, it was 0.5 percent per sortie. CBO, *Navy Budget Issues for Fiscal Year 1980*, p. 98. The number used here is thus quite conservative, exceeding the highest of these cases by a factor of over ten. The n-value of two shots per sortie is also conservative, especially against an attacker (the rapid deployment force) using FLIR technology, operating around the clock (at night), and approaching at low altitude a defender lacking a sophisticated look-down/shoot-down capability. The Soviet P_d value of 0.10 is very close to the 0.11 recorded by the U.S. AIM-7E in Vietnam. Benjamin F. Schemmer, "Pentagon, White House, and Congress Concerned over Tactical Aircraft Complexity and Readiness," p. 34.

e. A nominal rate for attack aircraft. James F. Dunnigan, *How to Make War*, p. 113. It is nonetheless assumed in order to minimize the virtual attrition that may be induced by those maintenance deferrals necessitated by higher sortie rates. That effect is modeled in Epstein, *Measuring Military Power*, where a further discussion of sortie rates and a more elaborate model of interdiction operations may be found.

Given some initial force, $F(0)$, $rF(0)$ are operationally ready. Of these, $(1 - P_d)^n rF(0)$ survive the first sortie. To be conservative, let us assume that all attrition manifests itself before the aircraft reaches its targets. Each of the $(1 - P_d)^n rF(0)$ aircraft that reaches its targets covers, in expected value, mP_K DGZs. Or,

$$rmP_K F(0)(1 - P_d)^n = \text{DGZs covered in the first sortie.}$$

Attrition proceeds, and we have

$$rmP_K F(0)(1 - P_d)^{2n} = \text{DGZs covered in the second sortie.}$$

In general,

$$rmP_K F(0)(1 - P_d)^{tn} = \text{DGZs covered in the } t\text{th sortie.}$$

Setting the sum of these terms equal to the requirement, $E(d)$, we obtain

$$rmP_K F(0) \sum_{t=1}^{sd} (1 - P_d)^{nt} = E(d),$$

where the upper bound, sd, is simply the total sorties executed; sorties per day (s) times days allotted (d). This equation in hand, the initial force required is easily obtained:

$$F(0) = \frac{E(d)}{rmP_K \sum_{t=1}^{sd} (1 - P_d)^{nt}}$$

To each judgment as to time urgency, d (days allotted), there corresponds a required initial force $(F(0))$. Simply applying the assumed values in the above equation, a range of choices for d yields the range of on-station air requirements shown in table A-3.

The first entry demonstrates the adequacy of two F-111 wings, as claimed in the text. Since each of the rapid deployment force's two F-111 wings possesses ninety, rather than the usual seventy-two, aircraft, this conclusion will not be substantially altered by assumptions even more conservative than those underlying this estimate.[1]

The sensitivity of the required force $(F(0))$ to variations in one's assumptions regarding payload (m) and accuracy (P_K) is given in table A-4.

It is apparent that, as noted in the text, an increase in the P_K, other things being equal, may be interpreted either as reducing the number of

---

1. The ninety-plane-per-wing figure is from Bowie, *Concepts of Operations*, p. 28.

Table A-3. *Air Requirements*

Time urgency (days) d	Force required (aircraft) F(0)	Time urgency (days) d	Force required (aircraft) F(0)
1	142	5	56
2	86	6	53
3	68	7	52
4	60		

Table A-4. *Sensitivity to Payload and Accuracy*

Assumptions	Day(s) allotted (d)						
	1	2	3	4	5	6	7
$m = 4, P_K = 0.5$	128	77	61	54	50	48	47
$m = 4, P_K = 0.6$	106	64	51	45	42	40	39
$m = 4, P_K = 0.7$	91	55	44	39	36	34	33
$m = 3, P_K = 0.5$	170	103	82	72	67	64	62
$m = 3, P_K = 0.6$	142	86	68	60	56	53	52
$m = 3, P_K = 0.7$	122	74	59	51	48	46	44

aircraft required or, at a fixed number of aircraft, as reducing the time required to execute the interdiction campaign. Selection of parameters corresponding more closely to different aircraft (for example, the F-16 or A-6) will allow the assessment of alternative basing and force-mix options.

Soviet Logistics Truck Requirements for the Battle of Khuzestan

IN THIS APPENDIX equations are developed that allow one to estimate the number of logistics trucks required to sustain a given force in combat at any specified distance from its supply base, or equivalently, to estimate the force that can be sustained in combat at a specified distance given a fixed pool of logistics trucks. The equations are applied below to estimate the Soviet ground force that can be sustained at full lethality in high-intensity combat at two distances—1,200 and 800 kilometers—from the USSR. These distances correspond to the two basic Soviet attack options (direct drive and northern Iran buildup) discussed in chapter 4.

	Variable	Assumed value
x	Number of Soviet divisions sustainable (at the assumed lethality) in Khuzestan	Value to be solved for
k	Short tons (STONs) of combat consumables required by each division per day	1,675 STONs[a]

a. The daily requirement of ammunition alone for the standard U.S. armored division on the defensive is 2,432.6 STONs. U.S. Department of the Army, *Staff Officers' Field Manual*, p. 7-5. When other classes of consumables—petroleum, oil, lubricants, spare parts, food, and so forth—are included the tonnage rises considerably. To account for these, I have rounded the U.S. figure up, to 2,500 STONs. Since I am rating the Soviet division at roughly two-thirds of a U.S. armored division equivalent (ADE), I take their daily tonnage requirement to be $0.67 \times 2,500 = 1,675$. This assumes implicitly that the Soviets obtain roughly the same lethality per ton of ordnance as does the United States, which, of the two, has certainly been the more vigorous in pursuing lighter, precision ordnance. The figure thus credits the Soviets with at least U.S. efficiency in this lethality/ton sense.

d	Average on-road distance from Soviet bases to line of engagement in Khuzestan	1,200 km (direct-drive attack); 800 km (northern Iran buildup)[b]
v	Average speed of logistics truck	25 km/hour[c]
u	Average operating time per truck per day (utilization rate)	15 hours/day[d]
a	Average truck availability	0.80[e]
c	Average fraction of truck capacity utilized	0.75[f]
p	Average payload per truck	4.0 STONs[g]
T	Table of Organization and Equipment (TO&E) trucks per division	1,350[h]
α	Daily truck attrition rate (virtual + actual attrition)	0
n	Duration of conflict in days	Varies with scenario
S	Theater pool of divisions	24[i]
β	Truck division equivalents (TDEs) per theater division (average fraction of 1,350 trucks in each of the theater divisions)	1.0

b. Estimates derived from Sahab Geographic and Drafting Institute, "Road Map of Iran."

c. U.S. Army estimate for poor roads. Department of the Army, *Staff Officers' Field Manual*, p. 7-17.

d. Average of minimum (10 hours) and maximum (20 hours) operating hours in U.S. practice. Ibid.

e. In the U.S. case, 83 percent is "maximum sustained effort; used only for all-out effort, and then only for periods of less than 30 days." Ibid., p. 7-16. The long-range planning figure is given as 75 percent. I have given the Soviets a value better than the average of the two.

f. According to the U.S. Army *Staff Officers' Field Manual*, "experience has shown that, due to cargo density and other factors, approximately two-thirds of the rated capacity is usually attained." Ibid., p. 7-17. I credit the Soviets with 75 percent of capacity utilized.

g. Based on interviews. Andrew Krepinevich of West Point uses 3.0 in his unpublished study "The U.S. Rapid Deployment Force and Protection of Persian Gulf Oil Supplies."

h. Jeffrey Record, *Sizing Up the Soviet Army*, p. 29. The assumption that all 1,350 are *logistics* trucks is favorable to the Soviets, since some would be troop transports and other nonconsumables carriers.

i. The theater pool comprises the 24 tank and motorized rifle divisions of the Transcaucasus, North Caucasus, and Turkestan military districts. International Institute for Strategic Studies, *The Military Balance, 1983–1984*, p. 16.

The in-theater supply of TDEs is, by definition,

(B-1) $\text{Supply} = S\beta.$

In the zero-attrition case, the engaged force's demand for TDEs is given by

(B-2) $\text{Demand} = \dfrac{xk(2d/v)}{(pc)(Ta)u}.$

This demand equation is the zero-delay equivalent of the U.S. Army's planning equation:[1]

$$\frac{\left(\begin{array}{c}\text{Daily tonnage}\\ \text{forward}\end{array}\right) \cdot \left(\dfrac{2 \cdot \text{distance}}{\text{rate}} + \text{delays}\right)}{\left(\begin{array}{c}\text{Tons per}\\ \text{vehicle}\end{array}\right) \cdot \left(\begin{array}{c}\text{Vehicles available}\\ \text{per company}\end{array}\right) \cdot \left(\begin{array}{c}\text{Operating}\\ \text{time per day}\end{array}\right)} = \begin{array}{c}\text{Truck companies}\\ \text{required.}\end{array}$$

Inclusion of a daily truck attrition term generalizes equation B-2 to

(B-3) $\text{Demand} = \dfrac{xk(2d/v)}{pcT(1 - \alpha)^n au}.$

Thus, in general, the demand-supply gap, or extratheater-penalty function, $P(x)$, is given by the difference of equations B-3 and B-1, or

(B-4) $P(x) = x\left(\dfrac{k(2d/v)}{pcT(1 - \alpha)^n au}\right) - S\beta.$

To determine the number of Soviet divisions sustainable in Khuzestan in a direct-drive attack from the USSR, we apply the values assumed above with d equal to 1,200 kilometers, obtaining

$$P(x) = 3.31x - 24.$$

Setting $P(x)$ equal to zero (no drawdown from outside the theater), we solve for x and find that a force of 7.25 Soviet divisions could be supported in a direct-drive attack.

To support the 24-division "threat" would entail an extratheater drawdown of 55 divisions, that is, when $x = 24$, $P(x) = 55$.

Applying the values assumed for the attack in which the Soviets take northern Iran first ($d = 800$ kilometers) yields a sustainable force of 10.88 divisions.

1. Department of the Army, *Staff Officers' Field Manual,* p. 4-13.

Figure B-1. *Soviet Simultaneous Contingency Penalty Function for Direct-Drive Attack*

Extratheater requirements, in truck
division equivalents (P(x))

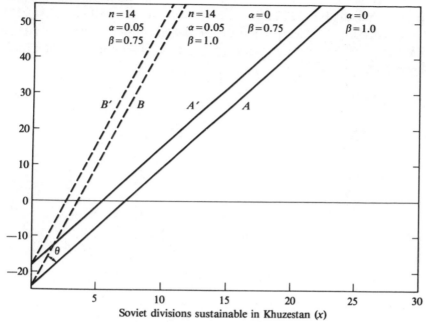

Soviet divisions sustainable in Khuzestan (x)

Two types of sensitivity should be distinguished. The extratheater penalty function for the direct-drive attack with no attrition ($\alpha = 0$) and with each in-theater division equipped with its full complement of trucks ($\beta = 1.0$) is graphed in figure B-1 as solid line A. Leaving attrition at zero ($\alpha = 0$), if we assume that the in-theater divisions, S, are equipped with less than their 100 percent complement of trucks, line A shifts leftward. At $\beta = 0.75$ (line A'), the theater pool is $S\beta = 24 \times 0.75 = 18$ TDEs and without an extratheater drawdown, only 5.44 divisions would be supportable in Khuzestan. Sensitivity to β is thus reflected in the $P(x)$-intercept.

At a fixed β, changes in other variables, while leaving the $P(x)$-intercept unaltered, will change the slope of the line. For example, on a two-week basis ($n = 14$) the assumption of a daily truck attrition of 5 percent ($\alpha = 0.05$) swings line A up through the angle θ to line B ($n = 14$, $\alpha = 0.05$, $\beta = 1.0$). On these assumptions, a force of but 3.55 divisions could be supported in Khuzestan without penalty to other contingencies. Or, equivalently, to support the 7.25 division force would require an extratheater drawdown of 25 TDEs.

One factor not reflected in the model is the status of the extratheater divisions themselves. If, for example, they are at the 75 percent level in trucks, then to obtain 25 TDEs from them would in fact denude $25/0.75 = 33.3$ divisions of their trucks. The actual constraint on other theaters imposed by a penalty expressed in TDEs may be far greater than has been discussed here.

An Adaptive Model of War: Ground and Close Air Engagement Equations

IN THIS APPENDIX the model's ground and close air support variables are defined.[1] Then the equations are presented and their development explained.

The numerical assumptions used for the battle of Khuzestan simulations discussed in chapter 4, along with the simulation results plotted in that chapter, and selected sensitivity analyses, are set out in appendix D.

Variables

Ground Forces

$A_g(t)$ Attacker's ground lethality surviving at start of tth day[2]

---

1. This model, developed by the author, was first published in Joshua M. Epstein, *The Calculus of Conventional War*.

2. The term *lethality* refers to the aggregate combat power of the force (based primarily on its weaponry) expressed in common numerical units. In the U.S. Army's so-called WEI/WUV system, described in chapter 4, the lethality of a force may be gauged by a weighted aggregation of the strength of its component units. The components are assigned weapon effectiveness indices (WEIs). These are then weighted and summed to obtain the force's weighted unit value (WUV). The WUV score of a standard U.S. armored division is 47,490. (This, by definition, is the WUV score of one armored division equivalent, or ADE. It can be used to convert ADEs to WUVs and vice versa.) For WUV scores, see William P. Mako, *U.S. Ground Forces and the Defense of Central Europe*.

$\alpha_g(t)$ Attacker's ground prosecution rate per day,[3] $0 \le \alpha_g(t) \lesssim 1$

$\alpha(t)$ Attacker's ground-to-ground lethality attrition rate per day (no-airpower case),[4] $0 \le \alpha(t) \le 1$

$\alpha_a(t)$ Attacker's total ground-lethality attrition rate per day (air- and ground-induced), $0 \le \alpha_a(t) \le 1$

α_{aT} Attacker's threshold, or equilibrium, attrition rate; the value of $\alpha_a(t)$ the Attacker seeks to achieve and sustain, $0 < \alpha_{aT} \le 1$

$D_g(t)$ Defender's ground lethality surviving at start of tth day

ρ Attacker's ground lethality killed per Defender's ground lethality killed (average ground-to-ground casualty-exchange ratio)[5]

α_{dT} Defender's threshold attrition rate; the value beyond which withdrawal begins, $0 \le \alpha_{dT} < 1$

$\alpha_d(t)$ Defender's total ground-lethality attrition rate per day (air- and ground-induced), $0 \le \alpha_d(t) \le 1$

$W(t)$ Defender's rate of withdrawal in kilometers per day

$W_{\max}$ Defender's maximum rate of withdrawal

t Time in days, $t = 1, 2, 3, \ldots$

Close Air Support Forces

$D_a(t)$ Defender's close air support (CAS) aircraft surviving at start of tth day

α_{da} Defender's CAS aircraft attrition rate per sortie, $0 \le \alpha_{da} \le 1$

S_d Defender's CAS daily sortie rate

3. As specified below, $\alpha_g(1)$ is set equal to some initial value less than α_{aT}. Technically, one could set $\alpha_g(1) = \alpha_{aT}$. But in that case the model degenerates into one in which the defender is adaptive but the attacker is not.

4. This is the attrition rate due only to defensive ground fire.

5. In this model ρ is interpreted as a constant, an average. (This is certainly no more problematic than Lanchester's treatment of his effectiveness coefficients as constants. See James G. Taylor, *Lanchester Models of Warfare*, vol. 1, pp. 111–12. For ease of reference, the Lanchester equations are summarized in appendix E at note 1.) More elaborate extensions of the present model could allow ρ to vary in time or space or both (for example, as a function of the position of the front, to reflect a sequence of progressively improving, or worsening, defensive positions prepared in depth). When the model is solved for ρ in the no-airpower case, ρ (a constant) equals the ratio of time-dependent variables (specifically, the differences). But this is not at all unusual; the ratio of time-dependent variables can be constant. The Lanchester linear variant illustrates the mathematical point; the differentials $dR(t)$ and $dB(t)$ are time-dependent. Their ratio nonetheless equals the constant b/r. (See appendix E for definitions.) There exists an infinitude of other examples.

For a number of historical exchange ratios, see Barry R. Posen, "Measuring the European Conventional Balance," pp. 56, 80–81.

K_d Attacker's armored fighting vehicles (AFVs) killed per Defender CAS sortie

$A_a(t)$ Attacker's CAS aircraft surviving at start of tth day

α_{aa} Attacker's CAS aircraft attrition rate per sortie, $0 \leq \alpha_{aa} \leq 1$

K_a Defender's AFVs killed per Attacker CAS sortie

S_a Attacker's CAS daily sortie rate

V AFVs per division equivalent (DE)

L Lethality points per DE[6]

$ACAS(t)$ Defensive ground lethality killed by Attacker's CAS on the tth day

$DCAS(t)$ Attacking ground lethality killed by Defender's CAS on the tth day

Equations

The general equations for the battle are simply

(C-1) $A_g(t) = A_g(t - 1)[1 - \alpha(t - 1)] - DCAS(t - 1)$

and

(C-2) $D_g(t) = D_g(t - 1) - \dfrac{\alpha(t - 1)}{\rho} A_g(t - 1) - ACAS(t - 1),$

where

(C-3) $$\alpha(t) = \alpha_g(t)\left(1 - \frac{W(t)}{W_{max}}\right)$$

and

(C-4) $W(t) = \begin{cases} 0 & \text{if } \alpha_d(t-1) \leq \alpha_{dT} \\[2mm] W(t-1) + \left(\dfrac{W_{max} - W(t-1)}{1 - \alpha_{dT}}\right)(\alpha_d(t-1) - \alpha_{dT}) & \text{if } \alpha_d(t-1) > \alpha_{dT} \end{cases}$

with

(C-5) $$\alpha_d(t) = \frac{D_g(t) - D_g(t + 1)}{D_g(t)}.$$

6. The lethality measure used in this book is weighted unit value, or WUV, discussed in note 2. The L value used is the WUV score of one armored division equivalent: 47,490. Mako, *U.S. Ground Forces*, p. 114.

We set $W(1) = 0$. On the attacker's side,

$$\text{(C-6)} \quad \alpha_g(t) = \alpha_g(t-1) - \left(\frac{\alpha_{aT} - \alpha_g(t-1)}{\alpha_{aT}}\right)(\alpha_a(t-1) - \alpha_{aT})$$

with

$$\text{(C-7)} \qquad\qquad \alpha_a(t) = \frac{A_g(t) - A_g(t+1)}{A_g(t)}.$$

We set $\alpha_g(1)$ equal to some initial value ($\alpha_g(1) < \alpha_{aT}$; see note 3).

One can leave airpower out by omitting the terms $DCAS(t)$ and $ACAS(t)$. In that case the state equation is

$$\text{(C-8)} \qquad\qquad \rho[D_g(1) - D_g(t)] = A_g(1) - A_g(t)$$

and the stalemate condition[7] is simply

$$\text{(C-9)} \qquad\qquad D_g(1) = \frac{A_g(1)}{\rho}.$$

7. This stalemate expression has the same algebraic form as the Lanchester linear stalemate condition (see note 1 of appendix E). Therefore, if the same numerical value is assigned to ρ as that assigned to *the ratio of* Lanchester linear coefficients, the two models will produce the same stalemate requirement. This is the only point of tangency between the two models (a point that ceases to exist if ρ is made time-dependent); and an infinitude of other models possesses stalemate conditions of the same algebraic form. This point of formal correspondence does not imply—nor is it the case—that my model is reducible to the Lanchester linear model (or conversely). The two make totally different estimates of daily attrition, the duration of the war, the movement of the front, and other dynamic factors; trajectories, in short, are different though stalemate conditions share—in a special case—an abstract algebraic form. In fact, for a fixed *ratio* of Lanchester linear coefficients (and hence a fixed stalemate condition), an infinitude of Lanchester linear trajectories exists, each depending on the *actual value* of the Red and Blue effectiveness coefficients, r and b. (The trajectory corresponding to $r = 1/2$ and $b = 1/4$ is different from that corresponding to $r = 1/8$ and $b = 1/16$; the ratio, r/b, however, and the stalemate condition corresponding to it are the same in both cases.) But the difference between my model and Lanchester's is much more fundamental than the difference between any pair of Lanchester linear simulations, or even between any pair of Lanchester models (for example, the square and linear variants). My model and Lanchester's are not intertranslatable. The table below illustrates why. Under L are listed the Lanchester ground variables (R and B are renamed A and D), and under E, some of the ground variables in my model.

L	E
$A(t)$	$A(t)$
$D(t)$	$D(t)$
r	ρ
b	α_{dT}
	α_{aT}

The tactical air terms are symmetrical with respect to offense and defense:

$$\text{(C-10)} \quad DCAS(t) = \frac{L}{V} D_a(1)(1 - \alpha_{da})^{S_d(t-1)} \left[K_d \sum_{i=1}^{S_d} (1 - \alpha_{da})^i \right]$$

and

$$\text{(C-11)} \quad ACAS(t) = \frac{L}{V} A_a(1)(1 - \alpha_{aa})^{S_a(t-1)} \left[K_a \sum_{i=1}^{S_a} (1 - \alpha_{aa})^i \right]$$

with

$$\text{(C-12)} \qquad\qquad D_a(t) = D_a(1)(1 - \alpha_{da})^{S_d(t-1)}$$

and

$$\text{(C-13)} \qquad\qquad A_a(t) = A_a(1)(1 - \alpha_{aa})^{S_a(t-1)}.$$

Equations C-10 and C-11 can be cleared of summation signs by applying a standard theorem on geometrical progressions[8] to yield, respectively,

$$DCAS(t) = \frac{L}{V} D_a(1)(1 - \alpha_{da})^{S_d(t-1)} K_d \left[\frac{1 - (1 - \alpha_{da})^{S_d+1}}{\alpha_{da}} - 1 \right]$$

and

$$ACAS(t) = \frac{L}{V} A_a(1)(1 - \alpha_{aa})^{S_a(t-1)} K_a \left[\frac{1 - (1 - \alpha_{aa})^{S_a+1}}{\alpha_{aa}} - 1 \right].$$

Leaving airpower aside for the moment, it is quite easy to see how the equations are developed.

The attacker's ground force on day t, $A_g(t)$, is his force on the preceding day, $A_g(t - 1)$, minus his attrition on the preceding day, $\alpha(t - 1)A_g(t - 1)$, where $\alpha(t - 1)$ is the attacker's attrition rate on day $(t - 1)$. Formally,

---

Each model estimates $A(t)$ and $D(t)$ for any time t. So the models' outputs can be compared. But no mapping can be constructed associating with each specific run of Lanchester (that is, a specific choice of r and b) a unique and corresponding run (a specific choice of ρ, α_{dT}, and α_{aT}) of my model. Put more formally, there exists no function H (independent of $A(t)$ and $D(t)$) mapping each pair (r, b) in Lanchester to a unique triplet $(\rho, \alpha_{dT}, \alpha_{aT})$ in my model, and conversely.

8. The basic theorem on geometrical progressions is that, with $q \neq 1$,

$$\sum_{i=0}^{n} aq^i = a \frac{1 - q^{n+1}}{1 - q}.$$

For a transparent proof, see Richard Courant and Herbert Robbins, *What Is Mathematics?* pp. 13–14. My result follows with $a = 1$ and $q = (1 - \alpha)$.

$$A_g(t) = A_g(t - 1) - \alpha(t - 1)A_g(t - 1),$$

which upon rearranging is equation C-1 above without air[

The defender's force on day t, $D_g(t)$, is his force on the pr[
$D_g(t - 1)$, minus his attrition on the preceding day. What is t[
ρ be the ratio of attackers lost to defenders lost, the defender[
day $(t - 1)$ are equal to $1/\rho$ times the attacker's losses on da[
From above, these latter are $\alpha(t - 1) A_g(t - 1)$, so the defender[
on day $(t - 1)$ are just $[\alpha(t - 1)/\rho] A_g(t - 1)$. Hence the defender[
on day t is given by

$$D_g(t) = D_g(t - 1) - \frac{\alpha(t - 1)}{\rho} A_g(t - 1),$$

which is precisely equation C-2 above without airpower.

Given ρ and the initial $(t = 1)$ values for attacker, A_g, and defend[
D_g, we require only the attacker's time-dependent attrition rate, $\alpha(t)$,
complete the dynamics. This we assume to depend on the attacker[
prosecution rate,[10] $\alpha_g(t)$, and on the defender's maximum and actua[
withdrawal rates, W_{max} and $W(t)$, respectively; we set $W(1) = 0$. As set
forth in equation C-3 above,

$$\alpha(t) = \alpha_g(t)\left(1 - \frac{W(t)}{W_{max}}\right).$$

Clearly, if the defender will not (or cannot) withdraw, then $W(t) = 0$
and the pace of war is left essentially at the discretion of the attacker.
As explained below, however, the defender can moderate his attrition
by withdrawing (at a rate $W(t)$ between zero and W_{max}). Indeed, this is
the basic rationale for withdrawal. As formalized in equation C-4 above,
withdrawal begins if a defensive attrition rate exceeding the movement
threshold, α_{dT}, is recorded. In this discrete-time model, the defender's
attrition rate for day t is calculable only *after* day t has elapsed (see

9. Factoring out the term $A_g(t - 1)$ we obtain

$$A_g(t) = A_g(t - 1) [1 - \alpha(t - 1)],$$

which is precisely equation C-1 without airpower.

10. As is discussed below, the *attacker's ground prosecution rate* is the rate of
ground attrition that the attacker himself is prepared to suffer in order to press the
combat at his chosen pace. This function captures the intensity with which the attacker
prosecutes the war, hence its name.

equation C-5 above). Hence the defender's rate of withdrawal *on* day t is a function of his attrition rate over the preceding day, $\alpha_d(t - 1)$.

We assume simply that the change in the defender's withdrawal rate $(W(t) - W(t - 1))$ depends on the difference between his actual attrition rate and his threshold value $(\alpha_d(t - 1) - \alpha_{dT})$. This difference is multiplied by a function designed to ensure that the defender's withdrawal rate approaches the maximum, W_{max}, should the defender's attrition rate approach 1.0. In short, we assume

$$W(t) = W(t - 1) + \left(\frac{W_{max} - W(t - 1)}{1 - \alpha_{dT}}\right)(\alpha_d(t - 1) - \alpha_{dT}).$$

The cyclical feedback character of the defender's behavior is depicted in the block diagram below:

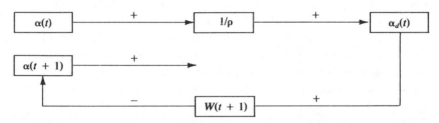

The attacker's attrition rate over day t, $\alpha(t)$, produces, via the inverse exchange ratio, $1/\rho$, a defensive attrition rate over day t, $\alpha_d(t)$. If this exceeds the defender's movement threshold, α_{dT}, then on the next day the defender withdraws at a rate $W(t + 1)$. This action reduces (that is, feeds back negatively on) the attacker's attrition rate $\alpha(t + 1)$.[11] In turn, this decrease in the attacker's attrition rate produces (again via $1/\rho$) a reduction in the defender's attrition rate $\alpha_d(t + 1)$, whose size relative to α_{dT} determines the rate of any subsequent withdrawal. If $\alpha_d(t + 1)$ is less than α_{dT}, no subsequent withdrawal occurs. The front then remains in place unless and until the attacker—by attempting to force the combat at his chosen pace—imposes on the defender an attrition rate exceeding his withdrawal threshold, and so on.[12] One might think of the defender

11. This negative feedback may not be sufficient to produce absolute reductions in the attacker's attrition rate if the attacker is simultaneously raising his prosecution rate.

12. As is illustrated by the simulations in appendix D, the model permits an attacker to pursue a withdrawing defender, and to subject him to further attrition. Indeed, the process of pursuit, closure, further attrition, and defensive withdrawal (if attrition exceeds the movement threshold) is built in and repeated iteratively in the model. Defensive withdrawal rates may rise, fall, or stay the same with each iteration.

as an adaptive system, with withdrawal rates as an attrition-regulating servomechanism.

All the while, the attacker, too, is adapting; the prosecution rate, $\alpha_g(t)$, is his servomechanism. Just as there is some threshold, α_{dT}, beyond which the defender will withdraw, so the attacker possesses an "equilibrium" attrition rate, α_{aT}. If on day $(t - 1)$ he records an attrition rate exceeding α_{aT}, the attacker reduces the pace at which he prosecutes the combat, $\alpha_g(t)$. If he records an attrition rate lower than α_{aT}, he accelerates by raising $\alpha_g(t)$. The magnitude of these changes in $\alpha_g(t)$ approach zero if the attacker's attrition rate approaches α_{aT}, the equilibrium rate. By a development symmetrical to the defender's, we assume[13]

$$\alpha_g(t) = \alpha_g(t - 1) - \left(\frac{\alpha_{aT} - \alpha_g(t - 1)}{\alpha_{aT}} \right) (\alpha_a(t - 1) - \alpha_{aT}).$$

Each side's adaptation may damp or amplify, penalize or reward, the adaptation of the other. *It is the interplay of the two adaptive systems, each searching for its equilibrium, which produces the observed dynamics*—the actual movement that occurs and the actual attrition suffered by each side.[14]

Airpower terms meanwhile calculate the additional daily reduction in each side's ground force that results from the adversary's close air operations. Sortie rates and per sortie attrition rates are applied; each sortie kills a certain number of armored fighting vehicles, each of which represents a given fraction of a division equivalent.[15] The close air

13. Notice that here the attacker's total ground-lethality attrition rate, $\alpha_a(t - 1)$, is used rather than the no-airpower rate, $\alpha(t - 1)$, from the preceding (no-airpower) discussion.

14. This overarching interaction of cyclical feedback structures is what I have attempted to capture. One may dispute whether the specific functional forms postulated in equations C-3, C-4, and C-6 precisely represent the inner dynamics of these feedback processes. But it is indisputable that the processes exist and interact; *no* such processes (and no such interactions) are postulated in Lanchester theory.

Thinking of war as a single self-regulating system, escalation might be seen as a case where the system exceeds the "elastic limits" of whatever servomechanisms (for example, defensive withdrawal) are operative. On feedback and cybernetics, see Norbert Wiener, *Cybernetics, or Control and Communication in the Animal and the Machine;* W. Ross Ashby, *Design for a Brain,* and *An Introduction to Cybernetics;* Michael A. Arbib, *Brains, Machines, and Mathematics,* chap. 4; and John D. Steinbruner, *The Cybernetic Theory of Decision.*

15. These division equivalents are expressed in units of lethality.

calculation simply cycles along until no planes are left or until one side's ground score sinks below the calculation's stopping point.[16]

In addition to addressing the problems noted in the critique of Lanchester theory set forth in appendix E, the equations have another property. Certain strategic decisions, affecting the way in which *given forces* are applied, can be represented explicitly in these equations. By contrast, in the Lanchester framework they are determined implicitly by the technical parameters of the force structure.

Specifically, *with a given force structure,* an offender may press his attack at a ferocious pace, suffering extraordinary attrition rates, if—for political, strategic, or operational reasons—a quick decision is paramount (this would be reflected in a high offensive equilibrium attrition rate, α_{aT}). Or, *with that same force structure,* he may choose to operate at a more restrained pace (a low α_{aT}). In the Lanchester framework, the pace is determined solely by the force structure $(r, R(0))$ itself.

Similarly, the tactical defender may be more or less stalwart in holding his positions. In guerrilla wars such as those in Afghanistan or Vietnam, larger forces seeking main force engagements have found themselves frustrated by guerrillas who withdraw—"disappear"—when even slight attrition is suffered. For such tactical defenders, the withdrawal-threshold attrition rate, α_{dT}, is very close to zero. At Verdun, by contrast, no attrition rate was high enough to dislodge the defenders from their entrenched positions: α_{dT} was effectively equal to one.

The adaptive model presented here thus yields guerrilla war and trench war as special cases, both possible with the *same* force structure. Its main contribution, however, lies in capturing the interaction of warfare's offensive and defensive feedback structures, which Lanchester theory cannot capture.

---

16. The calculations in this study stop when either side's ground lethality sinks to one-tenth of an armored division equivalent (a score of 4,749). A large number of natural extensions for the air and ground components of the model are possible. For example, submodels for the sortie rates and per sortie attrition rates of close air forces; decision rules for a defender's going over to the offense if his attrition is sufficiently low; generalizations of the exchange ratio, ρ, making it time- or position-dependent; sectoral variations in the prebattle force ratios; reinforcements; and more explicit breakthrough modeling (a surrogate would be to say that whenever a rate closely approaching W_{max} is sustained for a number of days, breakthrough has occurred). The equations will accommodate any breakpoint hypothesis one wishes to entertain. Little is known about the general phenomenon, however. See Robert L. Helmbold, *Decision in Battle.*

Battle of Khuzestan Assumptions, Simulations, and Sensitivity Analyses

THE NUMERICAL values given in table D-1 below are applied in the adaptive model of appendix C to produce the simulation results shown in tables D-2 through D-8. (These data were plotted as curves and discussed in chapter 4.) Selected sensitivity analyses follow.

Table D-1. Battle of Khuzestan: Numerical Assumptions for Cases 1–4A

| | Soviet direct drive | | | | Soviet northern buildup | | |
| | U.S. defends | USSR defends | | | U.S. defends | USSR defends | |
Variable[a]	Case 1	Case 2	Case 2A	Case 2B	Case 3	Case 4	Case 4A
$A_g(1)$	220,354[b]	203,732[c]	219,404[d]	235,550[e]	330,530[f]	203,732	292,538[g]
α_{aT}	0.075[h]	0.075	0.075	0.075	0.075	0.075	0.075
$D_g(1)$	203,732	220,354	220,354	220,354	203,732	330,530	330,530
ρ	1.500[i]	1.500	1.500	1.500	1.500	1.500	1.500
α_{dT}	0.050[j]	0.050	0.050	0.050	0.050	0.050	0.050
$\alpha_g(1)$	0.050	0.050	0.050	0.050	0.050	0.050	0.050
W_{max}	20[k]	20	20	20	20	20	20
$D_a(1)$	274[l]	245[m]	245	245	274	245	245
α_{da}	0.050[m]	0.050	0.050	0.050	0.050	0.050	0.050
S_d	1.500[o]	1.000[p]	1.000	1.000	1.500	1.000	1.000
K_d	0.500[q]	0.300[r]	0.300	0.300	0.500	0.300	0.300
$A_a(1)$	245	274	362[s]	361[t]	245	274	390[u]
α_{aa}	0.050[v]	0.050	0.050	0.050	0.050	0.050	0.050
K_a	0.250[w]	0.400[x]	0.400	0.400	0.250	0.400	0.400
S_a	1.000	1.500	2.000	1.500	1.000	1.500	1.500
V	1,200[y]	1,200	1,200	1,200	1,200	1,200	1,200
L	47,490[z]	47,490	47,490	47,490	47,490	47,490	47,490

a. See appendix C for definitions of variables.
b. Weighted unit value (WUV) score of the Soviet divisions sustainable from buildup points in the USSR; computed in appendix B and table 4-2.
c. WUV score of baseline U.S. rapid deployment force, detailed in table 4-1.
d. Consists of baseline RDF (4.29 armored division equivalents, or ADEs; see table 4-1) plus one Marine amphibious brigade (assumed to equal 0.33 ADE) for a total of 4.62 ADEs, or 219,404 WUV.
e. Consists of baseline RDF (4.29 ADEs; see table 4-1) plus two Marine amphibious brigades (0.67 ADE) for a total of 4.96 ADEs, or 235,550 WUV.
f. WUV score of the Soviet divisions sustainable from buildup points in northern Iran; computed in appendix B and table 4-2.
g. Consists of baseline RDF (4.29 ADEs; see table 4-1) plus two Marine amphibious brigades (0.67 ADE) and two light divisions (1.20 ADEs) for a total of 6.16 ADEs,

Table D-1 continued

or 292,538 WUV. The assumption of 0.60 ADE per light division credits each with the lethality of an armored division net of its tanks and M114A1 armored personnel carriers; at 53% of an armored division's manpower, the 10,000-man light divisions are favorably credited with 60% of the lethality. Yet even on these assumptions, the Reagan administration's planned 7⅓-division force falls short in case 4. Scores derived from William P. Mako, *U.S. Ground Forces and the Defense of Central Europe*, pp. 113–14.

h. Varied in the sensitivity analyses, this is a historically high rate assigned on the assumption that, when operating as the attacker, the U.S. and USSR would seek to force the combat at a high pace in hope of a speedy conclusion (see the sensitivity analyses for further discussion). The value assigned is equal to the "NATO-case" rate developed by Barry R. Posen in "Measuring the European Conventional Balance," p. 79.

i. As discussed in chapter 4 under Conservative Performance Numbers.

j. "Historically, short periods of very intense combat can be identified in which one side or both suffered 10 percent or worse attrition to armored fighting vehicles per day. On the other hand, rarely are battles of this intensity sustained for more than a few days." Posen, "Measuring the European Conventional Balance," pp. 55–56. Defenders willing to sustain such attrition rates have generally been defending their own territory. Even so, "engagements that continue until one side is wiped out are rare. Retreat begins when the number of casualties approaches the order of 10%." H. K. Weiss, "Requirements for a Theory of Combat," Memorandum Report 667, Ballistic Research Laboratories, Aberdeen Proving Ground, Maryland, April 1953 (AD 13 717), p. 16, as cited in James G. Taylor, *Lanchester Models of Warfare*, vol. 1, p. 113. When operating as the tactical defender in Iran, neither the U.S. nor the USSR would be defending its own territory. This study assumes their withdrawal threshold to be half the 10% figure noted above. The number is varied in the sensitivity analyses, where the issue is discussed at greater length.

k. William W. Kaufmann, "The Arithmetic of Force Planning," p. 213.

l. Consists of baseline RDF (391 aircraft; see table 4-1) at 0.7 overall readiness for close air. Assumes the same rate for helicopters and fixed-wing planes. The average mission-capability rate for the A-10 over fiscal years 1979–83 was 72.2. U.S. Department of the Air Force, Comptroller of the Air Force, *United States Air Force Summary, 1984*, p. D34. See also Joshua M. Epstein, *Measuring Military Power*, p. 28. Mission-capability rates for the AH-1 for fiscal years 1979–82 averaged 0.74. U.S. Department of Defense, *Annual Report to the Congress, Fiscal Year 1984*, p. 287.

m. 350 aircraft from table 4-2 at 0.7 overall readiness for close air, the same rate assumed under note l above for the United States.

n. This estimate is consistent with the assumption that each U.S. close air sortie would be subjected to two Soviet air defense shots, each with an overall kill probability of 0.025 (1 in 40) yielding a per sortie survival rate of $(1 - 0.025)^2 = 0.95$. By relevant historical standards, this assumed value is conservative. In what is generally regarded as the toughest close air environment since World War II—the Golan Heights in the 1973 Yom Kippur War—the Israelis suffered 1.5% attrition per sortie. Overall, the Israelis suffered 0.8% attrition per sortie. While the mission was clearly different, the U.S. Navy's value over North Vietnam from 1965 to 1973 was 0.1% per sortie; in Southeast Asia as a whole it was 0.5% per sortie for the same period. For these data, see U.S. Congressional Budget Office, *Navy Budget Issues for Fiscal Year 1980*, pp. 98 and 102–03.

o. A nominal sustained sortie rate for aircraft of medium complexity, operating in austere conditions. Equal to NATO's Phase II close air sortie rate, as defined and assumed by Posen in "Measuring the European Conventional Balance," table 1, p. 72.

p. Assumed to be lower than the U.S. value under note o above, due to the Soviets' relative inefficiency in the areas of ground support and battlefield maintenance, where flexibility and initiative count as heavily as in combat functions. For a detailed discussion of the Soviets' problems in the ground-support area, see Epstein, *Measuring Military Power*, chaps. 2 and 3. The value of 1.0 used here for Warsaw Pact close air systems by Posen, "Measuring the European Conventional Balance," table 1, p. 72.

q. Assuming eight TOW (tube-launched, optically tracked, wire-guided) antitank guided missiles per AH-1 sortie, an expected armored fighting vehicle (AFV) kill rate of 0.5 per sortie imputes to each TOW a kill probability of 0.06, which is conservative for modern precision ordnance. At 35 rounds per burst and 20 bursts per sortie, the same AFV kill rate of 0.5 per sortie, when assumed for the A-10, translates into an even more conservative kill probability of 0.025 per A-10 gunburst. Although alternative values can be entertained in sensitivity analyses, the assumption of 0.5 AFV kill per close air support sortie for both rotary and fixed-wing platforms (while that equality might be unrealistic) is not unduly favorable to the United States. Historically, the value is altogether plausible. During 1970, for example, in 1,486 sorties attacking trucks, the A-6 destroyed or damaged 977 vehicles, an average of 0.66 per sortie; in 2,332 sorties, the A-1 destroyed or damaged 1,271, for a rate of 0.55 per sortie. While trucks are relatively thin-skinned, the environment in which these data were recorded is a good deal less "target rich" than the one this study postulates in the Persian Gulf. Jack S. Ballard, *Development and Employment of Fixed-Wing Gunships, 1962–1972*, p. 149. See notes r and x below, where the U.S. value is degraded and the Soviet value raised when offense and defense roles are reversed.

r. Soviet close air effectiveness is assumed to rise by 20% (from the case 1 value of 0.25) when the Soviets go over to defense due to the exposure disadvantages of the offender. For the general point, though not the number, I thank analysts at Supreme Headquarters, Allied Powers Europe (SHAPE) Technical Center. Interview, Summer 1984.

s. Consists of baseline RDF (391 aircraft; see table 4-1) plus one Marine amphibious force complement of close air support (24 AH-1s and 38 AV-8Bs), for a total of 453 aircraft, at an increased readiness rate of 0.80.

t. Consists of baseline RDF (391 aircraft; see table 4-1) plus two Marine amphibious force complements of close air support (48 AH-1s and 76 AV-8Bs), for a total of 515 aircraft, at the original (case 1) readiness level of 0.70.

u. Consists of baseline RDF aircraft (391 aircraft; see table 4-1) plus aircraft associated with two Marine amphibious forces (76 AV-8Bs and 48 AH-1s) and two light divisions (42 AH-1s), for a total of 557 aircraft, all at the original (case 1) readiness level of 0.70. The light division AH-1 figure is from "U.S. Army Light Forces Initiative," Department of the Army briefing, 1983.

v. Same as assumed under note n for the United States.

w. One-half the U.S. rate assumed under note q. The A-10's 30mm cannon and the AH-1's TOW antitank guided missile are expected to outperform the Soviet's Swatter. See Posen, "Measuring the European Conventional Balance," p. 72. The Soviets' relative inexperience with the Su-25 Frogfoot—their *first* dedicated fixed-wing close air support plane—should also be taken into account. The 0.25 value nonetheless equals the per sortie rate at which trucks were damaged or destroyed by U.S. F-4s (not a specialized close air support system) in 6,310 sorties attacking trucks in May 1970 in Vietnam. Ballard, *Development and Employment*, p. 149. See notes r and x, where the U.S. value is degraded and the Soviet value raised when offense and defense roles are reversed.

x. U.S. close air effectiveness is assumed to degrade by 20% (from the case 1 value of 0.5) when the United States goes over to offense, due to the concealment advantages of the defender. Interview with analysts, SHAPE Technical Center, Summer 1984.

y. Figure for AFVs per division equivalent is from Posen, "Measuring the European Conventional Balance," p. 73.

z. Figure for WUV per armored division equivalent is from Mako, *U.S. Ground Forces*, p. 114.

D-2. Battle Simulation Results, Case 1: Soviet Direct Drive; United States Defends (Baseline RDF)

Day t	Defender's ground lethality (WUV) $D_g(t)$	Attacker's ground lethality (WUV) $A_g(t)$	Attacker's ground prosecution rate (percent) $\alpha_g(t)$	Attacker's attrition rate (percent) $\alpha_a(t)$	Defender's withdrawal rate (km/day) $W(t)$	Defender's attrition rate (percent) $\alpha_d(t)$	Displacement of the front (km) SUM W^a	Defender's aircraft $D_a(t)$	Attacker's aircraft $A_a(t)$
1	203,732	220,354	5.000	8.462	0.0	4.736	0.0	274	245
2	194,084	201,708	4.679	8.181	0.0	4.369	0.0	254	233
3	185,604	185,205	4.423	7.955	0.0	4.062	0.0	235	221
4	178,065	170,473	4.237	7.789	0.0	3.813	0.0	218	210
5	171,275	157,194	4.111	7.678	0.0	3.610	0.0	201	200
6	165,092	145,125	4.030	7.608	0.0	3.441	0.0	186	190
7	159,411	134,083	3.980	7.566	0.0	3.294	0.0	173	180
8	154,160	123,939	3.949	7.541	0.0	3.160	0.0	160	171
9	149,289	114,592	3.930	7.527	0.0	3.034	0.0	148	163
10	144,759	105,967	3.917	7.519	0.0	2.914	0.0	137	154
11	140,541	97,999	3.908	7.514	0.0	2.798	0.0	127	147
12	136,609	90,635	3.901	7.512	0.0	2.684	0.0	118	139
13	132,942	83,827	3.895	7.510	0.0	2.573	0.0	109	132
14	129,521	77,532	3.890	7.509	0.0	2.465	0.0	101	126
15	126,328	71,709	3.886	7.509	0.0	2.360	0.0	93	119
16	123,347	66,325	3.882	7.509	0.0	2.256	0.0	86	114
17	120,564	61,345	3.877	7.509	0.0	2.156	0.0	80	108
18	117,965	56,739	3.873	7.508	0.0	2.058	0.0	74	102
19	115,537	52,478	3.869	7.508	0.0	1.963	0.0	69	97
20	113,268	48,538	3.865	7.508	0.0	1.871	0.0	64	92
21	111,149	44,894	3.861	7.508	0.0	1.782	0.0	59	88
22	109,167	41,523	3.857	7.508	0.0	1.696	0.0	54	83
23	107,316	38,405	3.853	7.508	0.0	1.613	0.0	50	79

24	105,584	35,522	3.849	7.508	0.0	1.534	0.0	47	75
25	103,965	32,854	3.845	7.508	0.0	1.457	0.0	43	72
26	102,450	30,388	3.841	7.508	0.0	1.383	0.0	40	68
27	101,033	28,106	3.837	7.508	0.0	1.312	0.0	37	65
28	99,708	25,996	3.833	7.508	0.0	1.244	0.0	34	61
29	98,467	24,044	3.828	7.508	0.0	1.179	0.0	32	58
30	97,306	22,239	3.824	7.508	0.0	1.117	0.0	29	55
31	96,218	20,569	3.820	7.508	0.0	1.058	0.0	27	53
32	95,200	19,024	3.816	7.508	0.0	1.002	0.0	25	50
33	94,247	17,596	3.812	7.508	0.0	0.948	0.0	23	47
34	93,353	16,275	3.808	7.508	0.0	0.897	0.0	22	45
35	92,517	15,053	3.804	7.508	0.0	0.848	0.0	20	43
36	91,732	13,923	3.800	7.508	0.0	0.801	0.0	19	41
37	90,997	12,877	3.796	7.508	0.0	0.757	0.0	17	39
38	90,308	11,910	3.791	7.508	0.0	0.716	0.0	16	37
39	89,662	11,016	3.787	7.508	0.0	0.676	0.0	15	35
40	89,056	10,189	3.783	7.508	0.0	0.638	0.0	14	33
41	88,487	9,424	3.779	7.508	0.0	0.603	0.0	13	31
42	87,954	8,716	3.775	7.508	0.0	0.569	0.0	12	30
43	87,453	8,062	3.771	7.508	0.0	0.537	0.0	11	28
44	86,984	7,457	3.767	7.508	0.0	0.507	0.0	10	27
45	86,543	6,897	3.762	7.508	0.0	0.478	0.0	9	26
46	86,129	6,379	3.758	7.508	0.0	0.451	0.0	9	24
47	85,740	5,900	3.754	7.508	0.0	0.426	0.0	8	23
48	85,375	5,457	3.750	7.508	0.0	0.402	0.0	7	22
49	85,032	5,047	3.746	7.508	0.0	0.379	0.0	7	21
50[b]	84,709	4,668	3.742	0.000	0.0	0.000	0.0	6	20

a. SUM W is the cumulative displacement of the front, and equals the sum of the $W(t)$ values.
b. All calculations in this study stop when either side's ground lethality sinks to one-tenth of an ADE (a score of 4,749).

D-3. Battle Simulation Results, Case 2: Soviet Direct Drive; Soviets Defend (Baseline RDF)

Day t	Defender's ground lethality (WUV) $D_g(t)$	Attacker's ground lethality (WUV) $A_g(t)$	Attacker's ground prosecution rate (percent) $\alpha_g(t)$	Attacker's attrition rate (percent) $\alpha_a(t)$	Defender's withdrawal rate (km/day) $W(t)$	Defender's attrition rate (percent) $\alpha_d(t)$	Displacement of the front (km) SUM W	Defender's aircraft $D_a(t)$	Attacker's aircraft $A_a(t)$
1	220,354	203,732	5.000	6.356	0.0	5.851	0.0	245	274
2	207,460	190,782	5.381	6.709	0.2	5.993	0.2	233	254
3	195,026	177,983	5.605	6.898	0.4	6.027	0.6	221	235
4	183,272	165,706	5.757	7.014	0.6	6.010	1.2	210	218
5	172,258	154,083	5.870	7.094	0.8	5.964	2.0	200	201
6	161,984	143,152	5.958	7.154	1.0	5.899	3.0	190	186
7	152,429	132,911	6.029	7.202	1.2	5.821	4.1	180	173
8	143,555	123,339	6.088	7.244	1.3	5.734	5.5	171	160
9	135,324	114,404	6.136	7.282	1.5	5.638	7.0	163	148
10	127,694	106,073	6.175	7.320	1.6	5.536	8.6	154	137
11	120,625	98,309	6.207	7.358	1.7	5.427	10.3	147	127
12	114,078	91,075	6.232	7.398	1.8	5.314	12.1	139	118
13	108,017	84,337	6.249	7.439	1.9	5.195	14.0	132	109
14	102,405	78,063	6.259	7.484	1.9	5.072	15.8	126	101
15	97,212	72,221	6.262	7.531	1.9	4.944	17.8	119	93
16	92,406	66,783	6.257	8.174	0.0	5.097	17.8	114	86
17	87,696	61,324	6.145	8.122	0.0	4.894	17.8	108	80
18	83,404	56,343	6.033	8.083	0.0	4.695	17.8	102	74
19	79,488	51,789	5.919	8.038	0.0	4.493	17.8	97	69
20	75,917	47,626	5.805	7.995	0.0	4.291	17.8	92	64

21	72,659	43,819	5.693	7.954	0.0	4.092	17.8	88	59
22	69,686	40,333	5.584	7.917	0.0	3.895	17.8	83	54
23	66,971	37,140	5.477	7.885	0.0	3.702	17.8	79	50
24	64,492	34,212	5.374	7.856	0.0	3.513	17.8	75	47
25	62,226	31,524	5.273	7.832	0.0	3.328	17.8	72	43
26	60,155	29,055	5.174	7.812	0.0	3.148	17.8	68	40
27	58,262	26,785	5.077	7.796	0.0	2.973	17.8	65	37
28	56,529	24,697	4.982	7.783	0.0	2.803	17.8	61	34
29	54,945	22,775	4.887	7.772	0.0	2.639	17.8	58	32
30	53,495	21,005	4.792	7.764	0.0	2.480	17.8	55	29
31	52,169	19,374	4.696	7.758	0.0	2.326	17.8	53	27
32	50,955	17,871	4.600	7.753	0.0	2.178	17.8	50	25
33	49,845	16,485	4.502	7.749	0.0	2.037	17.8	47	23
34	48,830	15,208	4.403	7.746	0.0	1.901	17.8	45	22
35	47,902	14,030	4.301	7.744	0.0	1.771	17.8	43	20
36	47,054	12,943	4.197	7.742	0.0	1.647	17.8	41	19
37	46,278	11,941	4.090	7.741	0.0	1.530	17.8	39	17
38	45,570	11,017	3.980	7.740	0.0	1.419	17.8	37	16
39	44,924	10,164	3.868	7.739	0.0	1.313	17.8	35	15
40	44,334	9,377	3.752	7.738	0.0	1.214	17.8	33	14
41	43,796	8,652	3.633	7.737	0.0	1.120	17.8	31	13
42	43,305	7,982	3.510	7.737	0.0	1.033	17.8	30	12
43	42,858	7,365	3.384	7.736	0.0	0.950	17.8	28	11
44	42,451	6,795	3.255	7.736	0.0	0.873	17.8	27	10
45	42,080	6,269	3.121	7.735	0.0	0.801	17.8	26	9
46	41,743	5,784	2.984	7.735	0.0	0.734	17.8	24	9
47	41,436	5,337	2.843	7.734	0.0	0.672	17.8	23	8
48	41,158	4,924	2.698	7.734	0.0	0.614	17.8	22	7
49	40,905	4,543	2.548	0.000	0.0	0.000	17.8	21	7

D-4. Battle Simulation Results, Case 2A: Soviet Direct Drive; Soviets Defend (5-Division RDF with Close Air Enhancement)

Day t	Defender's ground lethality (WUV) $D_g(t)$	Attacker's ground lethality (WUV) $A_g(t)$	Attacker's ground prosecution rate (percent) $\alpha_g(t)$	Attacker's attrition rate (percent) $\alpha_a(t)$	Defender's withdrawal rate (km/day) $W(t)$	Defender's attrition rate (percent) $\alpha_d(t)$	Displacement of the front (km) SUM W	Defender's aircraft $D_a(t)$	Attacker's aircraft $A_a(t)$
1	220,354	219,404	5.000	6.259	0.0	8.137	0.0	245	362
2	202,425	205,670	5.414	6.511	0.7	8.279	0.7	233	327
3	185,667	192,279	5.689	6.608	1.3	8.324	2.0	221	295
4	170,212	179,573	5.904	6.639	2.0	8.326	4.0	210	266
5	156,041	167,652	6.087	6.635	2.6	8.304	6.6	200	240
6	143,083	156,529	6.250	6.611	3.2	8.267	9.8	190	217
7	131,254	146,180	6.398	6.574	3.8	8.220	13.6	180	196
8	120,465	136,570	6.534	6.528	4.3	8.164	17.9	171	177
9	110,630	127,654	6.659	6.476	4.9	8.100	22.8	163	159
10	101,669	119,388	6.774	6.418	5.4	8.030	28.2	154	144
11	93,505	111,725	6.879	6.356	5.8	7.953	34.0	147	130
12	86,068	104,624	6.974	6.291	6.3	7.871	40.2	139	117
13	79,294	98,042	7.059	6.224	6.7	7.784	46.9	132	106
14	73,122	91,940	7.134	6.154	7.1	7.691	54.0	126	95
15	67,498	86,282	7.199	6.084	7.4	7.594	61.4	119	86
16	62,372	81,033	7.256	6.013	7.8	7.493	69.2	114	78
17	57,699	76,160	7.304	5.943	8.1	7.388	77.3	108	70
18	53,436	71,634	7.345	5.873	8.4	7.280	85.7	102	63
19	49,545	67,427	7.379	5.805	8.7	7.170	94.4	97	57
20	45,993	63,513	7.406	5.738	8.9	7.058	103.3	92	52
21	42,747	59,869	7.428	5.674	9.2	6.945	112.5	88	47
22	39,778	56,472	7.446	5.613	9.4	6.831	121.9	83	42
23	37,061	53,302	7.459	5.555	9.6	6.716	131.5	79	38

24	34,572	50,341	7.470	5.500	9.8	6.602	141.3	75	34
25	32,289	47,572	7.478	5.449	10.0	6.489	151.3	72	31
26	30,194	44,980	7.484	5.401	10.1	6.377	161.4	68	28
27	28,269	42,550	7.488	5.357	10.3	6.266	171.7	65	25
28	26,498	40,271	7.492	5.316	10.4	6.157	182.0	61	23
29	24,866	38,130	7.494	5.279	10.5	6.050	192.6	58	20
30	23,362	36,117	7.496	5.246	10.6	5.945	203.2	55	18
31	21,973	34,222	7.497	5.216	10.7	5.842	213.9	53	17
32	20,689	32,437	7.498	5.190	10.8	5.742	224.7	50	15
33	19,501	30,754	7.499	5.166	10.9	5.644	235.5	47	14
34	18,401	29,165	7.499	5.146	10.9	5.549	246.5	45	12
35	17,379	27,664	7.499	5.130	11.0	5.457	257.4	43	11
36	16,431	26,245	7.500	5.116	11.0	5.368	268.5	41	10
37	15,549	24,902	7.500	5.105	11.1	5.281	279.5	39	9
38	14,728	23,631	7.500	5.097	11.1	5.197	290.6	37	8
39	13,963	22,427	7.500	5.092	11.1	5.115	301.7	35	7
40	13,248	21,285	7.500	5.090	11.1	5.037	312.8	33	7
41	12,581	20,201	7.500	5.090	11.1	4.960	323.9	31	6
42	11,957	19,173	7.500	9.260	0.0	9.341	323.9	30	5
43	10,840	17,398	7.500	8.999	0.9	8.975	324.8	28	5
44	9,867	15,832	7.500	8.781	1.7	8.642	326.5	27	4
45	9,015	14,442	7.500	8.598	2.4	8.334	329.0	26	4
46	8,263	13,200	7.500	8.445	3.0	8.047	332.0	24	4
47	7,598	12,085	7.500	8.319	3.6	7.778	335.6	23	3
48	7,007	11,080	7.500	8.217	4.1	7.523	339.6	22	3
49	6,480	10,170	7.500	8.137	4.5	7.280	344.1	21	3
50	6,008	9,342	7.500	8.076	4.9	7.047	349.0	20	2
51	5,585	8,588	7.500	8.034	5.2	6.823	354.1	19	2
52	5,204	7,898	7.500	8.009	5.5	6.606	359.6	18	2
53	4,860	7,265	7.500	8.001	5.7	6.394	365.3	17	2
54	4,549	6,684	7.500	0.000	5.9	0.000	371.2	16	2

D-5. Battle Simulation Results, Case 2B: Soviet Direct Drive; Soviets Defend (5⅓-Division RDF with Close Air Enhancement)

Day t	Defender's ground lethality (WUV) $D_g(t)$	Attacker's ground lethality (WUV) $A_g(t)$	Attacker's ground prosecution rate (percent) $\alpha_g(t)$	Attacker's attrition rate (percent) $\alpha_a(t)$	Defender's withdrawal rate (km/day) $W(t)$	Defender's attrition rate (percent) $\alpha_d(t)$	Displacement of the front (km) SUM W	Defender's aircraft $D_a(t)$	Attacker's aircraft $A_a(t)$
1	220,354	235,550	5.000	6.173	0.0	7.212	0.0	245	361
2	204,462	221,009	5.442	6.503	0.5	7.472	0.5	233	334
3	189,184	206,636	5.716	6.644	1.0	7.603	1.4	221	310
4	174,800	192,907	5.919	6.705	1.5	7.681	2.9	210	287
5	161,374	179,973	6.087	6.723	2.0	7.732	5.0	200	265
6	148,897	167,872	6.233	6.717	2.5	7.767	7.5	190	246
7	137,332	156,596	6.365	6.694	3.0	7.793	10.5	180	228
8	126,630	146,114	6.487	6.659	3.5	7.812	14.1	171	211
9	116,737	136,384	6.601	6.615	4.0	7.827	18.1	163	195
10	107,600	127,362	6.707	6.564	4.5	7.839	22.6	154	181
11	99,165	119,002	6.806	6.506	5.0	7.849	27.6	147	167
12	91,381	111,260	6.898	6.442	5.4	7.857	33.0	139	155
13	84,201	104,092	6.983	6.372	5.9	7.863	38.8	132	143
14	77,581	97,459	7.061	6.298	6.3	7.867	45.1	126	133
15	71,477	91,321	7.131	6.219	6.7	7.871	51.8	119	123
16	65,851	85,642	7.194	6.135	7.1	7.874	58.9	114	114
17	60,666	80,388	7.250	6.048	7.5	7.876	66.4	108	105
18	55,888	75,526	7.298	5.957	7.9	7.878	74.3	102	98
19	51,485	71,027	7.340	5.863	8.2	7.880	82.5	97	90
20	47,428	66,863	7.375	5.766	8.6	7.883	91.1	92	84

21	43,689	63,008	7.404	5.667	8.9	7.887	100.1	88	77
22	40,243	59,437	7.427	5.566	9.3	7.893	109.3	83	72
23	37,067	56,129	7.466	5.464	9.6	7.900	118.9	79	66
24	34,139	53,062	7.461	5.361	9.9	7.910	128.8	75	62
25	31,438	50,217	7.472	5.258	10.2	7.923	139.1	72	57
26	28,947	47,577	7.480	5.154	10.5	7.940	149.6	68	53
27	26,649	45,125	7.486	5.049	10.8	7.960	160.4	65	49
28	24,528	42,846	7.491	4.945	11.1	7.985	171.5	61	45
29	22,569	40,727	7.494	4.841	11.4	8.015	182.9	58	42
30	20,760	38,756	7.496	4.737	11.7	8.050	194.6	55	39
31	19,089	36,920	7.498	4.633	11.9	8.090	206.5	53	36
32	17,545	35,210	7.498	4.528	12.2	8.137	218.7	50	33
33	16,117	33,615	7.499	4.424	12.4	8.191	231.1	47	31
34	14,797	32,128	7.499	4.319	12.7	8.251	243.8	45	28
35	13,576	30,740	7.500	4.215	13.0	8.319	256.8	43	26
36	12,447	29,445	7.500	4.109	13.2	8.395	270.0	41	24
37	11,402	28,235	7.500	4.004	13.4	8.480	283.4	39	23
38	10,435	27,104	7.500	3.898	13.7	8.575	297.1	37	21
39	9,540	26,048	7.500	3.791	13.9	8.680	311.0	35	19
40	8,712	25,060	7.500	3.684	14.2	8.796	325.2	33	18
41	7,946	24,137	7.500	3.576	14.4	8.924	339.6	31	17
42	7,237	23,274	7.500	3.467	14.6	9.065	354.2	30	15
43	6,581	22,467	7.500	3.358	14.9	9.222	369.1	28	14
44	5,974	21,713	7.500	3.248	15.1	9.394	384.1	27	13
45	5,413	21,008	7.500	3.137	15.3	9.585	399.4	26	12
46	4,894	20,349	7.500	3.025	15.5	9.795	415.0	24	11
47	4,414	19,733	7.500	0.000	15.8	0.000	430.7	23	10

D-6. Battle Simulation Results, Case 3: Soviet Northern Buildup; United States Defends (Baseline RDF)

Day t	Defender's ground lethality (WUV) $D_g(t)$	Attacker's ground lethality (WUV) $A_g(t)$	Attacker's ground prosecution rate (percent) $\alpha_g(t)$	Attacker's attrition rate (percent) $\alpha_a(t)$	Defender's withdrawal rate (km/day) $W(t)$	Defender's attrition rate (percent) $\alpha_d(t)$	Displacement of the front (km) SUM W	Defender's aircraft $D_a(t)$	Attacker's aircraft $A_a(t)$
1	203,732	330,530	5.000	7.308	0.0	6.538	0.0	274	245
2	190,412	306,375	5.064	7.288	0.3	6.493	0.3	254	233
3	178,048	284,048	5.133	7.273	0.6	6.454	1.0	235	221
4	166,558	263,388	5.205	7.262	0.9	6.417	1.9	218	210
5	155,869	244,261	5.277	7.253	1.2	6.382	3.1	201	200
6	145,921	226,545	5.351	7.245	1.5	6.347	4.6	186	190
7	136,659	210,132	5.424	7.237	1.7	6.312	6.3	173	180
8	128,033	194,924	5.496	7.230	2.0	6.276	8.3	160	171
9	119,997	180,831	5.569	7.223	2.2	6.240	10.6	148	163
10	112,510	167,769	5.640	7.217	2.5	6.203	13.1	137	154
11	105,531	155,661	5.710	7.210	2.7	6.164	15.8	127	147
12	99,026	144,437	5.779	7.204	2.9	6.125	18.7	118	139
13	92,961	134,032	5.847	7.198	3.1	6.084	21.8	109	132
14	87,305	124,384	5.914	7.192	3.3	6.043	25.1	101	126
15	82,029	115,438	5.979	7.187	3.5	6.000	28.6	93	119
16	77,108	107,142	6.042	7.181	3.7	5.956	32.2	86	114
17	72,515	99,448	6.104	7.176	3.8	5.911	36.1	80	108
18	68,229	92,311	6.164	7.172	4.0	5.865	40.0	74	102
19	64,227	85,691	6.223	7.168	4.1	5.817	44.2	69	97
20	60,491	79,549	6.279	7.164	4.3	5.768	48.4	64	92
21	57,002	73,850	6.334	7.161	4.4	5.718	52.8	59	88
22	53,743	68,562	6.387	7.158	4.5	5.667	57.3	54	83
23	50,697	63,654	6.438	7.157	4.6	5.614	61.9	50	79
24	47,851	59,098	6.486	7.156	4.7	5.560	66.7	47	75
25	45,190	54,869	6.533	7.156	4.8	5.505	71.5	43	72

26	42,703	50,942	6.577	7.158	4.9	5.448	76.4	40	68
27	40,376	47,296	6.619	7.160	5.0	5.390	81.3	37	65
28	38,200	43,910	6.659	7.164	5.0	5.331	86.3	34	61
29	36,163	40,764	6.697	7.169	5.1	5.270	91.4	32	58
30	34,257	37,842	6.732	7.175	5.1	5.209	96.5	29	55
31	32,473	35,127	6.766	7.184	5.1	5.145	101.7	27	53
32	30,802	32,603	6.796	7.194	5.2	5.080	106.8	25	50
33	29,237	30,258	6.825	7.206	5.2	5.014	112.0	23	47
34	27,771	28,078	6.852	7.220	5.2	4.947	117.2	22	45
35	26,398	26,050	6.876	9.016	0.0	6.049	117.2	20	43
36	24,801	23,702	6.750	8.854	0.2	5.795	117.4	19	41
37	23,364	21,603	6.614	8.700	0.4	5.554	117.8	17	39
38	22,066	19,724	6.473	8.555	0.5	5.325	118.3	16	37
39	20,891	18,036	6.328	8.421	0.6	5.108	118.9	15	35
40	19,824	16,517	6.184	8.300	0.6	4.905	119.5	14	33
41	18,852	15,147	6.044	8.364	0.0	4.807	119.5	13	31
42	17,945	13,880	5.876	8.221	0.0	4.596	119.5	12	30
43	17,120	12,739	5.720	8.085	0.0	4.397	119.5	11	28
44	16,368	11,709	5.581	7.964	0.0	4.212	119.5	10	27
45	15,678	10,776	5.462	7.860	0.0	4.040	119.5	9	26
46	15,045	9,929	5.365	7.774	0.0	3.882	119.5	9	24
47	14,461	9,157	5.287	7.705	0.0	3.736	119.5	8	23
48	13,920	8,452	5.226	7.653	0.0	3.600	119.5	7	22
49	13,419	7,805	5.180	7.613	0.0	3.471	119.5	7	21
50	12,953	7,211	5.145	7.583	0.0	3.349	119.5	6	20
51	12,520	6,664	5.119	7.562	0.0	3.232	119.5	6	19
52	12,115	6,160	5.099	7.546	0.0	3.118	119.5	5	18
53	11,737	5,695	5.084	7.535	0.0	3.007	119.5	5	17
54	11,384	5,266	5.073	7.527	0.0	2.899	119.5	5	16
55	11,054	4,870	5.064	7.522	0.0	2.793	119.5	4	15
56	10,746	4,503	5.057	0.000	0.0	0.000	119.5	4	15

D-7. Battle Simulation Results, Case 4: Soviet Northern Buildup; Soviets Defend (Baseline RDF)

Day t	Defender's ground lethality (WUV) $D_g(t)$	Attacker's ground lethality (WUV) $A_g(t)$	Attacker's ground prosecution rate (percent) $\alpha_g(t)$	Attacker's attrition rate (percent) $\alpha_a(t)$	Defender's withdrawal rate (km/day) $W(t)$	Defender's attrition rate (percent) $\alpha_d(t)$	Displacement of the front (km) SUM W	Defender's aircraft $D_a(t)$	Attacker's aircraft $A_a(t)$
1	330,530	203,732	5.000	6.356	0.0	3.901	0.0	245	274
2	317,636	190,782	5.381	6.757	0.0	3.934	0.0	233	254
3	305,141	177,891	5.591	6.993	0.0	3.888	0.0	221	235
4	293,278	165,451	5.720	7.152	0.0	3.803	0.0	210	218
5	282,123	153,618	5.803	7.268	0.0	3.697	0.0	200	201
6	271,695	142,453	5.855	7.356	0.0	3.576	0.0	190	186
7	261,980	131,974	5.887	7.426	0.0	3.445	0.0	180	173
8	252,954	122,173	5.903	7.482	0.0	3.309	0.0	171	160
9	244,585	113,032	5.906	7.528	0.0	3.168	0.0	163	148
10	236,837	104,523	5.900	7.567	0.0	3.025	0.0	154	137
11	229,671	96,614	5.886	7.599	0.0	2.882	0.0	147	127
12	223,053	89,272	5.865	7.626	0.0	2.739	0.0	139	118
13	216,944	82,465	5.838	7.648	0.0	2.597	0.0	132	109
14	211,311	76,158	5.805	7.667	0.0	2.457	0.0	126	101
15	206,119	70,318	5.767	7.683	0.0	2.320	0.0	119	93
16	201,337	64,916	5.725	7.697	0.0	2.186	0.0	114	86
17	196,935	59,919	5.678	7.708	0.0	2.057	0.0	108	80
18	192,885	55,301	5.628	7.717	0.0	1.931	0.0	102	74
19	189,160	51,033	5.573	7.724	0.0	1.810	0.0	97	69
20	185,736	47,091	5.516	7.730	0.0	1.694	0.0	92	64

21	182,590	43,451	5.455	7.735	0.0	1.583	0.0	88	59
22	179,700	40,090	5.391	7.738	0.0	1.477	0.0	83	54
23	177,046	36,988	5.324	7.741	0.0	1.376	0.0	79	50
24	174,610	34,125	5.254	7.743	0.0	1.280	0.0	75	47
25	172,375	31,483	5.181	7.744	0.0	1.189	0.0	72	43
26	170,325	29,045	5.106	7.745	0.0	1.104	0.0	68	40
27	168,444	26,795	5.028	7.745	0.0	1.023	0.0	65	37
28	166,721	24,720	4.947	7.745	0.0	0.947	0.0	61	34
29	165,141	22,805	4.863	7.745	0.0	0.876	0.0	58	32
30	163,694	21,039	4.777	7.745	0.0	0.810	0.0	55	29
31	162,368	19,409	4.688	7.744	0.0	0.747	0.0	53	27
32	161,155	17,906	4.597	7.743	0.0	0.689	0.0	50	25
33	160,044	16,520	4.503	7.743	0.0	0.635	0.0	47	23
34	159,028	15,241	4.405	7.742	0.0	0.584	0.0	45	22
35	158,099	14,061	4.306	7.741	0.0	0.537	0.0	43	20
36	157,249	12,972	4.203	7.741	0.0	0.494	0.0	41	19
37	156,472	11,968	4.097	7.740	0.0	0.453	0.0	39	17
38	155,763	11,042	3.988	7.739	0.0	0.416	0.0	37	16
39	155,115	10,187	3.876	7.739	0.0	0.381	0.0	35	15
40	154,524	9,399	3.761	7.738	0.0	0.349	0.0	33	14
41	153,985	8,672	3.642	7.737	0.0	0.319	0.0	31	13
42	153,493	8,001	3.520	7.737	0.0	0.292	0.0	30	12
43	153,045	7,382	3.394	7.736	0.0	0.267	0.0	28	11
44	152,637	6,811	3.265	7.736	0.0	0.243	0.0	27	10
45	152,265	6,284	3.132	7.735	0.0	0.222	0.0	26	9
46	151,928	5,798	2.995	7.735	0.0	0.202	0.0	24	9
47	151,620	5,349	2.854	7.734	0.0	0.184	0.0	23	8
48	151,341	4,936	2.709	7.734	0.0	0.167	0.0	22	7
49	151,088	4,554	2.560	0.000	0.0	0.000	0.0	21	7

D-8. Battle Simulation Results, Case 4A: Soviet Northern Buildup; Soviets Defend (7⅓-Division RDF with Close Air Enhancement)

Day t	Defender's ground lethality (WUV) $D_g(t)$	Attacker's ground lethality (WUV) $A_g(t)$	Attacker's ground prosecution rate (percent) $\alpha_g(t)$	Attacker's attrition rate (percent) $\alpha_a(t)$	Defender's withdrawal rate (km/day) $W(t)$	Defender's attrition rate (percent) $\alpha_s(t)$	Displacement of the front (km) SUM W	Defender's aircraft $D_a(t)$	Attacker's aircraft $A_a(t)$
1	330,530	292,538	5.000	5.945	0.0	5.578	0.0	245	390
2	312,092	275,148	5.518	6.439	0.1	5.801	0.1	233	361
3	293,988	257,431	5.799	6.684	0.3	5.870	0.4	221	334
4	276,732	240,225	5.984	6.830	0.5	5.874	0.9	210	310
5	260,478	223,819	6.119	6.926	0.6	5.843	1.5	200	287
6	245,258	208,316	6.225	6.996	0.8	5.791	2.4	190	265
7	231,055	193,743	6.311	7.050	1.0	5.724	3.3	180	246
8	217,829	180,084	6.382	7.094	1.1	5.647	4.5	171	228
9	205,529	167,308	6.443	7.134	1.3	5.561	5.7	163	211
10	194,099	155,372	6.494	7.172	1.4	5.468	7.1	154	195
11	183,485	144,229	6.538	7.209	1.5	5.370	8.5	147	181
12	173,632	133,831	6.575	7.247	1.5	5.267	10.1	139	167
13	164,488	124,132	6.607	7.287	1.6	5.159	11.6	132	155
14	156,002	115,086	6.632	7.330	1.6	5.047	13.3	126	143
15	148,129	106,650	6.652	7.376	1.6	4.931	14.9	119	133
16	140,824	98,784	6.666	7.962	0.0	5.062	14.9	114	123
17	133,696	90,919	6.614	7.948	0.0	4.894	14.9	108	114
18	127,153	83,693	6.561	7.942	0.0	4.726	14.9	102	105
19	121,143	77,046	6.506	7.931	0.0	4.554	14.9	97	98
20	115,627	70,936	6.449	7.919	0.0	4.379	14.9	92	90
21	110,563	65,318	6.390	7.907	0.0	4.203	14.9	88	84
22	105,916	60,154	6.330	7.895	0.0	4.027	14.9	83	78
23	101,651	55,405	6.269	7.882	0.0	3.850	14.9	79	72

24	97,737	51,038	6.206	7.870	0.0	3.675	14.9	75	66
25	94,146	47,021	6.142	7.858	0.0	3.501	14.9	72	62
26	90,850	43,326	6.077	7.846	0.0	3.329	14.9	68	57
27	87,825	39,927	6.011	7.835	0.0	3.160	14.9	65	53
28	85,050	36,798	5.945	7.825	0.0	2.994	14.9	61	49
29	82,504	33,919	5.878	7.815	0.0	2.832	14.9	58	45
30	80,167	31,268	5.809	7.806	0.0	2.674	14.9	55	42
31	78,023	28,827	5.740	7.798	0.0	2.521	14.9	53	39
32	76,056	26,579	5.671	7.790	0.0	2.373	14.9	50	36
33	74,251	24,509	5.600	7.784	0.0	2.230	14.9	47	33
34	72,596	22,601	5.528	7.778	0.0	2.092	14.9	45	31
35	71,077	20,843	5.455	7.772	0.0	1.960	14.9	43	29
36	69,684	19,223	5.380	7.768	0.0	1.833	14.9	41	26
37	68,407	17,730	5.305	7.764	0.0	1.712	14.9	39	24
38	67,235	16,353	5.228	7.760	0.0	1.597	14.9	37	23
39	66,161	15,084	5.149	7.757	0.0	1.488	14.9	35	21
40	65,177	13,914	5.068	7.755	0.0	1.384	14.9	33	19
41	64,275	12,835	4.985	7.752	0.0	1.286	14.9	31	18
42	63,448	11,840	4.901	7.750	0.0	1.194	14.9	30	17
43	62,690	10,923	4.814	7.748	0.0	1.107	14.9	28	15
44	61,997	10,076	4.725	7.747	0.0	1.024	14.9	27	14
45	61,362	9,296	4.634	7.746	0.0	0.947	14.9	26	13
46	60,780	8,576	4.540	7.744	0.0	0.875	14.9	24	12
47	60,248	7,912	4.444	7.743	0.0	0.808	14.9	23	11
48	59,762	7,299	4.345	7.742	0.0	0.745	14.9	22	10
49	59,317	6,734	4.243	7.741	0.0	0.686	14.9	21	10
50	58,910	6,213	4.138	7.740	0.0	0.631	14.9	20	9
51	58,538	5,732	4.030	7.740	0.0	0.580	14.9	19	8
52	58,199	5,288	3.919	7.739	0.0	0.532	14.9	18	8
53	57,889	4,879	3.805	7.738	0.0	0.488	14.9	17	7
54	57,606	4,501	3.688	0.000	0.0	0.000	14.9	16	7

Selected Sensitivity Analyses

For most of the variables in the equations, it is clear how a change in the value will affect the results. For example, increases in the exchange ratio, ρ, will help the defender. Increases in either side's initial forces will be advantageous to that side. Higher tactical air readiness is always better than lower readiness, and so forth.

While demonstrating the general technique of sensitivity analysis to those who might wish to apply it further (to the above or other variables), this discussion is confined to the least transparent factors in the analysis, the threshold—or equilibrium—attrition rates, α_{aT} and α_{dT}.

Sensitivity to the Attacker's Equilibrium Attrition Rate (α_{aT})

For a variety of operational, strategic, or political reasons mentioned in chapter 4, each side, I have assumed, would be willing to sustain a historically very high attrition rate ($\alpha_{aT} = 0.075$, or 7.5 percent a day) when on the attack (in cases 1 and 3 for the USSR and cases 2 and 4 for the United States). It is appropriate, given the uncertainty surrounding α_{aT}, to examine alternatives holding all else fixed, in case the assignment of lower plausible values would drastically alter the main conclusions (that is, the main simulation results).

A reduction of α_{aT} to 0.06, for example, leaves winners and losers unaltered. The margins of victory are not substantially changed. However, reductions in α_{aT}, by cutting the pace of war, extend its duration, while reducing the displacement of the front, quite dramatically in case 3. These results are summarized in table D-9.

Sensitivity to the Defender's Threshold Attrition Rate (α_{dT})

The attrition rate at which withdrawal begins, α_{dT}, may vary between zero and one. For guerrilla defenders, α_{dT} can be very close to zero. For defenders engaged in trench warfare, by contrast, α_{dT} can be close to one.

While U.S. Special Forces operating in the Zagros Mountains of Iran (phase II) might resemble guerrillas, the battle of Khuzestan (phase III) would not be fought along the same lines; α_{dT} would be greater than zero.

However, since the defender (whether the United States or the Soviet Union) is not committed to a doctrine of forward defense, and is free to

D-9. *Sensitivity to Attacker's Equilibrium Attrition Rate*

Case	Assumed value	Winner	Winner's surviving ground lethality (WUV score)	Duration of war (days)	Displacement of front (km)
1	0.075	U.S.	84,709	50	0.0
	0.060	U.S.	83,833	63	0.0
2	0.075	USSR	40,905	49	17.8
	0.060	USSR	41,197	61	4.4
2A	0.075	U.S.	6,684	54	371.2
	0.060	U.S.	6,263	60	284.7
3	0.075	U.S.	10,746	56	119.5
	0.060	U.S.	10,089	70	9.1
4	0.075	USSR	151,088	49	0.0
	0.060	USSR	151,373	61	0.0
4A	0.075	USSR	57,606	54	14.9
	0.060	USSR	57,683	67	3.0

D-10. *Sensitivity to Defender's Threshold Attrition Rate*

Case	Assumed value	Winner	Winner's surviving ground lethality (WUV score)	Duration of war (days)	Displacement of front (km)
1	0.05	U.S.	84,709	50	0.0
	0.03	U.S.	84,710	50	8.7
2	0.05	USSR	40,905	49	17.8
	0.03	USSR	40,970	48	136.4
2A	0.05	U.S.	6,684	54	371.2
	0.03	U.S.	5,299	70	635.2
3	0.05	U.S.	10,746	56	119.5
	0.03	U.S.	10,060	67	426.3
4	0.05	USSR	151,088	49	0.0
	0.03	USSR	151,085	49	7.8
4A	0.05	USSR	57,606	54	14.9
	0.03	USSR	57,648	53	130.6

trade away space, I also assumed α_{dT} to be far less than 1.0. By historical standards, however, the assumed value of 5 percent a day is relatively high. That assumption is relaxed below.

The assignment of $\alpha_{dT} = 0.03$ would not alter winners, losers, or margins of victory. It has a large effect on the displacement of the front, however, as shown in table D-10.

APPENDIX E

Critique of Lanchester Theory

As NOTED IN chapter 1, the equations[1] developed by Frederick William Lanchester have for decades dominated the dynamic assessment of

1. Let $R(t)$ and $B(t)$ be the lethalities of engaged Red and Blue forces at time t, and let r and b (real numbers between zero and one) represent their respective effectiveness per unit. These so-called Lanchester coefficients are sometimes interpreted as overall damage probabilities per day. With constants c_1 through c_4 (between zero and one), the general Lanchester family equations are

$$\frac{dR}{dt} = -bB^{c_1}R^{c_2}$$

and

$$\frac{dB}{dt} = -rR^{c_3}B^{c_4}.$$

Applying the quotient form of the chain rule, the instantaneous casualty-exchange rate is obtained:

$$\frac{dR}{dB} = \frac{b}{r}B^{c_1-c_4}R^{c_2-c_3} = \frac{bB^{c_1-c_4}}{rR^{c_3-c_2}}.$$

Separating variables and integrating from terminal values to (higher) initial values, we obtain

$$r\int_{R(t)}^{R(0)} R^{c_3-c_2}dR = b\int_{B(t)}^{B(0)} B^{c_1-c_4}dB,$$

which yields the most general form of the Lanchester state equation:

$$\frac{r}{c_3-c_2+1}\left(R(0)^{c_3-c_2+1} - R(t)^{c_3-c_2+1}\right) = \frac{b}{c_1-c_4+1}\left(B(0)^{c_1-c_4+1} - B(t)^{c_1-c_4+1}\right).$$

The Lanchester square law, linear law, and other standard variants are then obtained as special cases determined by the c values, as shown below:

	c_1	c_2	c_3	c_4	State equation
Square law	1	0	1	0	$b[B(0)^2 - B(t)^2] = r[R(0)^2 - R(t)^2]$
Linear law	1	1	1	1	$b[B(0) - B(t)] = r[R(0) - R(t)]$
Logarithmic variant	0	1	0	1	$b\ln[B(0)/B(t)] = r\ln[R(0)/R(t)]$
Ambush variant	1	1	1	0	$b/2[B(0)^2 - B(t)^2] = r[R(0) - R(t)]$

146

conventional balances. My departure from them therefore warrants a brief explanation.

Lanchester theory suffers at least three serious problems.[2]

Problem 1: Why Withdraw?

A plausible model of ground war should capture the basic connection between attrition and the movement of the battle front. Historically, the basic rationale for withdrawal has been to reduce one's attrition; if a defender's attrition exceeds a certain threshold, he may withdraw, which action reduces his attrition. Not one of the Lanchester models (for example, the so-called square law or linear law) reflects this essential *feedback,* nor is it mathematically possible for them to. Not one of these equations can capture the effect *of* withdrawal—a response *to* attrition— *on* the rate of attrition itself.

Given the relevant state equation and other data, one's initial requirement can be obtained directly from the specified end states. Even this rather wide selection is but a special case. The inclusion of (a) reinforcements, (b) Red and Blue breakpoints, and (c) noninteger c values will expand the menu of homogeneous (apples versus apples) Lanchester equations immensely. Heterogeneous (apples versus oranges) generalizations are yet further possibilities. All of them suffer the first two fundamental problems discussed in this appendix; many suffer the third as well.

The single most comprehensive presentation of Lanchester equations is James G. Taylor, *Lanchester Models of Warfare,* 2 vols. For a more condensed version, see James G. Taylor, *Force-on-Force Attrition Modelling.* Other modern presentations are Philip M. Morse and George E. Kimball, *Methods of Operations Research,* pp. 63–77; Alan F. Karr, *Lanchester Attrition Processes and Theater-Level Combat Models;* and William W. Kaufmann, "The Arithmetic of Force Planning," pp. 208–16. The classic presentation of the square and linear variants is, of course, Lanchester's own: F. W. Lanchester, *Aircraft in Warfare.* Lanchester first published his equations in the British journal *Engineering* on October 2, 1914, in an article entitled "The Principle of Concentration." Soviet expositions may be found in Yu. V. Chuyev and Yu. B. Mikhaylov, *Forecasting in Military Affairs;* and Yu. V. Chuyev and others, *Fundamentals of Operations Research in Combat Materiel and Weaponry,* vol. 2, pp. 392–99.

2. This discussion is, of course, concerned specifically with problems beyond those encountered by *all models* (for example, the need to aggregate; to estimate effectiveness coefficients and other numbers; to idealize and simplify). A number of the aggregation and other problems that all models face are discussed in J. A. Stockfisch, *Models, Data, and War;* and U.S. General Accounting Office, *Models, Data, and War.* For further discussion of the goals, limits, and feasibility of quantitative contingency analysis, see Joshua M. Epstein, *Measuring Military Power,* preface and chap. 5. It should be noted that, though they are not discussed here, all probabilistic interpretations of the Lanchester equations are subject to the same fundamental criticisms lodged here. For probabilistic interpretations of Lanchester theory, see Taylor, *Lanchester Models,* vol. 1, chap. 4; and Morse and Kimball, *Methods of Operations Research,* pp. 67–71.

This is evident from Lanchester's attrition equations themselves. When solved for the opposing Red and Blue forces surviving at any time, t, the Lanchester square differential equations (see note 1) yield the following formulas:

$$(E\text{-}1a) \quad R(t) = \frac{1}{2}\left[\left(R(0) - \sqrt{\frac{b}{r}}B(0)\right)e^{\sqrt{rb}\cdot t}\right.$$
$$\left. + \left(R(0) + \sqrt{\frac{b}{r}}B(0)\right)e^{-\sqrt{rb}\cdot t}\right]$$

and

$$(E\text{-}1b) \quad B(t) = \frac{1}{2}\left[\left(B(0) - \sqrt{\frac{r}{b}}R(0)\right)e^{\sqrt{rb}\cdot t}\right.$$
$$\left. + \left(B(0) + \sqrt{\frac{r}{b}}R(0)\right)e^{-\sqrt{rb}\cdot t}\right].$$

$R(t)$ and $B(t)$ are the Red and Blue forces at time t, while r and b (real numbers between zero and one) are their respective Lanchester effectiveness coefficients.[3] Clearly, $R(t)$ and $B(t)$ depend *only* on r, b, t (time), and the initial Red and Blue forces. The rate of withdrawal does not appear; thus withdrawal does not affect the rate of attrition. The same is true for all other forms of the Lanchester equations.[4]

Formulas have been tendered to represent the velocity of the battle front as a function of the changing force ratios produced by the Lanchester attrition equations. Assuming Red to be a superior attacker, one procedure is to calculate the force ratio $x = R(t)/B(t)$ from the attrition formulas above and then to calculate the velocity of the front, $V(t)$, as a function of that ratio using the formula

$$(E\text{-}2) \qquad\qquad\qquad V(t) = \frac{V_{max}}{\sqrt{e^{(4/x)^2}}},$$

where V_{max} is the maximum feasible rate (in kilometers per day).[5] There are many alternative formulas positing velocity as a function of the force

3. These coefficients are sometimes interpreted as overall damage probabilities per day. For example, see William W. Kaufmann, "Nonnuclear Deterrence," p. 64.

4. Analytical solutions of the square and linear differential equations are derived in Taylor, *Lanchester Models*, vol. 1.

5. See Kaufmann, "Arithmetic of Force Planning," pp. 213–14.

ratio.[6] But these are implausible algorithms in that they are "one-way" calculations; movement is influenced by attrition, but not conversely. The movement of the front is *not* fed back into the ongoing attrition process, when the entire point of withdrawal was to affect that process— to reduce one's attrition rate.[7] Surely it is contradictory to assume *some benefit* in withdrawal (otherwise, why would anyone withdraw?) and then to reflect *no benefit* whatsoever in the ongoing attrition calculations. Yet all the original forms and contemporary extensions of the Lanchester equations suffer this glaring inconsistency.[8]

Problem 2: No Trading of Space for Time

Because there is no feedback *from* withdrawal rates *to* attrition rates, the Lanchester expression for the duration of the war (that is, the time

6. Alternative formulas are given in Taylor, *Lanchester Models,* vol. 2, p. 533; D. E. Emerson, *The New TAGS Theater Air-Ground Warfare Model* (*Incorporating Major Ground-Combat Revisions*), pp. 25–33; Philip E. Louer and Ralph E. Johnson, *Concepts Evaluation Model V* (*CEM V*), pt. 1: *Technical Description*; and Alan F. Karr, *On the CONAF Evaluation Model,* pp. 41–44.

7. It should be noted that withdrawal may be intended to lure the enemy into entrapment or ambush, though these tactical withdrawals would also have an effect on attrition that Lanchester's attrition equations cannot reflect. In the case of the traditional forced withdrawal, one may dispute whether it is the attrition rate specifically that the defender is seeking to reduce; it might be a complicated function of cumulative attrition, attrition rates, rates of change of attrition rates, and so forth. My general point is unchanged. Withdrawal seeks to alter (or to prevent from worsening) the pattern of defense death. No such effect will be evident from the Lanchester equations because withdrawal has no effect on attrition rates; there is *no feedback* from withdrawal to the course of attrition. Indeed, Lanchester's own exposition made no attempt whatsoever to estimate either the effect of attrition on movement or the effect of movement on attrition. Both of these are reflected in the equations offered in appendix C.

8. The only other interpretation is that the Lanchesterian framework is consistent, but is systematically biased in favor of the offense: the defender never gets any attrition-relief by withdrawing, though he vainly tries, because the offense always manages to stay in "full concentration" contact. That is, the offense perfectly anticipates the defender's tactical withdrawals, and always has the mobility, reconnaissance, and other capabilities necessary to keep attrition going as though no withdrawal were under way. This point applies to all—not just Lanchester—models that lack feedback from withdrawal to attrition.

One model that does attempt—although quite unsuccessfully—the interdependent computation of movement and attrition is the Lulejian-I combat model. Unfortunately, Lulejian-I erects a system of simultaneous equations that is literally insoluble in at least one instance and is of questionable plausibility on other grounds. This critique is convincingly set forth in Alan F. Karr, *Additional Remarks on Attrition and FEBA Movement Computations in the Lulejian-I Combat Model.* See also Alan F. Karr, *On the Lulejian-I Combat Model.* For a full exposition of the model, see Lulejian and Associates, *The Lulejian-I Theater-Level Model,* vol. 2: *Model Logic and Equations.*

elapsed) gives exactly the same answer whether the defender withdraws
a thousand miles or does not withdraw at all! The Lanchester duration
(time) is totally independent of the amount or rate of withdrawal (space)
and of the functional form chosen to calculate the velocity of the front.
This, too, is easily demonstrated.

Letting t_{end} stand for the time (in days) required by Red to annihilate
Blue, the square law duration will illustrate the general point. There are
various ways to write the duration; one is[9]

$$(E-3) \qquad t_{end} = \frac{1}{\sqrt{rb}} \ln \left(\frac{\sqrt{R_0^2 r} + \sqrt{B_0^2 b}}{\sqrt{R_0^2 r} - \sqrt{B_0^2 b}} \right)^{\frac{1}{2}}.$$

Here again t_{end} obviously depends only on r, b, and the initial Red and
Blue forces. The duration of the war, t_{end}, is totally independent of the
amount or rate of withdrawal. The same is true of the duration formulas
derived from other forms of the Lanchester differential equations. In
short, the Lanchester equations are incapable of representing perhaps
the most fundamental tactic in military history: trading space for time.
Given Blue and Red forces and effectiveness ratings, how much longer
does the war last if, rather than holding his ground, Blue (the defender)
trades away 100 kilometers? Or 500? Or 2,000? According to the
Lanchester equations, not one second longer. All else fixed, how much
longer does the war last if one adopts this movement function as against
that movement function? The Lanchester equations are incapable of
answering the question.

Problem 3: No Diminishing Marginal Returns

This point concerns the most famous and widely used result of
Lanchester theory, the square, or N^2, "law." Given Red and Blue forces,
Lanchester states his famous N^2 stalemate condition as follows: "the
fighting strengths of the two forces are equal when the *square of the
numerical strength multiplied by the fighting value of the individual units
are equal.*"[10] What he called *fighting values* are simply the Lanchester
coefficients, b and r. Thus in modern notation the square law says that a
Blue force, $B(0)$, will stalemate a Red force, $R(0)$, only if

---

9. See Kaufmann, "Arithmetic of Force Planning," p. 210.
10. Lanchester, *Aircraft in Warfare*, p. 48. Lanchester's emphasis. A stalemate is,
of course, a fight to the finish in which both sides are drawn to zero.

(E-4) $$bB(0)^2 = rR(0)^2.$$

Equivalently, the effectiveness ratio, b/r, must equal the square of the numerical ratio, $R(0)/B(0)$, for Blue to stalemate Red. So, for example, to stalemate an adversary three times one's size (in lethality units), it does *not* suffice to be three times as effective (per unit), or even six, seven, or eight times. Rather, one must be fully nine—or N^2—times as effective. There simply is no convincing evidence of this; indeed, there is impressive evidence to the contrary.[11]

Robert L. Helmbold's statistical study of ninety-two historical battles

11. By the same arithmetic, acceptance of the square law forces one to interpret given outcomes in questionable ways. For example, if one side stalemates (fights to zero-zero) an adversary five times as numerous—a feat approximated by Israel's Seventh Brigade on the Golan Heights in 1973—the Lanchesterite is mathematically compelled to conclude that the smaller force was twenty-five times as effective (that is, if stalemate occurred, then the effectiveness ratio equaled the square of the numerical ratio).

To counter that the equations are "technologically pessimistic" in the popular ("our weapons won't work") sense is simply wrong; the equations assert absolutely nothing about the relation of predicted weapon performance to actual weapon performance. Rather, they say that however the weapons perform (be that better than, worse than, or exactly as predicted), in order to stalemate, their effectiveness ratio, b/r, must stand in relation to their numerical ratio, R/B, as a number to its square.

While the plausibility of the N^2 relation is questionable in the homogeneous (apples fighting apples) cases, it is even less plausible that the matrix form (that is, the simple generalization) of the same underlying differential equations should govern conflict between heterogeneous forces (for example, air forces versus ground-based air defenses). Regarding the oft-claimed "elegance" of the equations, it might be added that the solution of the heterogeneous equations for the *daily numbers* of interacting air defense, close air, and ground units on each side is a rather unwieldy matrix equation (that is, a set of $2n$ separate equations, where n is the number of different types of units). The general heterogeneous expression for the duration of the war is correspondingly complex. The heterogeneous formulas for the initial forces needed to stalemate a given adversary are also far less neat than meets the eye. Given Red's air and ground forces and *given Blue's ground force*, it is easy to compute Blue's deficit and the close air required to fill it. But a different choice for Blue's ground force would yield a different deficit and a different close air requirement; yet a third Blue ground force would generate a third Blue deficit and close air requirement, and so forth. Indeed, given any specified end state (for example, stalemate), the equations admit an infinitude of Blue air-ground pairs (that is, a curve) that satisfies the requirement. Thus unless the Blue planner goes into the problem with all but one variable (for example, close air) fixed beforehand, the equations do not yield "an answer." But if the Blue planner *has* determined all but that one variable beforehand, he cannot be working on an optimal mix (since that would entail selecting the least-cost air-ground pair from the curve of air-ground pairs satisfying the specified end condition).

So not only are the Lanchester equations of questionable validity, they are also of rather narrow computational expedience, the latter property (expedience) being absolutely and irrevocably distinct from the former (validity) in any event.

not only fails to corroborate the Lanchester square equations, but also "suggests that victory in battle is primarily determined by factors other than numerical superiority, and challenges the ability of any model of combat which concentrates almost exclusively on numerical force size to yield a practically useful predictor of victory in battle."[12] Herbert K. Weiss's statistical study of Civil War data also offers no support for the Lanchester square law. Moreover, according to Weiss, "the phenomenon of losses increasing with force committed was observed by Richard H. Peterson at the Army Ballistic Research Laboratories in about 1950, in a study of tank battles. It was again observed by Willard and the present author has noted its appearance in the Battle of Britain data. It does not follow from either the linear or square Lanchester 'laws'."[13] The work referred to is D. Willard's *Lanchester as Force in History*, a statistical analysis on 1,500 land battles tabulated in G. Bodart's encyclopedic *Militär-historisches Kriegs-Lexicon (1618–1905)*. As Weiss observes, "The Willard study indicates that for the land battles given in Bodart, neither Lanchester law holds." Willard concludes, moreover, that "Lanchester's square law is the poorest among poor alternative choices of deterministic laws."[14]

As suggested above and noted explicitly below, one of the necessary (though not sufficient) conditions for any of the Lanchester equations to hold is that no movement (that is, defensive withdrawal) of the front be possible (since movement would have some effect on attrition rates, a feedback precluded in the Lanchester equations). What sorts of military engagements would qualify? Assaults on small, defended islands, for example.

The case of Iwo Jima—an island roughly five miles long, where the defender was basically surrounded, and where movement of the front was all but impossible—is among the special cases to which Lanchester equations may apply. It is the *only* case to my knowledge in which there is any statistical correspondence between events as they unfolded and as hypothesized by the Lanchester equations. Even if the statistical fit were good, there would be no basis for extrapolation to cases where movement is possible (for example, Europe). And, in fact, the fit is not good; J. H. Engel's famous "fit" of the Lanchester square equations to Iwo Jima is marred by insufficient data. Specifically, Lanchester's

12. Robert L. Helmbold, "Some Observations on the Use of Lanchester's Theory for Prediction," pp. 778–81.

13. Herbert K. Weiss, "Combat Models and Historical Data," p. 788.

14. Weiss, "Combat Models," p. 767; and Willard, *Lanchester as Force*, p. 4.

equations yield theoretical attrition curves for *each* side, defender and attacker. "Engel *assumed* that the attrition history of the defending [Japanese] forces was in accord with the Lanchester square-law predictions, since *no data* on observed attrition history for that force were available."[15] This is why, despite his tantalizing "fit" of the square equations to the U.S. data, Engel himself wrote, "The question might be raised: are there other forms of Lanchester's equations that might apply to the battle of Iwo Jima. . . . The answer to this question is 'yes'."[16] Commenting on the Engel study, James Busse notes that "there must be enough data from *both* sides (enemy and friendly) of the battle to allow a quantitative comparison between theory and 'experiment.' . . . Engel's theoretical fit to the American data is remarkably good, but nothing can be said about the fit of the missing Japanese data to the predictions of Lanchester's equations. In this respect, more data is needed before an adequate verification of Lanchester's theory will exist." Busse then attempted to fit the finite difference analogue of the Lanchester square equations to the Inchon-Seoul campaign. He found that they "are not satisfied by the data pertaining to this engagement."[17]

History's refusal to conform is not surprising when one notices that, at bottom, the Lanchester square equations deny a phenomenon to which virtually all social processes—including war—are subject: the phenomenon is diminishing marginal returns. To see this, a brief derivation is necessary.

The Lanchester square law is derived from the Lanchester square differential equations:

$$(E-5) \qquad \frac{dR}{dt} = -bB; \qquad \frac{dB}{dt} = -rR.$$

These equations say that the instantaneous rate of decrease in Red's

15. Helmbold, "Some Observations," p. 778. Emphasis added.

16. J. H. Engel, "A Verification of Lanchester's Law," pp. 170–71.

17. James J. Busse, "An Attempt to Verify Lanchester's Equations," pp. 587–97. Quotations are from pp. 587–88 and p. 596.

This noteworthy lack of statistical correspondence is not my sole—or even primary— basis for suggesting that the Lanchester equations be replaced with alternative force-planning tools. As discussed in chapter 4, the force planner wishes to arrive at a reasoned judgment about the wartime material adequacy of his or her force.

The methods employed in making such judgments must (a) be internally consistent and (b) offer a plausible representation of the dynamic interaction of dominant variables. On these grounds the equations offered in appendix C represent an advance over Lanchester's equations. For an extended discussion of the methodological distinction between conservatism and depictive precision in planning, see Epstein, *Measuring Military Power,* preface and chap. 5.

force (the time derivative, dR/dt) equals a constant (the Lanchester effectiveness coefficient, b) times Blue's strength (B), and analogously for Blue (the negative signs indicate that forces are decreasing). They imply the more revealing equation

(E-6)
$$\frac{dR}{dB} = \frac{bB}{rR},$$

from which the famous N^2 law is obtained directly by integration.[18]

Let us take a closer look at equation E-6, which *implies* the square law.[19] It asserts that the instantaneous casualty-exchange ratio, dR/dB—the limiting ratio of Reds killed per Blue killed—is a linear function of the force ratio, B/R, as graphed in the figure below.

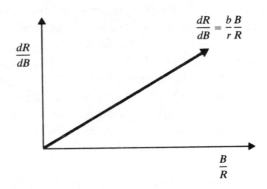

Thus the casualty-exchange rate, dR/dB, grows at a constant—*never*

18. Separating variables and integrating equation E-6, we obtain the Lanchester square state equation:

$$r\,(R(0)^2 - R(t)^2) = b\,(B(0)^2 - B(t)^2).$$

Setting $R(t) = B(t) = 0$, the familiar stalemate condition, or N^2 law, follows:

$$rR(0)^2 = bB(0)^2$$

or

$$\frac{b}{r} = \left(\frac{R(0)}{B(0)}\right)^2.$$

As noted in the text above, the effectiveness ratio, b/r, must equal the square of the numerical ratio, R/B, to stalemate.

19. In fact, equation E-6 both implies and is entailed by the Lanchester square state equation given in the above note; hence the two are equivalent.

marginally diminishing—rate, *b/r,* as the force ratio, *B/R,* grows.[20] No crowding, no force-to-space constraint, ever sets in to moderate the "concentratability" of Blue's force.[21] This is highly implausible; it is the essence of the Lanchester square law.

Some forms of the Lanchester differential equations do not imply a square relation (for example, the linear law), while others allow for asymmetrical solutions in which one side enjoys a square effect and the other does not (the so-called ambush variant).[22] Where (a) no diminishing marginal returns set in (for example, no force-to-space constraints apply) and (b) where movement of the front is precluded, certain forms may be more or less appealing. But as noted above, no form of the Lanchester equations registers, or can register, the effect *of* withdrawal (a response *to* attrition) *on* the rate of attrition itself. For that reason, they suffer the serious problems set forth at the outset. The equations presented in appendix C overcome these problems.

20. More rigorously, we can partially differentiate the instantaneous exchange ratio, *dR/dB,* in equation E-6 with respect to the force ratio, *B/R.* This yields

$$\frac{\partial}{\partial(B/R)}\left(\frac{dR}{dB}\right) = \frac{b}{r} > 0.$$

The casualty-exchange rate, *dR/dB,* thus grows at a constant—never marginally diminishing—rate, *b/r,* as the force ratio, *B/R,* increases. For a slightly different derivation, and a different interpretation, see Taylor, *Lanchester Models,* vol. 1, pp. 152–53. The effect pervades the dynamic interaction of engaged forces and cannot be altered by varying the density with which one chooses to populate the front (or by holding more or less force in reserve).

21. The absence of any diminishing marginal returns is the general point; no force-to-space constraints is simply one among many necessary conditions for it. Further conditions would have to be met to produce constant marginal returns. For example, one's command and control system would have to be able to manage an ever-increasing number of forces without any diminishing marginal returns in their effectiveness. Yet a third necessary condition for there to be no diminishing marginal returns is that each side's target acquisition probability (per shooter) not diminish marginally as the number of shooters increases; target acquisition and force levels are independent in the square law. Among the unrealistic features noted in the Soviet literature are these implicit assumptions that "the information on target damage arrives instantaneously; as soon as the combat unit of the enemy is annihilated, the victorious combat unit immediately transfers fire to another target." The Soviets refer to this as "a version of the so-called 'highly organized battle'" and go on to model "a battle during which there is no information on target damage and no transfer of fire." Chuyev and others, *Fundamentals of Operations Research,* vol. 2, p. 400.

22. This may well be the most plausible of all Lanchester variants, when applied to guerrilla engagements. See S. J. Deitchman, "A Lanchester Model of Guerrilla Warfare," pp. 818–27; and Taylor, *Lanchester Models,* vol. 1, pp. 169–81.

Bibliography

Books, Articles, and Monographs

Arbib, Michael A. *Brains, Machines, and Mathematics*. New York: McGraw-Hill, 1964.

Arnhold, Klaus. *Zur Problematik Eines Vergleichs der Konventionellen Landstreitkräfte von NATO und Warschauer Pakt in Europa*. Arbeitspapier. Ebenhausen, F.R. Ger.: Stiftung Wissenschaft und Politik, 1983.

Ashby, W. Ross. *Design for a Brain*. 2d ed. 1960. Reprint. London: Chapman and Hall, 1978.

————. *An Introduction to Cybernetics*. London: Chapman and Hall, 1956.

Ball, Desmond. *Targeting for Strategic Deterrence*. Adelphi Paper 185. London: International Institute for Strategic Studies, 1983.

Berman, Robert P. *Soviet Air Power in Transition*. Washington, D.C.: Brookings Institution, 1978.

Betts, Richard K. *Surprise Attack: Lessons for Defense Planning*. Washington, D.C.: Brookings Institution, 1982.

Blechman, Barry M., and Edward N. Luttwak, eds. *International Security Yearbook 1983/84*. New York: St. Martin's Press for the Georgetown University Center for Strategic and International Studies, 1984.

Bodart, Gaston. *Militär-historisches Kriegs-Lexicon (1618–1905)*. Vienna and Leipzig: C. W. Stern, 1908.

Bowie, Christopher J. *Concepts of Operations and USAF Planning for Southwest Asia*. R-3125-AF. Prepared for the U.S. Air Force. Santa Monica, Calif.: Rand Corporation, 1984.

Brodie, Bernard. *Escalation and the Nuclear Option*. Princeton: Princeton University Press, 1966.

Brown, Harold. *Thinking about National Security: Defense and Foreign Policy in a Dangerous World*. Boulder, Colo.: Westview Press, 1983.

Busse, James J. "An Attempt to Verify Lanchester's Equations." In Benjamin Avi-itzhak, ed., *Developments in Operations Research*, vol. 2. New York: Gordon and Breach Science Publishers, 1971.

Canby, Stephen L., and Edward N. Luttwak. *The Control of Arms Transfers and Perceived Security Needs*. Prepared for the U.S. Arms Control and Disarmament Agency. Potomac, Md.: C and L Associates, 1980.

Clausewitz, Carl von. *On War*. Edited and translated by Michael Howard and Peter Paret. Princeton: Princeton University Press, 1976.

Cochran, Thomas B., William M. Arkin, and Milton M. Hoenig. *Nuclear Weapons Databook*. Vol. 1: *U.S. Nuclear Forces and Capabilities*. Cambridge, Mass.: Ballinger, 1984.

Collins, John M. *U.S.-Soviet Military Balance: Concepts and Capabilities, 1960–1980*. New York: McGraw-Hill, 1980.

Cordesman, Anthony H. *The Gulf and the Search for Strategic Stability: Saudi Arabia, the Military Balance in the Gulf, and Trends in the Arab-Israeli Military Balance*. Boulder, Colo.: Westview Press, 1984.

Cotter, Donald R. "Potential Future Roles for Conventional and Nuclear Forces in Defense of Western Europe." In European Security Study (ESECS), *Strengthening Conventional Deterrence in Europe: Proposals for the 1980s*. New York: St. Martin's Press, 1983.

Courant, Richard, and Herbert Robbins. *What Is Mathematics? An Elementary Approach to Ideas and Methods*. New York: Oxford University Press, 1941.

Deitchman, S. J. "A Lanchester Model of Guerrilla Warfare." *Operations Research*, vol. 10 (November–December 1962).

deLeon, Peter. *The Peacetime Evaluation of the Pilot Skill Factor in Air-to-Air Combat*. R-2070-PR. Prepared for the U.S. Air Force. Santa Monica, Calif.: Rand Corporation, 1977.

Dunnigan, James F. *How to Make War*. New York: Quill, 1982.

Dupuy, Col. T. N. *Numbers, Predictions and War: Using History to Evaluate Combat Factors and Predict the Outcome of Battles*. Indianapolis: Bobbs-Merrill, 1979.

Emerson, D. E. *The New TAGS Theater Air-Ground Warfare Model (Incorporating Major Ground-Combat Revisions): A Description and Operating Instructions*. R-1576-PR. Prepared for the U.S. Air Force. Santa Monica, Calif.: Rand Corporation, 1974.

Engel, J. H. "A Verification of Lanchester's Law." *Operations Research*, vol. 2 (May 1954).

Epstein, Joshua M. *The Calculus of Conventional War: Dynamic Analysis without Lanchester Theory*. Washington, D.C.: Brookings Institution, 1985.

———. "Improving Soviet Airlift." *Military Logistics Forum*, vol. 2 (October 1985).

———. *Measuring Military Power: The Soviet Air Threat to Europe*. Princeton: Princeton University Press, 1984.

———. *The 1987 Defense Budget*. Washington, D.C.: Brookings Institution, 1986.

Gaddis, John Lewis. "Containment: Its Past and Future." *International Security*, vol. 5 (Spring 1981).

———. *Strategies of Containment: A Critical Appraisal of Postwar American National Security Policy*. New York: Oxford University Press, 1982.

Guensberg, Gerold, trans. *Soviet Command Study of Iran (Moscow 1941): Draft Translation and Brief Analysis*. Prepared for the Office of the Secretary of Defense. Arlington, Va.: SRI International, 1980.

Hackett, Sir John. "Protecting Oil Supplies: The Military Requirements." Paper presented to the International Institute for Strategic Studies, 22d Annual Conference, Stresa, Italy, September 1980.

Halperin, Morton H. *Defense Strategies for the Seventies*. Boston: Little, Brown, 1971.

Hamilton, Andrew. "Redressing the Conventional Balance: NATO's Reserve Military Manpower." *International Security*, vol. 10 (Summer 1985).

Healy, Melissa. "Lehman: We'll Sink Their Subs." *Defense Week*, vol. 6 (May 13, 1985).

———. "War Game Sends Subs Surging." *Defense Week*, vol. 6 (September 3, 1985).

Heiman, Leo. "Soviet Invasion Weaknesses." *Military Review*, vol. 49 (August 1969).

Heller, Mark, ed. *The Middle East Military Balance, 1983*. Tel Aviv, Israel: Tel Aviv University, Jaffee Center for Strategic Studies, 1983.

Helmbold, Robert L. *Decision in Battle: Breakpoint Hypotheses and Engagement Termination Data*. R-772-PR. Prepared for the U.S. Air Force. Santa Monica, Calif.: Rand Corporation, 1971.

———. "Some Observations on the Use of Lanchester's Theory for Prediction." Letter to the Editor. *Operations Research*, vol. 12 (September–October 1964).

Herzog, Chaim. *The Arab-Israeli Wars: War and Peace in the Middle East*. New York: Random House, 1982.

Hewett, Ed A. *Energy, Economics, and Foreign Policy in the Soviet Union*. Washington, D.C.: Brookings Institution, 1984.

Huntington, Samuel P. "The Renewal of Strategy." In Huntington, ed., *The Strategic Imperative: New Policies for American Security*. Cambridge, Mass.: Ballinger, 1982.

Iklé, Fred Charles. *Every War Must End*. New York: Columbia University Press, 1971.

International Institute for Strategic Studies. *The Military Balance*. London, IISS. Annual.

Isby, David C. *Weapons and Tactics of the Soviet Army*. London: Jane's Publishing Co., 1981.

Jane's Weapon Systems. London, Jane's Publishing Co. Annual.

Jefferson, Thomas. *The Living Thoughts of Thomas Jefferson*. Presented by John Dewey. New York: Longmans, Green, 1940.

Jervis, Robert. *Perception and Misperception in International Politics*. Princeton: Princeton University Press, 1976.

Kahn, Herman. *On Escalation: Metaphors and Scenarios*. New York: Praeger, 1965.

Kaplan, Fred. *The Wizards of Armageddon*. New York: Simon and Schuster, 1983.

Karr, Alan F. *Additional Remarks on Attrition and FEBA Movement Computations in the Lulejian-I Combat Model*. P-1277. Arlington, Va.: Institute for Defense Analyses, 1977.

——. *Lanchester Attrition Processes and Theater-Level Combat Models.* P-1528. Arlington, Va.: Institute for Defense Analyses, 1981.

——. *On the CONAF Evaluation Model.* P-1210. Arlington, Va.: Institute for Defense Analyses, 1976.

——. *On the Lulejian-I Combat Model.* P-1182. Arlington, Va.: Institute for Defense Analyses, 1976.

Kaufmann, William W. "The Arithmetic of Force Planning," "Nonnuclear Deterrence," and "Nuclear Deterrence in Central Europe." In John D. Steinbruner and Leon V. Sigal, eds., *Alliance Security: NATO and the No-First-Use Question.* Washington, D.C.: Brookings Institution, 1983.

——. "The Defense Budget." In Joseph A. Pechman, ed., *Setting National Priorities: The 1982 Budget.* Washington, D.C.: Brookings Institution, 1981.

——. "The Defense Budget." In Joseph A. Pechman, ed., *Setting National Priorities: The 1983 Budget.* Washington, D.C.: Brookings Institution, 1982.

——. "Defense Policy." In Joseph A. Pechman, ed., *Setting National Priorities: Agenda for the 1980s.* Washington, D.C.: Brookings Institution, 1980.

——. "Limited Warfare" and "The Requirements of Deterrence." In Kaufmann, ed., *Military Policy and National Security.* Princeton: Princeton University Press, 1956.

Kelleher, Catherine McArdle. "Thresholds and Theologies: The Need for Critical Reassessment." *Survival,* vol. 26 (July–August 1984).

Kingston, Lt. Gen. Robert C. "C³I and the U.S. Central Command." *Signal,* vol. 38 (November 1983).

Komer, Robert W. "Maritime Strategy vs. Coalition Defense." *Foreign Affairs,* vol. 60 (Summer 1982).

Krepinevich, Andrew. "The U.S. Rapid Deployment Force and Protection of Persian Gulf Oil Supplies." Cambridge, Mass.: Harvard University, Kennedy School of Government, 1979.

Kuzmack, Arnold M. "Where Does the Navy Go from Here?" *Military Review,* vol. 52 (February 1972). Brookings Reprint 226.

Lanchester, Frederick William. *Aircraft in Warfare: The Dawn of the Fourth Arm.* London: Constable, 1916. The seminal chapters, 5 and 6, are reprinted as "Mathematics in Warfare," in James R. Newman, ed., *The World of Mathematics,* vol. 4. New York: Simon and Schuster, 1956.

Lulejian and Associates. *The Lulejian-I Theater-Level Model.* Vol. 2: *Model Logic and Equations.* WSEG Report 259. Arlington, Va.: Weapons Systems Evaluation Group, 1974.

Luttwak, Edward N. "Delusions of Soviet Weakness." *Commentary,* vol. 79 (January 1985).

McNamara, Robert S. "The Military Role of Nuclear Weapons: Perceptions and Misperceptions." *Foreign Affairs,* vol. 62 (Fall 1983).

McNaugher, Thomas L. *Arms and Oil: U.S. Military Strategy and the Persian Gulf.* Washington, D.C.: Brookings Institution, 1985.

Mako, William P. *U.S. Ground Forces and the Defense of Central Europe.* Washington, D.C.: Brookings Institution, 1983.

Morse, Philip M., and George E. Kimball. *Methods of Operations Research.* Cambridge, Mass.: Technology Press of Massachusetts Institute of Technology, 1951; New York: Wiley, 1951.

Newman, James R. "Commentary on Frederick William Lanchester." In Newman, ed., *The World of Mathematics,* vol. 4. New York: Simon and Schuster, 1956.

Perry, Robert, Mark A. Lorell, and Kevin N. Lewis. *Second-Area Operations: A Strategy Option.* R-2992-USDP. Prepared for the Office of the Under Secretary of Defense for Policy. Santa Monica, Calif.: Rand Corporation, 1984.

Posen, Barry R. "Inadvertent Nuclear War? Escalation and NATO's Northern Flank." *International Security,* vol. 7 (Fall 1982).

———. "Measuring the European Conventional Balance: Coping with Complexity in Threat Assessment." *International Security,* vol. 9 (Winter 1984–85).

———. *The Sources of Military Doctrine: France, Britain, and Germany between the World Wars.* Ithaca, N.Y.: Cornell University Press, 1984.

Record, Jeffrey. *The Rapid Deployment Force and U.S. Military Intervention in the Persian Gulf.* Cambridge, Mass.: Institute for Foreign Policy Analysis, 1981.

———. *Sizing Up the Soviet Army.* Washington, D.C.: Brookings Institution, 1975.

Rosen, Steven J. "What the Next Arab-Israeli War Might Look Like." *International Security,* vol. 2 (Spring 1978).

Sahab Geographic and Drafting Institute. "Road Map of Iran." Tehran, Iran: Sahab, 1977.

Schelling, Thomas C. *Arms and Influence.* New Haven: Yale University Press, 1966.

———. *The Strategy of Conflict.* Cambridge, Mass.: Harvard University Press, 1960.

Schemmer, Benjamin F. "Pentagon, White House, and Congress Concerned over Tactical Aircraft Complexity and Readiness." *Armed Forces Journal International,* vol. 117 (May 1980).

Schwartz, David N. "A Historical Perspective." In John D. Steinbruner and Leon V. Sigal, eds., *Alliance Security: NATO and the No-First-Use Question.* Washington, D.C.: Brookings Institution, 1983.

———. *Nato's Nuclear Dilemmas.* Washington, D.C.: Brookings Institution, 1983.

Shirer, William L. *The Rise and Fall of the Third Reich: A History of Nazi Germany.* New York: Simon and Schuster, 1960.

Sigal, Leon V. *Nuclear Forces in Europe: Enduring Dilemmas, Present Prospects.* Washington, D.C.: Brookings Institution, 1984.

Smoke, Richard. *War: Controlling Escalation.* Cambridge, Mass.: Harvard University Press, 1977.

"Soviet Naval Presence Doubles in Indian Ocean, Lacks Support." *Aviation Week and Space Technology,* vol. 114 (April 6, 1981).

Steinbruner, John D. "Alliance Security." In John D. Steinbruner and Leon V. Sigal, eds., *Alliance Security: NATO and the No-First-Use Question*. Washington, D.C.: Brookings Institution, 1983.

———. *The Cybernetic Theory of Decision: New Dimensions of Political Analysis*. Princeton: Princeton University Press, 1974.

Stockfisch, J. A. *Models, Data, and War: A Critique of the Study of Conventional Forces*. R-1526-PR. Prepared for the U.S. Air Force. Santa Monica, Calif.: Rand Corporation, 1975.

Taylor, James G. *Force-on-Force Attrition Modelling*. Arlington, Va.: Operations Research Society of America, 1981.

———. *Lanchester Models of Warfare*. 2 vols. Arlington, Va.: Operations Research Society of America, 1983.

Trachtenberg, Marc, ed. "Documentation: White House Tapes and Minutes of the Cuban Missile Crisis." *International Security*, vol. 10 (Summer 1985).

Valenta, Jiri. "From Prague to Kabul: The Soviet Style of Invasion." *International Security*, vol. 5 (Fall 1980).

Van Evera, Stephen. "The Cult of the Offensive and the Origins of the First World War." *International Security*, vol. 9 (Summer 1984).

Waltz, Kenneth N. "A Strategy for the Rapid Deployment Force." *International Security*, vol. 5 (Spring 1981).

Watkins, Adm. James D. "The Maritime Strategy." In *The Maritime Strategy*. Annapolis, Md.: U.S. Naval Institute, 1986.

Weiss, Herbert K. "Combat Models and Historical Data: The U.S. Civil War." *Operations Research*, vol. 14 (September–October 1966).

Wiener, Norbert. *Cybernetics, or Control and Communication in the Animal and the Machine*. New York: Wiley, 1948.

Willard, D. *Lanchester as Force in History: An Analysis of Land Battles of the Years 1618–1905*. RAC-TP-74. Bethesda, Md.: Research Analysis Corporation, 1962.

Government Publications

Babayev, Gen.-Col. Aleksandr Ivanovich. "Flight and the Combat Maneuver." Translated by U.S. Air Force Intelligence Service, Directorate of Soviet Affairs. *Soviet Press Selected Translations* (Bolling Air Force Base, Washington, D.C.), April 1977. (Originally published in *Krasnaya Zvezda*, December 23, 1976.)

Ballard, Jack S. *Development and Employment of Fixed-Wing Gunships, 1962–1972*. The United States Air Force in Southeast Asia Series. Washington, D.C.: Government Printing Office, 1982.

Bonder, Seth. "Issues Facing Model Developers-I." In U.S. Department of Commerce, National Bureau of Standards, *Utility and Use of Large-Scale Mathematical Models*, NBS Special Publication 534. Washington, D.C.: Government Printing Office, 1979.

Chuyev, Yu. V., and Yu. B. Mikhaylov. *Forecasting in Military Affairs: A Soviet View*. Washington, D.C.: Government Printing Office, 1980.

Chuyev, Yu. V., and others. *Fundamentals of Operations Research in Combat Materiel and Weaponry*, vol. 2. Translated by Foreign Technology Division, Wright Patterson Air Force Base, Ohio, 1968.

Konstantinov, Gen.-Col. Anatoliy Ustinovich. "Thorough Knowledge of Affairs." Translated by U.S. Air Force Intelligence Service, Directorate of Soviet Affairs. *Soviet Press Selected Translations* (Bolling Air Force Base, Washington, D.C.), June 1977. (Originally published in *Krasnaya Zvezda*, March 13, 1977.)

Lavalle, Maj. A. J. C. *The Tale of Two Bridges and the Battle for the Skies over North Vietnam*. USAF Southeast Asia Monograph Series, vol. 1, monographs 1 and 2. Washington, D.C.: Government Printing Office, 1980.

Leighton, Richard M., and Robert W. Coakley. *United States Army in World War II, the War Department: Global Logistics and Strategy, 1940–1943*. Washington, D.C.: U.S. Department of the Army, Office of the Chief of Military History, 1955.

Leonard, Capt. Henry, and Jeffrey Scott. "Methodology for Estimating Movement Rates of Ground Forces in Mountainous Terrain with and without Defensive Obstacles: First Draft." Prepared for Office of the Assistant Secretary of Defense, Program Analysis and Evaluation, Regional Programs, Special Regional Studies. Washington, D.C., 1979.

Louer, Philip E., and Ralph E. Johnson. *Concepts Evaluation Model V (CEM V)*. Part 1: *Technical Description*. CAA-D-80-3. Bethesda, Md.: U.S. Army Concepts Analysis Agency, 1980.

Motter, T. H. Vail. *United States Army in World War II, the Middle East Theater: The Persian Corridor and Aid to Russia*. Washington, D.C.: U.S. Department of the Army, Office of the Chief of Military History, 1952.

Pavlov, Gen.-Lt. G. "Inexhaustible Reserve." Translated by U.S. Air Force Intelligence Service, Directorate of Soviet Affairs. *Soviet Press Selected Translations* (Bolling Air Force Base, Washington, D.C.), April 1977. (Originally published in *Krasnaya Zvezda*, August 4, 1976.)

Public Papers of the Presidents: Jimmy Carter, 1980–81, vol. 1. Washington, D.C.: Government Printing Office, 1981.

Rapid Deployment Joint Task Force. Headquarters. Public Affairs Office. "Fact Sheet." MacDill Air Force Base, Fla., January 1981.

"United States Central Command." Public affairs document. MacDill Air Force Base, Fla.: CENTCOM, January 1983.

Uryzhnikov, V. A. "In a Complex Situation." Translated by U.S. Air Force Intelligence Service, Directorate of Soviet Affairs. *Soviet Press Selected Translations* (Bolling Air Force Base, Washington, D.C.), April 1977. (Originally published in *Krasnaya Zvezda*, January 7, 1977.)

U.S. Central Intelligence Agency. *The International Energy Situation: Outlook to 1985*. ER77-102YOU. Washington, D.C.: CIA, 1977.

———. "Map of Iran." Washington, D.C.: CIA, 1978.

U.S. Congress. House. Committee on Appropriations. *Department of Defense*

Appropriations for 1980. Hearings. 96 Cong. 1 sess. Washington, D.C.: Government Printing Office, 1979.

———. ———. Committee on Government Operations. *The Implementation of the NATO Long-Term Defense Program (LTDP).* H. Rept. 97-37. 97 Cong. 1 sess. Washington, D.C.: Government Printing Office, 1981.

———. Senate. Committee on Appropriations. *Department of Defense Appropriations for Fiscal Year 1984.* Hearings. 98 Cong. 1 sess. Washington, D.C.: Government Printing Office, 1984.

———. ———. Committee on Armed Services. *Department of Defense Authorization for Appropriations for Fiscal Year 1981.* Hearings. 96 Cong. 2 sess. Washington, D.C.: Government Printing Office, 1980.

U.S. Congressional Budget Office. *Navy Budget Issues for Fiscal Year 1980.* Washington, D.C.: CBO, 1979.

———. *Rapid Deployment Forces: Policy and Budgetary Implications.* Washington, D.C.: CBO, 1983.

———. *U.S. Airlift Forces: Enhancement Alternatives for NATO and Non-NATO Contingencies.* Washington, D.C.: CBO, 1979.

———. *U.S. Projection Forces: Requirements, Scenarios, and Options.* Washington, D.C.: CBO, 1978.

———. *The U.S. Sea Control Mission: Forces, Capabilities, and Requirements.* Washington, D.C.: CBO, 1977.

U.S. Department of Defense. *Annual Report to the Congress.* Washington, D.C.: Government Printing Office. Annual for fiscal years.

———. *Soviet Military Power.* 5th ed. Washington, D.C.: Government Printing Office, 1986.

U.S. Department of the Air Force. *Soviet Aerospace Handbook.* AF Pamphlet 200-21, May 1978. Washington, D.C.: Government Printing Office, 1977.

———. Comptroller of the Air Force. *United States Air Force Summary, 1984.* Washington, D.C.: USAF, 1984.

U.S. Department of the Army. *Maneuver Control.* FM 105-5, December 1973. Washington, D.C.: Government Printing Office, 1975.

———. *Operations.* FM 100-5, July 1976. Washington, D.C.: Government Printing Office, 1977.

———. *Staff Officers' Field Manual: Organizational, Technical and Logistical Data.* FM 101-10-1, July 1976. Washington, D.C.: Government Printing Office, 1976.

———. *Soviet Army Operations.* IAG-13-U-78, April 1978. Washington, D.C.: Government Printing Office, 1983.

———. *U.S. Army Reference Data.* Vol. 1: *The Army Division.* Vol. 2: *Non-Divisional Organizations.* ST-17-1-1. Fort Knox, Ky.: U.S. Army Armor School, 1981.

———. Concepts Analysis Agency. War Gaming Directorate. *Final Report: Weapon Effectiveness Indices/Weighted Unit Values (WEI/WUV).* Vol. 1: *Executive Summary.* Study Report CAA-SR-73-18. Bethesda, Md.: Department of the Army, 1974.

U.S. Department of the Navy. "Sea Plan 2000: Naval Force Planning Study, Unclassified Executive Summary." Undated.

U.S. General Accounting Office. *Models, Data, and War: A Critique of the Foundation for Defense Analyses*. PAD-80-21. Washington, D.C.: Government Printing Office, 1980.

U.S. Organization of the Joint Chiefs of Staff. *United States Military Posture for FY 1987*. Washington, D.C.: JCS, 1986.

Voigt, Karsten, rapporteur. "Draft Interim Report of the Sub-Committee on Conventional Defence in Europe." North Atlantic Assembly, Military Committee, MC/CD (84) 1, May 1984.

Declassified Government Documents

Coleridge, Capt. R. D. "Assistance to Persia." Letter to General Gruenther. July 8, 1984. Records of the Army Staff. Record Group 319. P&O 091 Jan TS 1948 F/W 15. National Archives, Modern Military Branch, Washington, D.C.

McNamara, Robert S. "Draft Memorandum for the President on Theater Nuclear Forces." October 1965.

———. "Draft Memorandum for the President on Theater Nuclear Forces." January 6, 1967.

———. "Draft Memorandum for the President on Theater Nuclear Forces." Revised January 11, 1968.

———. "Draft Memorandum for the President on Theater Nuclear Forces." January 15, 1969.

Maddocks, Maj. Gen. Ray T. "Memorandum for the Chief of Staff, U.S. Army: Joint U.S.-British Policy with Respect to Iran." P&O 091 Iran TS, July 13, 1948. P&O 091 Jan TS 1948 F/W 15. Records of the Army Staff. Record Group 319. National Archives, Modern Military Branch, Washington, D.C.

"Memorandum by the Chief of Naval Operations for the Joint Chiefs of Staff on Operation Plan No. ABA 1-49 (Neckpiece)." JCS-2034/6, March 15, 1950. CCS 381 (3-14-49), sec. 1. Records of the U.S. Joint Chiefs of Staff. Record Group 218. National Archives, Modern Military Branch, Washington, D.C.

"United States Naval Forces: Eastern Atlantic and Mediterranean." Appendix to "Note by the Secretaries to the Joint Chiefs of Staff on Targets for Attack by U.S. Strategic Air Forces in Support of Operations in the Mediterranean-Middle East." JCS 2034/2, October 11, 1949. CCS 381 (3-14-49), sec. 1. Records of the U.S. Joint Chiefs of Staff. Record Group 218. National Archives, Modern Military Branch, Washington, D.C.

U.S. Joint Chiefs of Staff. "Decision on J.C.S. 1920/1, Long-Range Plans for War with the USSR—Development of a Joint Outline Plan for Use in the Event of War in 1957." JCS 1920/1, May 6, 1949. CCS 381 U.S.S.R. (3-2-46), sec. 28. Records of the U.S. Joint Chiefs of Staff. Record Group 218. National Archives, Modern Military Branch, Washington, D.C.

U.S. Joint Intelligence Staff. "Overland Lines of Communication." Appendix

A to "Service Members, Joint Intelligence Staff: Intelligence Estimate of Specific Areas in Southern Europe, the Middle and Near East, and Northern Africa (Overland Lines of Communication)." JIS 267/1/"A", October 24, 1946. CCS 381 U.S.S.R. (3-2-46), sec. 3. "A" Team. Records of the U.S. Joint Chiefs of Staff. Record Group 218. National Archives, Modern Military Branch, Washington, D.C.

U.S. Joint Logistics Plans Committee. "Directive—Comments on Logistical Aspects of Dropshot." JLPC 416/26/D. October 19, 1948. CCS 381 U.S.S.R. (3-2-46) sec. 22. Records of the U.S. Joint Chiefs of Staff. Record Group 218. National Archives, Modern Military Branch, Washington, D.C.

U.S. Joint Strategic Plans Committee. "Brief of Joint Outline Emergency War Plan (Short Title: Offtackle)." JSPC 877/59, May 26, 1949. CCS 381 U.S.S.R. (3-2-46), sec. 32. Records of the U.S. Joint Chiefs of Staff. Record Group 218. National Archives, Modern Military Branch, Washington, D.C.

U.S. Joint Strategic Plans Group. "Crankshaft." JSPG 496/10, May 11, 1948. CCS 381 U.S.S.R. (3-2-46), sec. 14. Records of the U.S. Joint Chiefs of Staff. Record Group 218. National Archives, Modern Military Branch, Washington, D.C.

———. "Proposed Guidance for an Alternative Plan to 'Bushwacker.' " JSPG 500/3, March 8, 1948. CCS 381 U.S.S.R. (3-2-46), sec. 11. Records of the U.S. Joint Chiefs of Staff. Record Group 218. National Archives, Modern Military Branch, Washington, D.C.

U.S. Joint War Plans Committee. "Overland Lines of Communication." Annex D to Appendix to "Joint War Plans Committee: Strategic Study of the Area between the Alps and the Himalayas, Short Title 'Caldron.' " JWPC 475/1, November 2, 1946. CCS 381 U.S.S.R. (3-2-46), sec. 3, pt. 1. Records of the U.S. Joint Chiefs of Staff. Record Group 218. National Archives, Modern Military Branch, Washington, D.C.

U.S. National Security Council. "NSC 73/4: Note by the Executive Secretary to the National Security Council on the Position and Actions of the United States with Respect to Possible Further Soviet Moves in the Light of the Korean Situation," August 25, 1950. In U.S. Department of State, *Foreign Relations of the United States, 1950*. Vol. 1: *National Security Affairs; Foreign Economic Policy*. Washington, D.C.: Government Printing Office, 1977.

Index

A-*4* aircraft, 70
A-*6* aircraft, 111, 129n
A-*7* aircraft, 83n, 95
A-*10* aircraft, 70, 83n, 128n, 129n
Afghanistan, Soviet invasion of, 61–62, 98, 102, 125
AH-*1* helicopter, 70, 83n, 120n, 129n
AIM-*7* missile, 94, 109n
AIM-*54*A missile, 94
Air Force, U.S., readiness, 83n, 128–29. *See also* Air interdiction campaigns, U.S.
Air interdiction campaigns, U.S., 54–56, 107–11
An-*22* aircraft, 64
An-*124* aircraft, 64
Anderson, Jack, 51n
Arbib, Michael A., 124n
Arkin, William M., 21n
Army, U.S., Weapon Effectiveness Indices/Weighted Unit Values (WEI/WUV) system, 69–71, 77, 117
Arnhold, Klaus, 71n
Ashby, W. Ross, 124n
Asymmetrical response, 1, 98–99. *See also* Horizontal escalation strategy; Vertical escalation strategy
Atomic demolition munitions (ADMs), 15–16, 21, 22, 51
AV-*8*A/B/C aircraft, 83n, 129n
AWACS aircraft, 92

B-*52* bomber, 54–55, 96
Babayev, Gen.-Col. Aleksandr Ivanovich, 90n
Backfire bomber, 94, 95
Ball, Desmond, 16n
Ballard, Jack S., 129n
Bean counting. *See* Input measures
Bear bomber, 96n
Berman, Robert P., 90n
Betts, Richard K., 12n
Blechman, Barry M., 32n, 44n
Bodart, Gaston, 152

Bonder, Seth, 9n
Bowie, Christopher J., 83n, 108n, 110n
Brodie, Bernard, 24n
Brown, Harold, 3
Burt, Richard, 16n, 51n
Busse, James J., 153

C-*5* aircraft, 63, 64, 65
Canby, Stephen L., 107n
Carter, Jimmy, 2, 16
Carter administration, 15, 99
Carter Doctrine, 2, 6, 11, 16, 102
Central Command, U.S. (CENTCOM): combat forces available to, 7, 8, 32, 44, 52, 69; created, 2
Chuyev, Yu. V., 147n, 155n
Clark, William P., 32
Clausewitz, Carl von, 48, 49n, 74, 79, 80
Claytor, W. Graham, 95
Coakley, Robert W., 76n
Cochran, Thomas B., 21n
Coleridge, Capt. R. D., 57n
Collins, John M., 92n
Command, control, and communications (C³), 25; command, control, communications, and intelligence (C³I), 25
Conservatism, of assumptions, 73–78
Cordesman, Anthony H., 24n
Cotter, Donald R., 74n
Courant, Richard, 121n
Crisis management, 100–02
Cuba, value to Soviets, 37, 39
Czechoslovakia, Soviet invasion of, 61, 62, 65–66, 72

Deitchman, S. J., 155n
deLeon, Peter, 91n
Delta-Bravo-Romeo target categories, 13–17
Deterrence, 4, 29, 41, 42, 44, 62–63, 98
Diego Garcia, 24, 96–97
Diplomacy, horizontal escalation and, 40–42
Draft Presidential Memoranda. on theater

nuclear forces, 6, 12, 14, 18, 19, 20, 22, 25, 98–99
Dudney, Robert S., 7
Dunnigan, James F., 75n, 109n
Dupuy, Col. T. N., 52n
Dynamic analysis, 9–10, 68–80, 117–25, 126–45. *See also* Lanchester theory

E-2B/C aircraft, 94
EA-6B aircraft, 91
Ellis, Gen. Richard H., 55
Emerson, D. E., 149n
Engel, J. H., 152–53, 153n
Epstein, Joshua M., 9n, 10n, 36n, 64n, 69n, 78n, 85n, 90n, 91n, 92n, 109n, 128n, 147n, 153n

F-4 aircraft, 83n, 90, 94–95, 129n
F-14 aircraft, 94, 95, 96
F-15 aircraft, 89n
F-16 aircraft, 89n, 111
F-111 aircraft, 54, 83n, 108–11
F/A-18 aircraft, 95
Forrest, Nathan Bedford, 68
Forward-looking infrared (FLIR) technology, 92, 108n, 109n

Gabriel, Gen. Charles A., 89n
Gaddis, John Lewis, 1n, 11n
GBU-15 bomb, 108n, 109n
Gelb, Leslie H., 31n
Geographical escalation. *See* Horizontal escalation strategy
Getler, Michael, 11n
Ground-controlled intercept (GCI), 91–92
Guensberg, Gerold, 8n, 45n, 48n, 49n, 50n, 56n, 77n, 88n

Hackett, Sir John, 63n
Halloran, Richard, 4n, 32n, 38n, 41n, 65n
Halperin, Morton H., 19n
Hamilton, Andrew, 71n
Hart, B. H. Liddell, 75n
Hayward, Adm. Thomas B., 94
Healy, Melissa, 37n
Heiman, Leo, 66n
Heller, Mark, 66n
Helmbold, Robert L., 125n, 151, 152n, 153n
Herzog, Chaim, 91n
Hewett, Ed A., 4n
Hoenig, Milton M., 21n
Horizontal escalation strategy, 6–7, 98; counterhorizontal escalation risks, 39–40, 99; credibility, 42–43, 99; diplomatic costs, 40–41; goals, 33–35; and

nuclear risks, 36, 38–39, 41–42, 43; Reagan administration and, 30–33; target selection problems, 35. *See also* Asymmetrical response
Huntington, Samuel P., 38n

Iklé, Fred Charles, 37n, 41, 42
Input measures, 41, 69–72; and relation to outputs, 25–26, 73–80. *See also* Output measures
Iran, potential Soviet-U.S. conflict, 103–05; contingency defined, 2–6; phase I, 47–56, 62, 107–11; phase II, 56–63; phase III, 63–89, 112–16; simulations, 80–89, 126–45; Soviet attack options, 65–67, 68, 89–92, 112–16; Soviet logistical constraints, 65–67, 102, 112–16; U.S. carrier defense against Soviet bomber attack, 92–97. *See also* Horizontal escalation strategy; Vertical escalation strategy
Iranian armed forces, 57
Isby, David C., 71n
Israeli air force, 90, 91, 109n, 128n

Jefferson, Thomas, 40
Jervis, Robert, 22
Johnson, Lyndon B., 14
Johnson, Ralph E., 149n
Joint Chiefs of Staff (JCS), 8, 13, 15, 32, 50, 51n, 86–87, 102–03
Joint Intelligence Staff, 49
Joint Logistics Plans Committee, 51n
Joint Strategic Plans Committee, 56n, 57n
Joint Strategic Plans Group, 57n, 76
Joint War Plans Committee, 49, 50, 53n
Jones, Gen. David C., 92

Kahn, Herman, 27n, 39n
Kaplan, Fred, 13n, 15n
Karr, Alan F., 147n, 149n
Kaufmann, William W., 19n, 23n, 32n, 41n, 43n, 61n, 128n, 147n, 148n, 150n
Kelleher, Catherine McArdle, 20
Khomeini, Ayatollah R. M., 3
Khrushchev, Nikita, 39
Kimball, George E., 147n
Kingston, Lt. Gen. Robert C., 25n
Kissinger, Henry, 15
Komer, Robert W., 32n, 37n
Konstantinov, Gen.-Col. Anatoliy U., 90n
Korean War, 91
Krepinevich, Andrew, 113n
Kuzmack, Arnold M., 36n

Lanchester, Frederick William, 9, 147n, 150n

Lanchester theory, 9–10, 78, 118n, 120–21n, 124, 125, 146–55
Lavalle, Maj. A. J. C., 108n, 109n
Lehman, John, 31n, 41n
Leighton, Richard M., 76n
Leonard, Capt. Henry, 15n, 51n, 58n, 67n
Lewis, Kevin N., 31n
Long, Adm. Robert, 17
Lorell, Mark A., 31n
Louer, Philip E., 149n
Luttwak, Edward N., 7, 32n, 44n, 107n

M-*118*, 108n
MacArthur, Gen. Douglas, 41
McNamara, Robert S., 6, 12, 14n, 18n, 19n, 20n, 22n, 25n, 29n
McNaugher, Thomas L., 44n, 52n, 59n, 63n, 64n, 85n
Maddocks, Maj. Gen. Ray T., 57n
Mako, William P., 69n, 70n, 71n, 72n, 117n, 119n, 128n, 129n
Massive retaliation, 11, 12, 43
Mi-*24* helicopter, 71n
MiG-*21* aircraft, 90, 91n, 96n
MiG-*23* aircraft, 91n, 96n
Mikhaylov, Yu. B., 147n
MK-*83*, 108n
MK-*84*, 108n
Morse, Philip M., 147n
Motter, T. H. Vail, 76n
Motti tactics, 56, 61

National Security Council, 56; NSC *73/4*, 56
National Security Decision Memorandum (NSDM)-*242*, 15
Navy, U.S., 55, 109n; carrier vulnerability, 24, 92–97; and horizontal escalation, 31, 34, 36; Pacific Fleet, 17
Newman, James R., 9n
North Atlantic Treaty Organization (NATO), 29n, 100,104; compensation for diversion of U.S. forces, 5; consultation in, 101–02; credibility of U.S. commitment, 28–29; flexible response, 6, 11, 99; Long-Term Defense Program, 102; and nuclear tripwire strategy, 12
Nuclear proliferation, 27–28. *See also* Vertical escalation strategy

Output measures, 72–73; and relation to inputs, 25–26, 73–80. *See also* Input measures

Pavlov, Gen.-Lt. G., 90n
Perry, Robert, 31n
Perry, William J., 16
Peterson, Richard H., 152
Pilot skill, U.S. and Soviet, 90–91
Poland, Soviet mobilization for, 61
Posen, Barry R., 22n, 36, 72, 75n, 118n, 128n, 129n

Rapid deployment forces (RDFs), simulated performance, 80–89, 97, 99–100, 126–43. *See also* Central Command, U.S. (CENTCOM); Rapid Deployment Joint Task Force
Rapid Deployment Joint Task Force, 2n, 7, 17
Reagan administration, 30–33, 35, 84, 99
Record, Jeffrey, 7, 64n, 113n
Robbins, Herbert, 121n
Rosen, Steven J., 90n
Rusk, Dean, 39n

Samuel, Peter, 34n
Schelling, Thomas C., 22, 23n, 27n, 43
Schemmer, Benjamin F., 109n
Schwartz, David N., 11n, 29n
Scott, Jeffrey, 15n, 51n, 58n, 67n
Sea lines of communication (SLOC), 55, 63, 76
Shirer, William L., 103n
Sigal, Leon V., 19n, 29n
SL-*7* fast sealift ship, 64
Smoke, Richard, 27n
Soviet Command Study of Iran, 8, 45, 46, 47, 48n, 49n, 50, 56n, 77n, 88n, 104
Soviet-Finnish Winter War, 56
Soviet military doctrine, 74, 93
Steinbruner, John D., 19n, 124n
Stockfisch, J. A., 71n, 147n
Strategic Air Command, 13, 64
Strategic ballistic missile submarines (SSBNs), 36
Strategic Projection Force (Spif), 54, 96n
Su-*22* aircraft, 91n
Su-*24* aircraft, 91
Su-*25* aircraft, 129n

Taylor, James G., 118n, 128n, 147n, 148n, 149n, 155n
Turner, Adm. Stansfield, 2

Uryzhnikov, Col. V. A., 91n
USSR Long-Range Aviation (LRA), 93
USSR Naval Aviation, 93, 94

Valenta, Jiri, 61n
Van Evera, Stephen, 101n
Vertical escalation strategy, 6–7, 30; battlefield nuclear exchanges, 18–20; credibility, 28–29, 98–99; and nuclear proliferation, 27–28; nuclear targeting options, 13–18; operational pressures, 20–27. *See also* Asymmetrical response
Vietnam War, 72–73, 90, 125, 129n; attrition rate per sortie, 109n; exchange ratios, 91; Operation Linebacker, 109n
Voigt, Karsten, 74n

Walleye II bomb, 108n
Waltz, Kenneth N., 12, 16n
Warning time, 92, 94, 96, 97

Warsaw Pact, 4, 28, 34
War-widening strategy. *See* Horizontal escalation strategy
Watkins, Adm. James D., 36n
Weapon Effectiveness Indices/Weighted Unit Values (WEI/WUV) system, 69–71, 77, 117
Weinberger, Caspar W., 4, 7, 30, 31n, 36, 38, 40, 42, 64
Weiss, Herbert K., 128n, 152
Wiener, Norbert, 124n
Willard, D., 152
Wilson, George C., 30n, 31n, 32n, 37n, 40n, 54n, 55n, 89n, 96n
World War I, 22, 101
World War II, 22, 75n, 76, 125